CLUB CULTURES

CLUB CULTURES

Music, Media and Subcultural Capital

SARAH THORNTON

Wesleyan University Press
Middletown, Connecticut

To Jeremy

Published by Wesleyan University Press, Middletown, CT 06459
www.wesleyan.edu/wespress

First published in 1995 by Polity Press in association with
Blackwell Publishers Ltd.
First U.S. edition 1996

Library of Congress Catalog Card Number: 95–61500
ISBN 978–0–8195–5291–4 (cl.)
ISBN 978–0–8195–6297–5 (pa.)

Printed in the United States of America
10 9 8 7 6

Contents

List of Plates   vii
List of Figures   viii
Acknowledgements   ix

1 The Distinctions of Cultures Without Distinction
    Introduction   1
    Youth and their Social Spaces   14

2 Authenticities from Record Hops to Raves
    (and the History of Disc Culture)
    The Authentication of a Mass Medium   26
    Industrial Forces, Musician Resistance and 'Live'
        Ideology   34
    'Real' Events and Altered Spaces   51
    Disc Jockeys and Social Sounds   58
    The Authenticities of Dance Genres   66
    The Response of the 'Live' Gig   76
    Conclusion   85

3 Exploring the Meaning of the Mainstream
    (or why Sharon and Tracy Dance around their Handbags)
    A Night of Research   87

Academic Accounts of the Cultural Organization
   of Youth   92
The Social Logic of Subcultural Capital   98
Participation versus Observation of Dance Crowds   105
Conclusion   114

4 The Media Development of 'Subcultures'
   (or the Sensational Story of 'Acid House')
   The Underground versus the Overexposed   116
   Mass Media: 'Selling Out' and 'Moral Panic'   122
   Micro-Media: Flyers, Listings, Fanzines, Pirates   137
   Niche Media: the Editorial Search for Subcultures   151
   Conclusion   161

Afterword   163

Bibliography   169

Index   188

List of Plates

Plates 1 and 2 Two 'mould-breaking' raves held just ten
miles apart on 26–7 August 1989
(Photographs: David Swindells)   23

Plate 3 One of the first instances of records made
specifically for the public dancefloor
(Reproduced by kind permission of the Musicians' Union)   40

Plate 4 The death of vinyl
(Reproduced by kind permission of DJ *magazine)*   64

Plate 5 Front-page coverage of the rave scene, June 1989
(Reproduced by kind permission of the Sun*)*   133

Plate 6 A selection of flyers from 1989
(Photograph: David Swindells)   142

Plate 7 DJ Danny Rampling and his devotees at Shoom
(Photograph: David Swindells)   144

List of Figures

Figure 1 Dance versus other entertainments 1979–94
(Source: Leisure Consultants)   15

Figure 2 Axes of authenticity   31

Figure 3 The academic divides of youth culture   97

Publishers' note: Every effort has been made to trace all the copyright holders, but if any have been inadvertently overlooked, the publishers will be pleased to make the necessary arrangement at the first opportunity.

Acknowledgements

I would like to acknowledge the financial support of the Association of Commonwealth Universities and the British Council (for funding my postgraduate research at the John Logie Baird Centre, Strathclyde University, Glasgow) and of the Coca-Cola Foundation (for financing a research fellowship at the Center for Humanities, Wesleyan University, Connecticut).

I am very grateful to many people for their advice and support during the writing of this book and the PhD dissertation from which it derives. First, my thanks go to those interviewees, informants and guides who spent time with me, on and off the dancefloor, sharing their experience of, and insights into, British dance culture. Thanks also to Andy Linehan at the National Sound Archive for his help with research and to David Swindells at *Time Out* for kindly allowing me to reproduce his photographs. Second, I want to express my profound appreciation to the following friends, students and mentors for their constructive comments on various chapters and drafts of the book. In alphabetical order, they are: José Arroyo, Brian Austin, Jacob Bricca, Matt Callaghan, Stephi Donald, Alan Durant, Leslie Felperin, Wendy Fonarow, Andrew Goodwin, Reesa Greenberg, Larry Grossberg, Dave Hesmondhalgh, Kate Lacey, Rachel Malik, Martin Montgomery, Mica Nava, Keith Negus, Richard Ohmann, Patria Roman, Kitty Scott, Roger Silverstone, Paul

Theberge and John Thompson. I would especially like to thank Angela McRobbie and my dissertation supervisor, Simon Frith, for their invaluable and enduring guidance.

Finally, this book would not have been written without the steadfast support of my parents, Glenda and Monte Thornton, and my *ad hoc* editor and partner, Jeremy Silver.

I

The Distinctions of Cultures Without Distinction

Introduction

Nothing could better signify the 'complete disappearance of a culture of meaning and aesthetic sensibility,' says postmodern cultural commentator Jean Baudrillard, than 'a spinning of strobe lights and gyroscopes streaking the space whose moving pedestal is created by the crowd' (Baudrillard 1982: 5). Baudrillard's dismissal of the discotheque as the lowest form of contemporary entertainment reiterates a well-established view. Dance cultures have long been seen to epitomize mass culture at its worst. Dance music has been considered to be standardized, mindless and banal, while dancers have been regarded as narcotized, conformist and easily manipulated. Even Theodor Adorno, an early theorist of mass culture, reserved some of his most damning prose for the 'rhythmic obedience' of jitterbug dancers, arguing that the 'music immediately expressed their desire to obey' and that its regular beat suggested 'coordinated battalions of mechanical collectivity . . . Thus do the obedient inherit the earth' (Adorno 1941/1990: 312).

For many years, discotheques and dance music have even been excluded from popular music's own canons. Rock criticism and much pop scholarship have tended to privilege 'listening' over dance musics, visibly performing musicians over behind-the-scenes producers, the rhetorically 'live' over the 'recorded' and hence guitars over synthesizers and samplers. Until the mid-eighties, successive genres of dance music tended to be dismissed as irrelevant fads or evoked as symbols of all that was not radical or innovative in music. Although these ideas are no longer held by as many music critics as they once were, the old rock canon persists in many spheres. For example, the following entry on disco music from the 1989 edition of the *Penguin Encyclopedia of Popular Music* typifies the opinion of the old guard:

> Dance fad of the 70s with profound and unfortunate influence on popular music . . . it had a disastrous effect on music for two related reasons, the producers and the technology . . . producers, who already had too much power, used drum machines, synthesizers and other gimmicks at the expense of musical values . . . most disco hitmakers were virtually anonymous, and the anonymity has translated into the sameness of pop music in the 80s. (Clarke 1989: 344)

The purpose of this book is *not* to celebrate the creativity of dance culture (it seems to me that this needs no proving), nor to canonize dance music nor elevate the status of discotheques. In fact, except for some discussion of the taste war between disc-dancers and the Musicians' Union in the first chapter, I don't investigate in depth the values of people outside dance culture. Instead, I am concerned with the attitudes and ideals of the youthful insiders whose social lives revolve around clubs and raves.

Despite having once been an avid clubber, I was an outsider to the cultures in which I conducted research for several reasons. First and foremost, I was *working* in a cultural space in which everyone else (except the DJs, door and bar staff, and perhaps the odd journalist) was at their *leisure*. Not only did I have intents and purposes that were alien to the rest of the crowd, but also for the most part I tried to maintain an analytical frame of mind that is truly anathema to the 'lose yourself' and 'let the rhythm take control' ethos of clubs and raves.* Two demographic factors – my age and nationality – further contributed to this detachment. I began my research when I was

---

* There is no shortage of superb insider accounts of clubbing. (See magazines like *i-D*, *The Face*, *Time Out* and *DJ* or, for more confessional tales, the many fanzines which come and go.)

twenty-three and slowly aged out of the peer group I was studying, acquiring increments of analytical distance with each passing year. As a North American investigating British clubs and raves, I was also, quite literally, a stranger in a strange land. Although club culture is a global phenomenon, it is at the same time firmly rooted in the local. Dance records and club clothes may be easily imported and exported, but dance crowds tend to be municipal, regional and national. Dance styles, for example, which need to be *embodied* rather than just bought, are much less transnational than other aspects of the culture.

'Club culture' is the colloquial expression given to youth cultures for whom dance clubs and their eighties offshoot, raves, are the symbolic axis and working social hub. The sense of place afforded by these events is such that regular attenders take on the name of the spaces they frequent, becoming 'clubbers' and 'ravers'. The territorial affiliations of most post-war youth subcultures have been more ambiguous and numerous than club cultures, even if we envision hippies at rock festivals, skinheads on football terraces and punks at small 'live' gigs. Club cultures, by contrast, are persistently associated with a specific space which is both continually transforming its sounds and styles and regularly bearing witness to the apogees and excesses of youth cultures.

Club cultures are *taste cultures*. Club crowds generally congregate on the basis of their shared taste in music, their consumption of common media and, most importantly, their preference for people with similar tastes to themselves. Taking part in club cultures builds, in turn, further affinities, socializing participants into a knowledge of (and frequently a belief in) the likes and dislikes, meanings and values of the culture. Clubs and raves, therefore, house *ad hoc* communities with fluid boundaries which may come together and dissolve in a single summer or endure for a few years. Crucially, club cultures embrace their own hierarchies of what is authentic and legitimate in popular culture – embodied understanding of which can make one 'hip'. These distinctions – their cultural logics and socio-economic roots – are the main subject of this book.

Club cultures are riddled with cultural hierarchies. My intention is to explore three principal, overarching distinctions which can be briefly designated as: the authentic versus the phoney, the 'hip' versus the 'mainstream', and the 'underground' versus 'the media'. Each distinction opens up a world of meanings and values which is explored in a separate and self-contained chapter. Each chapter, in turn, excavates the sociological sources and pursues the cultural ramifications of the distinction in question. As such, the three ensuing chapters enter into slightly different debates about youth, music, media and culture. However, they are all unified by an unbroken concern with the problem of cultural status.

In the first part of the book, I explore the distinction between the authentic and the inauthentic, the 'real' happening and the non-event, original dance records and formula pop. Although the authenticities of 'live' performance have been comprehensively researched, little has been written about the new authenticities attributed to records and recorded events. Even though they enjoy many affinities, club cultures espouse dynamics of distinction sufficiently different from those of live music cultures to justify coining a new term and discussing them as *disc cultures*. For example, within disc cultures, recording and performance have swapped statuses: records are the original, whereas live music has become an exercise in reproduction. Club cultures celebrate technologies that have rendered some traditional kinds of musicianship obsolete and have led to the formation of new aesthetics and judgements of value. Producers, sound engineers, remixers and DJs – not song-writing guitarists – are the creative heroes of dance genres. As a result, when a 'performance' is called for, it may entail hiring a model and dancers to lip-synch to the sampled vocals while the track's composer prances behind a computer keyboard or DJ console at the back of the stage. The clubber consensus is that these kinds of appearance are often laughably inauthentic attempts to visualize something which is usually best left in its pure sonic state.

The history of these shifting authenticities between the 'live' and the *quintessentially recorded* is primarily dependent on changing modes of music consumption. The story goes back to the 'record hops' of the 1950s and involves the rise of the discotheque and the decline of live music for public dancing. Discotheques institutionalized the practice of dancing to discs; they were crucial to the enculturation of records, the material process upon which their authentication is predicated. This history therefore entails not just sounds, but changing finances and labour relations, novel locations and transformed architectural environments, new 'youth' audiences and new music professions. I explore these in order to grasp the issue of musical authenticity *not* just as a vague sensibility or aesthetic, but as a cultural value anchored in concrete, historical practices of production and consumption.

The second distinction I investigate is one principally discussed as that between the 'hip' world of the dance crowd in question and its perpetually absent, denigrated *other* – the 'mainstream'. This contrast between 'us' and the 'mainstream' is more directly related to the process of envisioning social worlds and discriminating between social groups. Its veiled elitism and separatism enlist and reaffirm binary oppositions such as the alternative and the straight, the diverse and the homogeneous, the radical and the conformist, the distinguished and the common. The mainstream is a trope which, once prised open, reveals the complex and cryptic relations between age and the social structure.

The mainstream is the entity against which the *majority* of clubbers define themselves. Can the mainstream be a majority? What is its exact status? Is it a minority, a myth, neither or both? More to the point, how does the 'mainstream' function for those who invoke it? What are the social differences implied by clubber discourses about the mainstream? And, what problems or possibilities does the belief pose for researchers investigating the cultural organization of youth?

To some degree, the mainstream stands in for the masses – discursive distance from which is a measure of a clubber's cultural worth. Youthful clubber and raver ideologies are almost as *anti-mass culture* as the discourses of the artworld. Both criticize the mainstream/masses for being derivative, superficial and *femme* (Huyssen 1986). Both conspicuously admire innovative artists, but show disdain for those who have too high a profile as being charlatans or overrated media-sluts. Of course, they differ in many ways. Crucially, rather than the artworld's dread of 'trickle down', the problem for *underground subcultures* is a popularization by a gushing *up* to the mainstream. These metaphors are not arbitrary; they betray a sense of social place. Subcultural ideology implicitly gives alternative interpretations and values to young people's, particularly young men's, subordinate status; it re-interprets the social world.

In the final section of the book, I examine the distinction between the 'underground' and 'the media' which encompasses a series of further contrasts including the esoteric versus the exposed, the exclusive versus the accessible, the pure versus the corrupted, the 'independent' versus the 'sold out'. Club undergrounds see themselves as renegade cultures opposed to, and continually in flight from, the colonizing co-opting media. To be 'hip' is to be privy to insider knowledges that are threatened by the general distribution and easy access of mass media. Like the mainstream, *'the* media' is therefore a vague monolith against which subcultural credibilities are measured.

But the relations between various media and club cultures – as well as clubber and raver discourses about individual media – are complex and varied. To make any sense of their dynamics, one needs to differentiate between *micro, niche* and *mass* media, then to consider the disparate consequences of affirmative or critical, explicit or allusive coverage within each of these spheres. For example, disapproving 'moral panic' stories in mass circulation tabloid newspapers often have the effect of certifying transgression and legitimizing youth cultures. How else might youthful leisure be turned into revolt, lifestyle into social upheaval, difference into defiance? Approving reports in mass media like tabloids or television, however, are the subcultural kiss of death. Nevertheless both kinds of coverage tend to lead to a quick abandonment of the key insignia of the culture. For example, Smiley-face T-shirts were cast off as uncool and the word 'acid' was dropped from club names and music genre classifications as soon as 'acid house' became a term familiar to general readers of national newspapers.

Disparagement of the inauthentic, the mainstream and the media is prevalent amongst all kinds of club cultures. Interest in authenticity and distinction would seem to be the norm. Nevertheless, the subcultural ideologies I investigate are those of predominantly straight and white club and rave cultures. Similar 'underground' discourses operate in gay and lesbian clubs but, as the alternative values involved in exploring sex and sexuality complicate the situation beyond easy generalization, I concentrate on their heterosexual manifestation. Moreover, 'campness' rather than 'hipness' may be a more appropriate way to characterize the prevailing cultural values of these communities (cf. Sontag 1966; Savage 1988).* And, although I did substantial research in Afro-Caribbean and mixed-race clubs, the book more thoroughly (but not exclusively) analyses the cultural worlds of the white majority. Despite the fact that black and white youth cultures share many of the same attitudes and some of the same musics, race is still a conspicuous divider.

Over the past few decades, there has been much productive inquiry into the divide between high and popular culture. Some work has attempted to deconstruct the elitist assumptions that lie behind high theorists' denigration of 'mass culture' and has considered the problem in the light of debates about modernism and postmodernism (cf. Huyssen 1986; MacCabe 1986). Other studies have traced the upward or downward mobility of artistic figures and forms, like the transformation of Shakespeare from a people's playwright into a cultural deity or the process by which jazz was 'elevated' from being a music of nightclubs to one of university music departments (cf. Levine 1988; Ross 1989). Some research has examined the relation between cultural hierarchies and social ones, attempting to demonstrate that personal taste is not the result of an individual's immanent nature, but of family background, education and class (cf. Gans 1974; Bourdieu 1984). Still other investigations have found that cultural forms, previously considered trivial, actually threaten the social order in significant ways and theories of the symbolic 'resistances' of the popular to 'dominant' culture have been developed (cf. Hall and Jefferson 1976; Hebdige 1979).

Comparatively little attention, however, has been paid to the hierarchies *within* popular culture. Although judgements of value are made as a matter of course, few scholars have empirically examined the systems of social and cultural distinction that divide and demarcate contemporary culture, particularly youth culture.[†] Feminist analyses are a general exception to this rule, but they tend to

---

* There is substantial literature on the importance of dance clubs to the gay liberation movement in the USA (see Hooker 1969; Humphreys 1972; Krieger 1983) and to the congregation of gays and lesbians before and after the decriminalization of male homosexuality in Britain in 1966 (see Burton 1985; Weeks 1985; Wilson 1988).

[†] Exceptional considerations of youth's cultural hierarchies include: Becker 1963, Christenson and Peterson 1988, Clarke 1990, Frith 1981c, 1986 and 1987c, Frith and Horne 1987, Hebdige 1988 and Lewis 1992.

restrict their inquiry to criticizing the devaluation of the feminine and to examining the subordinate position of girls (cf. McRobbie 1991). They have not extended this insight to a general examination of the way youth cultures are stratified within themselves or the manner in which young people seek out and accumulate cultural goods and experiences for strategic use within their own social worlds. The analysis of these cultural pursuits as forms of power brokering is essential to our understanding not only of youth and music cultures in particular but of the dynamics of popular culture in general.

Studies of popular culture have tended to embrace anthropological notions of culture as a *way of life* but have spurned art-oriented definitions of culture which relate to *standards of excellence* (cf. Williams, 1976 and 1981). High culture is generally conceived in terms of aesthetic values, hierarchies and canons, while popular culture is portrayed as a curiously flat folk culture. One is depicted as vertically ordered, the other as horizontally organized. Of course, consumers of popular culture have been depicted as discerning, with definite likes and dislikes, but these tastes are rarely charted systematically as ranked standards.

In Britain and to a lesser extent North America and Australia, studies of popular culture – particularly studies of youth sub-cultures – have been dominated by a tradition associated with the 1970s work of the Centre for Contemporary Cultural Studies, University of Birmingham, England. Given that so many years have passed, it should come as no surprise that this study is indebted to their work but is nevertheless distinctly 'post-Birmingham' in several ways. First, this book doesn't adopt their theoretical definitions of 'subcultures' for the main reason that I found them to be empirically unworkable (cf. chapter 4). Instead, I use the term 'subcultures' to identify those taste cultures which are labelled by media as subcultures and the word 'subcultural' as a synonym for those practices that clubbers call 'underground'.

In this respect, my work harks back to the studies of Chicago School sociologists whose concern for researching empirical social groups always took precedence over their elaboration of theory. In fact, Howard Becker offers a compelling analysis of 'distinction' under another name in his study of a 'deviant' culture of musicians in the 1940s (published in *Outsiders*, 1963). The white jazz musicians in Becker's study saw themselves as possessing a mysterious attitude called 'hip' and dismissed other people, particularly their audience, as ignorant 'squares'. Similarly, in the early sixties, Ned Polsky researched the social world of Greenwich Village Beatniks, finding that the Beats distinguished not only between being 'hip' and 'square', but added a third category of the 'hipster' who shared the Beatnik's fondness for drugs and jazz, but was said to be a 'mannered show off regarding his hipness' (Polsky 1967: 149). The overwhelming majority of Beats were neither exhibitionists nor publicity seekers but precisely the opposite. According to Polsky, 'the cool world [was] an iceberg, mostly underwater' (Polsky 1967: 151).

Second, the classic Birmingham subcultural studies tended to banish media and commerce from their definitions of authentic culture. In *Resistance Through Rituals*, the authors position the media in opposition to and after the fact of subculture (cf. Hall and Jefferson 1976). In *Subculture: The Meaning of Style*, Dick Hebdige sees media and commerce as 'incorporating' subcultures into the hegemony, swallowing them up and effectively dismantling them. (Hebdige 1979). In *Profane Culture*, Paul Willis argues that violent acts of appropriation are necessary to transform the 'shit of capitalist production' into the sacred objects of authentic youth subcultures (Willis 1978: 170). By contrast, I attempt to problematize the notion of authenticity and see various media and businesses as integral to the authentication of cultural practices. Here, commercial culture and popular culture are not only inextricable in practice, but also in theory.

Third, the book does not offer a synchronic interpretation of subcultures or textual analysis of their sounds and styles, but an analysis explicitly concerned with cultural change. (For all their concern for rebellion and resistance, this tradition gave little consideration to social change!) The book explores cultural transformations in two periods: through archival research, it recounts a history of the evolving authenticities of records and recorded events since the Second World War; and through ethnographic research, it examines the complex cultural and media processes by which acid house 'subculture' crystallized and turned into the rave 'movement' between 1988 and 1992.

Finally, this book is not about dominant ideologies and subvers-

ive subcultures, but about subcultural ideologies. It treats the discourses of dance cultures, not as innocent accounts of the way
things really are, but as ideologies which fulfil the specific cultural
agendas of their beholders. Subcultural ideologies are a means by
which youth imagine their own and other social groups, assert their
distinctive character and affirm that they are not anonymous members of an undifferentiated mass. In this way, I am not simply
researching the beliefs of a cluster of communities, but investigating
the way they make 'meaning in the service of power' – however
modest these powers may be (Thompson 1990: 7). Distinctions are
never just assertions of equal difference; they usually entail some
claim to authority and presume the inferiority of *others*.

In trying to make sense of the values and hierarchies of club
culture, I've drawn from the work of the French sociologist Pierre
Bourdieu, particularly his book *Distinction* (1984) and related essays
on the links between taste and the social structure. Bourdieu writes
extensively about what he calls *cultural capital* or knowledge that is
accumulated through upbringing and education which confers
social status. Cultural capital is the linchpin of a system of distinction in which cultural hierarchies correspond to social ones and
people's tastes are predominantly a marker of class. For instance, in
Britain, accent has long been a key indicator of cultural capital, and
university degrees have long been cultural capital in institutionalized form. Cultural capital is different from *economic capital*. High
levels of income and property often correlate with high levels of
cultural capital, but the two can also conflict. Comments about the
'*nouveau riche*' or the 'flash' disclose the possible frictions between
those rich in cultural capital but relatively poor in economic capital
(like artists or academics) and those rich in economic capital but less
affluent in cultural capital (like business executives and professional football players).

One of the many advantages of Bourdieu's schema is that it
moves away from rigidly vertical models of the social structure.
Bourdieu locates social groups in a highly complex multi-dimensional space rather than on a linear scale or ladder. His theoretical
framework even includes discussion of a third category – *social
capital* – which stems not so much from *what* you know as *who* you
know (and who knows you). Connections in the form of friends,
relations, associates and acquaintances can all bestow status. The

aristocracy has always privileged social over other forms of capital, as have many private members' clubs and old boys' networks. The notion of social capital is also useful in explaining the power of fame or of being known by those one doesn't know, particularly when the famous consolidate their social capital in marriage (hence the stop-press news coverage of the marital merger of Michael Jackson and Lisa Marie Presley).

In addition to these three major types of capital – cultural, economic and social – Bourdieu elaborates many subcategories of capital which operate within particular fields such as 'linguistic', 'academic', 'intellectual', 'information' and 'artistic' capital. One characteristic that unifies these capitals is that they are all at play within Bourdieu's own field, within *his* social world of players with high volumes of institutionalized cultural capital. However, it is possible to observe subspecies of capital operating within other less privileged domains. In thinking through Bourdieu's theories in relation to the terrain of youth culture, I've come to conceive of 'hipness' as a form of *subcultural capital*.

Although subcultural capital is a term that I've coined in relation to my own research, it is one that accords reasonably well with Bourdieu's system of thought. In his essay, 'Did you say Popular?', he contends that 'the deep-seated "intention" of slang vocabulary is above all the assertion of an aristocratic distinction' (Bourdieu 1991: 94). Nevertheless, Bourdieu does not talk about these popular 'distinctions' as 'capitals'. (Perhaps he sees them as too paradoxical in their effects to warrant the term?) However, I would argue that clubs are refuges for the young where their rules hold sway and that, inside and to some extent outside these spaces, subcultural distinctions have significant consequences.

Subcultural capital confers status on its owner in the eyes of the relevant beholder. In many ways it affects the standing of the young like its adult equivalent. Subcultural capital can be *objectified* or *embodied*. Just as books and paintings display cultural capital in the family home, so subcultural capital is objectified in the form of fashionable haircuts and well-assembled record collections (full of well-chosen, limited edition 'white label' twelve-inches and the like). Just as cultural capital is personified in 'good' manners and urbane conversation, so subcultural capital is embodied in the form of being 'in the know', using (but not over-using) current slang and looking as if you were born to perform the latest dance styles. Both cultural and subcultural capital put a premium on the 'second nature' of their knowledges. Nothing depletes capital more than the sight of someone trying too hard. For example, fledgeling clubbers of fifteen or sixteen wishing to get into what they perceive as a sophisticated dance club will often reveal their inexperience by over-dressing or confusing 'coolness' with an exaggerated cold blank stare.

It has been argued that what ultimately defines cultural capital as capital is its 'convertibility' into economic capital (Garnham and Williams 1986: 123). While subcultural capital may not convert into economic capital with the same ease or financial reward as cultural capital, a variety of occupations and incomes can be gained as result of 'hipness'. DJs, club organizers, clothes designers, music and style journalists and various record industry professionals all make a living from their subcultural capital. Moreover, within club cultures, people in these professions often enjoy a lot of respect not only because of their high volume of subcultural capital, but also from their role in defining and creating it. In knowing, owning and playing the music, DJs, in particular, are sometimes positioned as the masters of the scene, although they can be overshadowed by club organisers whose job it is to know who's who and gather the right crowd.

Although it converts into economic capital, subcultural capital is not as class-bound as cultural capital. This is not to say that class is irrelevant, simply that it does not correlate in any one-to-one way with levels of youthful subcultural capital. In fact, class is wilfully obfuscated by subcultural distinctions. For instance, it is not uncommon for public-school-educated youth to adopt working-class accents during their clubbing years. Subcultural capitals fuel rebellion against, or rather escape from, the trappings of parental class. The assertion of subcultural distinction relies, in part, on a fantasy of classlessness. This may be one reason why music is the cultural form privileged within youth's subcultural worlds. Age is the most significant demographic when it comes to taste in music, to the extent that playing music in the family home is the most common source of generational conflict (after arguments over the clothes that sons and daughters choose to wear) (cf. Euromonitor 1989b). In contrast the relation between class and musical taste is much more difficult to chart. The most clearly up-market genre, classical music, is also the least disliked of all types of music by most sectors of the population, hence its abundant use in television commercials to advertise products of all kinds, from butter and baked beans to BMWs.

One reason why subcultural capital clouds class backgrounds is that it has long defined itself as extra-curricular, as knowledge one cannot learn in school.* As a result, after age, the social difference along which it is aligned most systematically is, in fact, gender. On average, girls invest more of their time and identity in doing well at school. Boys, by contrast, spend more time with (and money on) leisure activities such as going out, listening to records and reading music magazines (Mintel 1988c; Euromonitor 1989b). But this doesn't mean that girls do not participate in the economy of subcultural capital. On the contrary, if girls opt out of the game of 'hipness', they will often defend their tastes (particularly their taste for pop music) with expressions like 'It's crap but I like it'. In so doing, they acknowledge the subcultural hierarchy and accept their lowly position within it. If, on the other hand, they refuse this defeatism, female clubbers and ravers are usually careful to distance themselves from the degraded pop culture of 'Sharon and Tracy'. (This is a long story which is explored in chapter 3 on the feminization of the mainstream.)

A critical difference between subcultural capital (as I explore it) and cultural capital (as Bourdieu develops it) is that the media are a primary factor governing the circulation of the former. Several writers have remarked upon the absence of television and radio from Bourdieu's theories of cultural hierarchy (cf. Frow 1987; Garnham 1993). Another scholar has argued that they are absent from his schema because 'the cultural distinctions of particular taste publics collapse in the common cultural domain of broadcasting' (Scannell 1989: 155). I would argue that it is impossible to understand the distinctions of youth cultures without some systematic investigation of their media consumption. For, within the economy of subcultural capital, the media are not simply another symbolic good or marker of distinction (which is the way Bourdieu describes films

---

* Certain kinds of higher education may be exceptions to this rule. For an analysis of the significance of art schools to the values of music culture, see Frith and Horne 1987.

and newspapers *vis-à-vis* cultural capital), but a network crucial to the definition and distribution of cultural knowledge. In other words, the difference between being *in* or *out* of fashion, high or low in subcultural capital, correlates in complex ways with degrees of media coverage, creation and exposure.

The idea that concern for cultural value and status is common in popular cultures seemingly devoid of them is one which, once stated, seems obvious. However, the many ramifications of the idea are less clear and little explored. This book contributes to the shift away from stale celebrations to more critical analyses of popular culture. A great deal of extant research on youth subcultures has both over-politicized their leisure and at the same time ignored the subtle relations of power at play within them. This inquiry into subcultural distinctions – which concentrates on the three problems of the persistent value of authenticity, the useful myth of the mainstream and the symbiotic relations between cultural kudos and the media – attempts to give fuller representation to the complex politics of popular culture.

Youth and their Social Spaces

Why are discotheques, particularly their recent incarnations as clubs and raves*, so central to British youth culture? How do dance clubs fit into the larger context of youth's social spaces and leisure activities? What exactly are the appeals of the institution? How do they fulfil youth's cultural agendas? The following social geography of youth goes some way towards explaining the existence of club cultures. It maps the empirical terrain upon which dance cultures rest as a necessary preface to an analysis of their distinctions.

Because clubbing and raving are done by a narrow segment of the population after most other people have gone to bed, the scale of the social phenomenon often goes unnoticed. Admissions to dance events are substantially higher than those to sporting events, cine-

---

* Raves are clubs held outside established dance venues in unconventional places which tend to feature certain genres of dance music, including house, acid house, techno and jungle music.

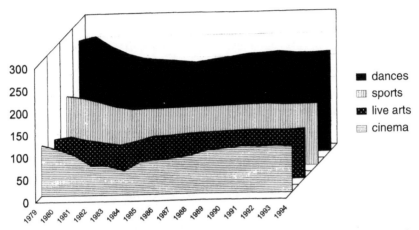

Figure 1 Dance versus other entertainments 1979–94 (million admissions)
(*Source*: Leisure Consultants)

mas and all the 'live' arts combined. In financial terms, the value of the club market (called 'nightclubs' by the leisure industry to avoid the fashion connotations of words like 'club' or 'rave' and to convince shareholders that such establishments are a stable investment) was estimated as being £1,968 million in 1992 (Mintel 1992). Although data on raves is even more in the realm of the 'guesstimate', the value of the rave market was calculated to be £1.8 billion ($2.7b) in 1993. A survey by the Henley Centre for Forecasting found that attendance at rave events was over fifty million a year in Britain, with each person spending an average of £35 ($52) on admission charges, soft drinks and recreational drugs (*Music and Copyright* 10 November 1993).

Going out dancing crosses boundaries of class, race, ethnicity, gender and sexuality, but *not* differences of age. The most avid clubbers and ravers are between fifteen and nineteen, followed by those aged twenty to twenty-four. The age boundaries of clubbing are tight, framed on the younger end of the scale by practical factors such as being allowed out of the house after eleven, having enough money to pay the substantial entrance fees, and successfully negotiating a loosely enforced drinking age of eighteen. A loss of interest in clubbing coincides with moving out of the parental home, which has repercussions for young people's desire to get out of the house and escape the family. Most importantly, however, clubbing declines when people form partnerships by either living together or marrying. Market research repeatedly finds that single people are ten times more likely to be frequent clubbers than married people (Mintel 1990 and 1992).

For a broad spectrum of British youth, then, going to dance clubs is an integral part of growing up. It is a rite of passage which marks adolescent independence with the freedom to stay out late with friends beyond the neighbourhood in a space which is relatively their own. Clubs allow their patrons to indulge in the 'adult' activities of flirtation, sex, drink and drugs, and explore cultural forms (like music and clothes) which confer autonomous and distinct identities.

The widespread significance of dance clubs to growing up may be unique to Britain. In America, bars and clubs are important to the gay rite of passage called 'coming out', but are peripheral to heterosexual adolescence. In so-called 'Middle America' (i.e. straight, white suburbia), acquiring a driver's licence and access to a car offer the sense of freedom, mobility and independence that British youth find at clubs and raves. In Britain, fewer young people have a driver's licence, let alone a car. 'Joyriding', which was subject to 'moral panic' in America in the 1950s, was considered a 'new' juvenile crime in Britain in the 1990s. Although car ownership is on the increase* (and ravers are dependent on cars to the extent that the events sometimes take place in remote areas of the countryside), British youth have yet to participate fully in American-style 'driving' or 'parking culture'. The illicit activities of the back seat are vicariously understood from Hollywood films and American song lyrics, rather than from common personal experience.

This marginal position of the car is something that British youth cultures (in general) share with American youth cultures of the inner city (in particular). In fact, in older American cities with a surviving centre and a public transport system like New York, the dance club scenes are analogous to those of Britain. Edith Folb argues, however, that cars are a potent symbol even for American

---

* The number of British households owning a car in 1989 was sixty-eight per cent, while ownership of two or more cars was only twenty per cent (Kinsman 1990: 43).

youth from low income backgrounds for whom cars are a luxury. In Afro-American youth culture, for example, cars 'not only afford mobility and prestige, but they become total environments to themselves. They are literally like mobile homes.' This is accentuated by the practice of 'freaking off' cars, in other words, fixing them up and lavishly decorating their interiors (Folb 1980: 84).

One can make a parallel between cars and clubs in their respective national contexts. The centrality of the car to American leisure is the main reason behind a strictly enforced legal drinking age of twenty-one. Conversely, in Britain, the drinking age of eighteen is seldom enforced – partly because British lawmakers haven't needed to worry about commensurate road fatalities. As a result, by the age it is legal to go to clubs in the United States, youth in the United Kingdom have started to lose interest in the activity.

Just as British youth have less access to the 'home away from home' of the car, so they enjoy less personal space within the home itself. Britain has a lower standard of living and a higher population density. Even with the decline in family sizes, overcrowding is still standard. Moreover, due to a decline in the average youth wage and to the increased participation of youth in education or training, a greater number of young people have had to delay 'leaving home' (cf. Smith 1992). Although the campus (with its residences, student unions, lounges, cafeterias and other semi-public spaces) is the cultural focus of a privileged but still substantial number of Americans, it has been and still is accessible to fewer Britons.* Moreover, even though there have been great increases in the number of students in higher education, most of the new universities do not have campuses in the traditional sense and can ill afford to provide student-only space.

Not only is there limited cubic space, but the average British home enjoys less of the extensive if virtual social space afforded by the telephone. British youth are less likely to have their own extension, let alone their own line (which is becoming an upper-middle-class norm in the States) and, without that privacy, the phone is of limited social use. Moreover, because one has traditionally paid by the minute for local calls, the kind of social life where one spends

---

* For a comparison of British and American youth that concentrates on differences in education and class consciousness, see Mays 1965: 172–9.

hours talking to friends has been prohibitively expensive for all but the most affluent. For this reason, young people's outgoing calls tend to be strictly regulated by their parents (cf. Silverstone and Morley 1990).

Youth often seek independence from the 'tyranny of the home' through their management of time (cf. Douglas 1991). Synchrony is crucial to the order and integration of the home. Youth therefore often adopt 'anti-social' strategies of time-use such as schedules whereby they stay up late and wake up late to avoid parental scrutiny and control. Domesticity is anathema to many youth cultures. It is not surprising, then, that youth watch less of that domestic medium, television, than any other age-group except newborn babies (cf. BBC Broadcasting Research 1990). Moreover, youth television programming follows this logic of de-synchronization. Many youth-orientated shows are scheduled before and after prime time partly because, in single television households, youth can then watch alone, but also because youth are likely to be out in the middle of the evening. In fact, youth's absence from the home has led satellite services like MTV Europe to argue that ratings should take into account out-of-home viewing in pubs and cafés which they have tried to promote to potential advertisers as the 'O.O.H. factor' (cf. *Broadcast* 14 May 1993).

British youth spend considerable time on the street. By night, young people often congregate outside pubs and clubs, and around hubs of public transportation. In fact, because late-night buses are intermittent and tend to leave from a single square in the city centre, after-hours scenes develop at bus shelters where vendors sell hotdogs to youth on their way home under the surveillance of police, bus and taxi drivers. Eating out for British youth has long meant eating on the street, for high streets have been more likely to have fish-and-chip and kebab take-aways than sit-down fast-food restaurants. This too relates to the high cost of space. Outdoor shopping is also a norm. Youth-oriented shopping streets (like Carnaby Street and parts of the King's Road) and weekend clothes markets (like Camden Town, said to be the largest street market in Europe) are places for the spectacular congregation of subcultural youth. But limited opening hours mean that these are daytime territories. The indoor malls, vital to the assembly of American youth, are relatively few and far between. Moreover, most close at

5.30 p.m. and are consequently less significant to British youth culture.

Young people go to more films than any other age-group, but the cinema is not central to the distinct culture of British youth (cf. Docherty et al. 1987). Jon Lewis asserts that films are the 'principal mass mediated discourse of youth' and positions rock'n'roll as a 'corollary narrative' (Lewis 1992: 2–3). This may have been true of British youth culture in the 1950s, but it is certainly not the case in the 1990s. The cinema is a significant option for an evening's entertainment, but it only occasionally prevails over youth styles, tastes and activities outside screen time. In the United States, movies are probably more central to youth culture, first, because rates of cinema-going are higher and, second, because Hollywood depicts American youth (cf. Austin 1989). The much less prolific British film industry, however, concentrates on literary adaptations, period and 'art' films rather than 'teenpics' and, as a result, portrays British youth only sporadically and then generally in an historical setting (e.g. *Absolute Beginners* and *Young Soul Rebels*).

The cultural form closest to the lives of the majority of British youth is, in fact, music. Youth subcultures tend to be music subcultures. Youth buy more CDs and tapes and listen to more recorded music than anyone else. Youth television is to a large extent music television, while young men's magazines are predominantly music magazines. Youth leisure and identity often revolve around music. Even market research repeatedly finds that 'young adults are under a certain amount of peer pressure to keep abreast of trends in modern music which forms an important part of their active socializing with people of the same age group attending concerts, dances, pubs, clubs and raves' (Mintel 1993).

One of the main ways in which youth carve out virtual, and claim actual, space is by *filling* it with *their* music. Walls of sound are used to block out the clatter of family and flatmates, to seclude the private space of the bedroom with records and radio and even to isolate 'head space' with personal stereos like the Walkman. The Walkman often affords a feeling of autonomy and empowerment by cutting the wearers off from unwanted communication and distancing them from their surroundings (cf. Hosokawa 1984). For this reason, portable personal stereos are used mainly by young people: 40 per cent of 15–19-year-olds and 22 per cent of 20–24-year-olds listen to Walkmans, compared to only 5 per cent of those over 35 (Mintel 1993).

Conversely, adults can get rid of young people by playing music that grates on their taste. For example, in an attempt to deter teenagers from hanging-out in their stores, the American 7-Eleven chain began playing 'easy listening' music from loudspeakers outside their shops. Having experimented with many tactics, they found this method to be most effective. 'It really worked well,' said a spokeswoman, 'the kids found it was uncool to be anywhere near that kind of elevator music' (The *Guardian* 27 August 1990). Youth tend to have specialist music tastes, with strong preferences for hiphop, indie or hardcore dance. Less than a third of 15–24-year-olds say they really like 'pop', which is not surprising given that it is the overwhelming favourite of children and pre-teens between eight and fourteen (Euromonitor 1989).

As meeting people is a prime motivation behind youthful leisure activities, however, communal listening is still paramount. Previously British youth subcultures might have found their consummate expression in 'live' music events. Although 'live' events still thrive in relation to certain genres, since punk, increasing numbers of British youth cultures have revolved around records rather than performance. This has a complicated history which is recounted in the next chapter. Suffice it to say here that the long-term decline of 'live' music and the slow rise of the discotheque in its many incarnations from record hops to raves has led to a situation whereby the majority of British music cultures could be described as disc cultures.

Comparison with that quintessentially British institution, the public house or pub, is particularly revealing about the appeal of dance clubs. Although young people go to pubs more often than any other place outside the home, pubs have not accrued the same symbolic or social significance as clubs and raves (cf. Mintel 1990). The reasons are manifold. Firstly, there is a simple legal determinant. Since 1953, having a dancefloor of a certain size specification has been the cheapest and surest way to acquire the music and dancing licence that has rendered premises eligible for a late liquor licence. As a result, dance clubs are one of the few spaces open when the pubs close at 11 p.m. in England and Wales and midnight in Scotland.

Alcohol is the most widely used intoxicant of club cultures, if only because it is legal, easily available and inexpensive.* However, 'uppers' like speed and cocaine have long been club drugs, while Ecstasy (sometimes pharmaceutical MDMA, often a cocktail of amphetamines and LSD) was the prototypical drug of the late-eighties/nineties rave scene. Research shows that many clubbers are often polydrug users who tend to abstain from drugs other than marijuana outside clubs and raves (cf. Newcombe 1992). Much like the hippie cultures that Jock Young analysed in the late sixties, it would seem that legal drugs like alcohol are used by clubbers to 'symbolize the achievement of adult status', while illicit drugs are used to signify a rejection of adult culture (Young 1971: 147).

A second reason for the popularity of clubs over pubs is that the latter are continuous with their locality and tend to use the cosy decorative rhetoric of the home (often the Victorian home). Clubs, however, offer other-worldly environments in which to escape; they act as interior havens with such presence that the dancers forget local time and place and sometimes even participate in an imaginary global village of dance sounds. Clubs achieve these effects with loud music, distracting interior design and lighting effects. British clubs rarely have windows through which to look into or out of the club. Classically, they have long winding corridors punctuated by a series of thresholds which separate inside from outside, private from public, the dictates of dance abandon from the routine rules of school, work and parental home.

In fact, so powerful are the feelings of 'liberation' afforded by the dance club that the most common argument about contemporary social dancing is that it empowers girls and women (cf. Blum 1966, Rust 1969, McRobbie 1984, Griffiths 1988, Gotfrit 1988). However, these studies tend to conflate the *feeling* of freedom fostered by the discotheque environment with substantive political rights and freedoms. Youthful discourses about clubbing and raving themselves promote this confusion. The lyrics of dance tracks, which raid the speeches of political figures like Martin Luther King and feature

* Rates of alcohol consumption in Britain are similar to the United States and Canada, slightly lower than Australia and substantially lower than most continental European countries such as France and Germany (see Plant and Plant 1992).

female vocalists singing 'I got the power' and 'I feel free', work to blur the boundaries between affective and political freedom. However, one shouldn't forget that these records tend to be segued between tracks which incite the dancer to 'let the music take control' or recommend that their ultimate goal should be 'total ecstasy'.

A third cause behind the preference for clubs over pubs is that the latter tend to cross age and style boundaries, whereas clubs target youth and keep up with their fads and fashions by frequently changing their music playlists, decor and names. Their adaptability is facilitated by the distinction between 'clubs', which operate on one night of the week, and their 'venues', the licence-holding architectural spaces which they inhabit. By these means, permanent venues attempt to cope with fast-changing fashions, try to avoid identification with any particular scene, prolong their life and defer costly refurbishment.

When raves moved clubs out of traditional dance venues into new sites like disused warehouses, aircraft hangars, municipal pools and tents in farmers' fields, it was partly in pursuit of forbidden and unpredictable senses of place. An organizer of clubs and raves explains the distinction as he perceives it:

> The difference between a rave and a club is the same as [that] between a holiday resort that no one goes to – you've discovered this beautiful place – and going back five years later to find they've built twenty-five high-rise hotels along the beach. Raves explore new territory, while clubs are the same old predictable places. (Leo Paskin, interview: 19 March 1993)

Finally, in addition to having the advantages mentioned above, clubs facilitate the congregation of people with like tastes – be they musical, sartorial or sexual. Clubs have larger catchment areas, narrower demographics and taste specializations than pubs. Through the use of flyers, listings, telephone lines and flyposting, club organizers aim to deliver a particular crowd to a specified venue on a given night. To a large degree, then, club crowds come pre-sorted and pre-selected. The door policies which sometimes restrict entry are simply a last measure. If access to information about the club and taste in music fail to segregate the crowd, the bouncers will ensure the semi-private

Plates 1 and 2 Two 'mould-breaking' raves held just ten miles apart on 26–7 August 1989. (1) Five thousand ravers at World Dance party just before sunrise (2) A few hours later eight hundred clubbers greet the dawn at Boy's Own party near East Grinstead.
(*Photographs*: David Swindells)

nature of these public spaces by refusing admission to 'those who don't belong'.

This institutional state of affairs is arguably the precondition for that oft-celebrated experience of social harmony, the thrill of belonging afforded by clubs. In other words, although some clubbers complain about the gatekeeping practices which assemble, construct and limit the crowd, these practices are undoubtedly a problematic part of their appeal. Moreover, discriminatory admission policies are actually recommended by many local governments as a means of crowd control (and clubs need to heed their suggestions if they want to maintain their licences). For example, the now defunct, left-wing Greater London Council was one of the few local governments actually to publish a code of practice for discotheques. Despite being much out-of-date, it is worth quoting here because of its explicitness:

> The type of person admitted to discos determines the standard conduct on the premises and the likelihood of violence occurring. Licensees should have a clear policy on the *sort of people* they want to see on their premises. Steps should be taken to *exclude anyone considered to be undesirable. Management can turn anyone away without explanation.* If in doubt they should refuse entry.
>   Management should have a clear policy on the following:
> 1. Type of dress permitted
> 2. Searching people at the door.
> 3. Whether there should be an equal balance of the sexes.
> 4. How drunks and *other undesirables* should be excluded.
> 5. Whether to keep a list of barred people.
> 6. Time at which admission to the premises ends.
> 7. Whether to adopt a price policy to discourage people who have been drinking elsewhere from coming towards the end of the disco.
> 8. Whether to fix a minimum age of admission.
>   (GLC 1979: 5; my italics)

Clubs, by popular demand and government recommendation, segregate. This segregation is sometimes condemned for being elitist or racist. At other times it is celebrated for guaranteeing subcultural autonomy and permitting subordinate social groups to control and define their own cultural space. The latter proposition was theorized by subculturalists in the Birmingham tradition as a heroic 'winning of space' and resistant maintenance of subcultural boundaries. In *Resistance Through Rituals,* for example, Clarke et al. contend that subcultures *'win space* for the young: cultural space in the neighbourhood and institutions ... actual room on the street or street corner. They serve to *mark out* and *appropriate* territory in the localities' (Clarke et al. 1976: 46; my italics). While they identify space as an important social issue, there are at least two problems with this formulation. First, ideas of 'winning' and defiantly 'appropriating' mystify more than they reveal. To a large extent, places are 'won' when social groups are recognized as profitable markets. Venue owners hire club organizers (or club organizers hire venues) to target, promote and advertise to both 'rebellious' and 'conforming' youth. Crucially, in the case of dance clubs and raves, their marketing has been most successful when youth feel they have 'won' it for themselves. Second, discotheques may house alternative cultures, but they tend to duplicate structures of exclusion and stratification found elsewhere. Black men, in particular, find themselves barred or, more usually, subject to maximum quotas. This ongoing fact should not be forgotten in the face of the utopian 'everybody welcome' discourses in which dance clubs are intermittently enveloped. For example, despite their discourses of liberty, fraternity and harmony, raves had distinct demographics – chiefly white, working-class, heterosexual and dominated by the lads. Raves may have involved large numbers of people and they may have trespassed on new territories, finding new spaces for youthful leisure, but they did little to rearrange its social affairs.

As a semi-private, musical environment which adapts to diverse fashions, proffers escape (sometimes with added transgressional thrills) and regulates who's in and who's out of the crowd, the dance club fulfils many youth cultural agendas. Like youth subcultures themselves, the institution has developed since the Second World War and multiplied in kind and style since the seventies. In accommodating the social activities of a few fleeting years of youth, discotheques have become a lasting cultural establishment. However, the popularity of the discotheque was not automatic. For years, it was considered a second-rate institution, a lowly entertainment, a cheap night out. The next chapter considers the slow process by which the discotheque distinguished itself.

2

Authenticities from Record Hop to Raves (and the History of Disc Culture)

The Authentication of a Mass Medium

Authenticity is arguably the most important value ascribed to popular music. It is found in different kinds of music by diverse musicians, critics and fans, but it is rarely analysed and is persistently mystified. Music is perceived as authentic when it *rings true* or *feels real*, when it has *credibility* and comes across as *genuine*. In an age of endless representations and global mediation, the experience of musical authenticity is perceived as a cure both for alienation (because it offers feelings of community) and dissimulation (because it extends a sense of the really 'real'). As such, it is valued as a balm for media fatigue and as an antidote to commercial hype. In sum, authenticity is to music what happy endings are to Hollywood cinema – the reassuring reward for suspending disbelief.

While authenticity is attributed to many different sounds, between the mid-fifties and mid-eighties, its main site was the live gig. In this period, 'liveness' dominated notions of authenticity. The essence or truth of music was located in its performance by musicians in front of an audience. Interestingly, the ascent of 'liveness' as a distinct musical value coincided with the decline of performance as both the dominant medium of music and the prototype for recording. Only when records began to be taken for music itself (rather than as 'records' in the strict sense of the word) did performed music really start to exploit the specificities of its 'liveness', emphasizing presence, visibility and spontaneity.

In fact, the demand for live gigs was arguably roused by the proliferation of recordings, which had the effect of intensifying the desire for the 'original' performer. Steve Connor contends that 'increasingly high fidelity reproduction stimulates the itch for more, for closer reproductions, and the yearning to move closer to the original' (Connor 1987: 130). Similarly, Andrew Goodwin argues that 'aura' has been transferred from the art object to its maker; it has taken up residence in the physical presence of the star (Goodwin 1990: 269). Walter Benjamin, the theorist who first explored this terrain in the 1930s, hoped that 'the work of art in the age of mechanical reproduction' would be liberated from this kind of worship. He believed that the awe reserved for unique objects would decline in a democratized world of mass-produced cultural goods. However, he knew this process would be difficult, for 'cult value does not give way without resistance' and was even suspicious that it would 'retire into an ultimate retrenchment: the human countenance' (Benjamin 1955/1970: 227–8).

What Benjamin did not and could not foresee was the formation of new authenticities specific to recorded entertainment, for these were dependent on historical changes in the circumstances of both the production and consumption of music. Initially, records transcribed, reproduced, copied, represented, derived from and sounded like performances. But, as the composition of popular music increasingly took place in the studio rather than, say, off stage, records came to carry sounds and musics that neither originated in nor referred to actual performances. In the 1960s, with the increased use of magnetic tape, producers began to edit their wares into 'records of ideal, not real, events' (Frith 1987a: 65). Moreover, in the 1970s and 1980s, new instruments such as synthesizers and samplers meant that sounds were recorded from the start. Accordingly, the record shifted from being a secondary or derivative form to a primary, original one.

In the process of becoming originals, records accrued their own authenticities. Recording technologies did not, therefore, corrode or demystify 'aura' as much as disperse and re-locate it. Degrees of aura came to be attributed to *new, exclusive* and *rare* records. In becoming the source of sounds, records underwent the mystification usually reserved for *unique* art objects. Under these conditions, it would seem that the mass-produced cultural commodity is not necessarily imitative or artificial, but plausibly archetypal and authentic. These values are related to but different from the 'mystical veil' or 'magic' described by Marx in his short essay, 'The fetishism of commodities and the secret thereof'. Commodity fetishism would seem to account accurately for the obsessions of record collectors who call themselves 'vinyl junkies', but it does not explain the inversion of original and copy.

The proliferation of 'cover' bands from the 1950s to the mid-1970s probably best demonstrates this transposition of values. These live groups reproduced the tunes of the latest hit records and were evaluated on the basis of their proximity to the original record, hence their choice of names like 'Disc Doubles' and 'Personality Platters'. By the eighties, these types of rock and pop cover bands were all but defunct, being superseded for the most part by records and to a lesser extent by tribute bands which specialized in the repertoire of specific dead or disbanded acts. (For example, the Australian Abba imitators, Bjorn Again, who played more university gigs in Britain than any other live act in the 1992–93 academic year, emulate not just records but the clothing and dance styles depicted on album covers and in film and video clips.)

Changes in music consumption were also essential to the development of the new authenticities of the disc. Records were not automatically absorbed into a static system called popular culture. Nor did they simply replace performance just because they resembled and reproduced music. The public acceptance of records for dancing was slow, selective and generational. For many years, records were considered a form of entertainment inferior to performance; they were not regarded as the 'real' thing or as capable of delivering an authentic experience of musical community. Records had to undergo a complex process of assimilation or integration, which involved transformations in the circulation, structure, meaning and value of both records and music cultures. This gradual enculturation of records is signalled by the changing names of the institution in which people danced to discs. The *record hops, disc sessions* and *discotheques* of the 1950s and 1960s specifically refer to the recorded nature of their entertainment. In the 1970s, transition is signalled with the shortened, familiar *disco*. In the 1980s, with *clubs* and *raves*, enculturation is complete and it is 'live' venues that must announce their difference.

The ultimate end of a technology's enculturation is authentication. In other words, a musical form is authentic when it is rendered essential to subculture or integral to community. Equally, technologies are *naturalized* by enculturation. At first, new technologies seem foreign, artificial, inauthentic. Once absorbed into culture, they seem indigenous and organic. Simon Frith has been most productive in analysing the discourses of subcultural authenticity crucial to music culture (cf. Frith 1981c, 1986, 1988a). Frith argues that new music technologies tend to be opposed to nature and community. They are considered false and falsifying and, as such, threaten the authenticity or the 'truth of music' (Frith 1986: 265). Behind the discursive oppositions, however, lurks the fact that technological developments make new concepts of authenticity possible. In the early days of the microphone, for example, crooners were said to have a pseudo-public presence and to betray false emotions. Later, however, the extended intimacies of the microphone became a guarantor of new forms of authenticity; 'it made stars knowable, by shifting conventions of personality, making singers sound sexy in new ways . . . moving the focus from the song to the singer' (Frith 1986: 270). Similarly, when electric guitars were first introduced, they were said to alienate music from its folk roots. Later, however, when they were fully integrated into rock culture, the sound of the electric guitar became *the* seal of rock credibility. Records have taken an analogous, if more circuitous route, to become an authentic musical instrument of club and rave culture.

In the 1990s, records have been enculturated within the night life of British dance clubs to the extent that it makes sense to talk about *disc cultures* whose values are markedly different from those of live music cultures. What authenticates contemporary dance cultures is the buzz or energy which results from the interaction of records, DJ and crowd. 'Liveness' is displaced from the stage to the dancefloor, from the worship of the performer to a veneration of 'atmosphere' or 'vibe'. The DJ and dancers share the spotlight as *de facto* performers; the crowd becomes a self-conscious cultural phenomenon – one which generates moods immune to reproduction, for which you have to be there. This is even more pronounced when it comes to raves, the latest incarnation of the discotheque, which are conceived as one-off rather than weekly events, some of which have attained the status of unique happenings on a scale that was once the lone preserve of the live rock festival.

Subcultural authenticities are often inflected by issues of nation, race and ethnicity. Gage Averill examines the significance of being *'natif natal'* or native born and truly national to the perceived authenticity of Haitian music (cf. Averill 1989). While Paul Gilroy considers the trans-Atlantic circulation of discourses about racial roots and 'authentic blackness' to the meaning of post-war popular music (cf. Gilroy 1993). So, black British disc cultures often emphasize the strength of community ties outside the dance club, seeing the 'vibe' as an affirmation of a politicized black identity. Sexuality similarly informs and inflects disc cultural values. In gay clubs, which have long been spaces to escape straight surveillance, the celebratory expression of one's 'true' sexuality often overrides other authenticities.

Between the production and consumption of records discussed here, two kinds of authenticity are at play. The first sort of authenticity involves issues of originality and aura; this value is held most strongly by DJs. The second kind of authenticity is about being natural to the community or organic to subculture; this is the more widespread ideal. These two kinds of authenticity can be related to two basic definitions of culture: the first draws upon definitions of culture as art, the second relates to culture in the anthropological sense of a 'whole way of life' (cf. Williams 1961 and 1976). With live music ideologies, the artistic and subcultural authenticities collide (and are often confused) at the point of authorship. Artistic authenticity is anchored by the performing author in so far as s/he is assumed to be the unique origin of the sound, while subcultural authenticity is grounded in the performer in so far as s/he represents the community. Within disc cultures, however, the two authenticities diverge. The record is an authentic source and the crowd makes it a 'living' culture. DJs bridge the gap in that they are professional collectors and players of 'originals' as well as mediators and orchestrators of the crowd, but not to the extent that they seem to embody authenticity (like live music performers).

Live and disc authenticities, though distinct, still have a lot in common. Both emphasize the cultural importance of being genuine and sincere and both seek to elevate their cultures above the realm of mass culture, media and commerce. Moreover, much popular music is entangled with both sets of values. Bands like the Rolling Stones are caught up in the logic of disc culture even if the dominant strains of their myth are about Mick Jagger as dramatic performer, Keith Richards as virtuoso guitarist and a legacy of gigging and live stadium shows. Similarly, even hardcore disc cultures, like house or techno, sometimes espouse residual variants of live ideology, celebrating star producer-DJs and singing divas. Some clubs and raves include 'personal appearances' (or 'PAs') by these dance 'stars', while others have made a purist selling point of the fact that they have 'no PAs'. Live and recorded authenticities are therefore not mutually exclusive categories, but part of a continuum.

The development of disc cultures, the enculturation of records for dancing and the cultural ramifications of the supremacy of recording are the key issues addressed in this chapter. Most academic work on recording technology examines its effects on music production, in either its industrial or artistic guise. The main currents of debate consider whether it is democratizing or hierarchizing, rationalizing or disruptive of production processes, commodifying or challenging to legal definitions of property, inhibiting or

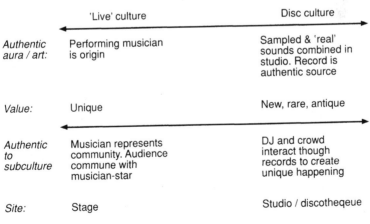

	'Live' culture	Disc culture
Authentic aura / art:	Performing musician is origin	Sampled & 'real' sounds combined in studio. Record is authentic source
Value:	Unique	New, rare, antique
Authentic to subculture	Musician represents community. Audience commune with musician-star	DJ and crowd interact though records to create unique happening
Site:	Stage	Studio / discotheqeue

Figure 2 Axes of authenticity

enabling of new creativities and sites of authorship.* While this chapter touches upon these issues, it concentrates on the less investigated relationship between recording technology and consumption.

The following chapter is divided into five sections, each of which recounts the history of the enculturation and ultimate authentication of records from a different angle. The first section is a political economy (an analysis of the production of music consumption) which traces the economically-determined routes by which records entered the field of popular entertainments, tracking the rise of records and decline of performance in certain kinds of time and place. It also considers the obstacles put in the path of this 'industrial revolution' by the Musicians' Union, with its exploitation of rights' legislation and campaign to keep music 'live'.

The rest of the chapter considers the integration of records into music culture from more social and cultural perspectives. The second section examines how the social spaces of dancing changed to accommodate recorded music. It considers how the new social alliances and architectural designs contributed to the eventual subcultural authenticity of records. The third focuses on how record formats were modified in response to their increasing public use, detailing the formatting experiments of the 1960s, the development of twelve-inch singles in the 1970s and finally concentrating on the changing status of the DJ. The fourth section explores the specificities of recording and the kinds of music most at home with the medium. It considers how changes in the way popular music was recorded and disseminated contributed to transformations in the meaning and value of records and ponders why certain music genres came to be perceived as quintessentially and authentically recorded while others did not. The final section looks at changes to the shape and meaning of the live gig during the period in question. It identifies two seemingly contradictory tendencies. On the one hand, performances increasingly exploit those features which might distinguish them from records, retrieving spontaneity, making a

---

* This rich body of work includes: Cutler 1984, Durant 1991, Eisenberg 1987, Frith 1987a and 1987b and 1988b and 1992a, Gelatt 1977, Goodwin 1990 and 1992a, Grossberg 1992, Hayward 1991, Kealy 1979, Laing 1986 and 1990, Langlois 1992, Middleton 1990, Mowitt 1987, Negus 1992, Porcello 1991, Qualen 1986, Read and Welch 1976, Straw 1990, Struthers 1987, Theberge 1989 and 1991.

theatrical happening, magnifying the presence and personality of the star. On the other hand, many performers adopted high technologies, pre-recording and even lip-synching to entertain the massive audiences they had accumulated through records, radio and other media.

Until recently, media scholars tended to overlook enculturation. Marshall McLuhan, for instance, does not identify the process *per se* because he sees media technologies as already cybernetic 'extensions of man'. His analysis starts with the natural and human qualities attributed to technologies once they are fully enculturated, but doesn't problematize them (cf. McLuhan 1964). Jean Baudrillard, to give another example, ignores the distinct statuses and effects of techniques of reproduction because he assumes that technologies which *simulate* are not in need of any form of *assimilation*. Although well-known in anthropology, the issue of enculturation is relatively new to Media Studies, having been put on the agenda by the collection, *Consuming Technologies*, which addresses the integration of media and information technologies into the home (cf. Silverstone and Hirsch 1992). In their opening essay, Silverstone, Hirsch and Morley identify four overlapping phases in the process of a technology's integration into the home: appropriation (by ownership); objectification (within the decorative space of the home); incorporation (into the temporal structure of everyday lives); and conversion (into topics of conversation and cultural bonds) (cf. Silverstone et al. 1992). These categories can be used, by analogy, to clarify important dynamics in the enculturation of records into the public sphere of dancing. For example, I examine something akin to 'incorporation' into temporal structures (in discussing the development of new kinds of dance event) and 'objectification' in spatial structures (in relation to the interior design of discotheques). Moreover, their category of 'conversion' is an important dimension of what I include under the more encompassing historical but more specifically aesthetic category of 'authentication'.

One needs to be wary of superimposing models generated by study of domestic contexts on to the public domain, particularly in light of the fact that one of the main hypotheses about recording technology is that it necessarily privatizes or domesticates music consumption. In his book *The Recording Angel*, for example, Evan Eisenberg reduces his otherwise compelling argument about the art of 'phonography' because, for him, 'a record is heard in the home' and its tendency is essentially private (Eisenberg 1987: 99). Shuhei Hosokawa's discussion of the Walkman, for another example, slips into positioning the personal stereo as the culmination of recording's relentless logic of individuation (cf. Hosokawa 1984). By ignoring broader contexts, these theorists fail to see the contradictory effects of music technology and the diverse significance of recorded music. Recorded music is as much a feature of public houses, shops, factories, lifts, restaurants and karaoke bars as it is an attribute of the private home.

Another hypothesis against which this chapter offers substantial evidence is that records engender cultural homogeneity. Recording technology informed Theodor Adorno's conviction that popular music was characterized by a standardization that aimed at standard reactions (Adorno 1968/1988). While disciples of Adorno, like Jacques Attali, continue to contend that mass-reproduced music is 'a powerful factor in consumer integration, interclass levelling, cultural homogenization. It becomes a factor in centralization, cultural normalization, and the disappearance of distinctive cultures' (Attali 1985: 111). However, the discotheque is an institution which caters for neither individual nor mass consumption, but the collective consumption of the small group. Rather than homogenizing tastes, dance clubs nurture cultural segmentation.

Authenticity is regularly mentioned in studies of popular music but (other than the studies already cited) it tends to be discussed in terms of nebulous free-floating beliefs. Even when it is subject to thorough examination, it can still be indeterminate and unanchored. But these cryptic cultural values have material foundations; they relate to the economic, social, cultural and media conditions in which they were generated. The main aim of this chapter is, therefore, to ground the changing values of authenticity in transformed processes of music production and consumption.

Industrial Forces, Musician Resistance and 'Live' Ideology

Records were selectively enculturated into music culture: they moved from the private to the public sphere, from background accompaniment to specially featured entertainment, from minor occasions to momentous events, from modest locations to prominent places. Their movement is partly explained by an economic logic by which they replaced performance in the times and places with the youngest patrons and lowest budgets. Their progressive colonization of public spaces, however, was actively fought by the Musicians' Union which was the first (and for a long time the only) body to see the practice as a serious cultural development. At the outset, the Union wanted to eradicate the practice; then it was satisfied with regulating it; later, it was appeased by receiving a percentage of the millions of pounds accrued in performance rights; finally, it resigned itself to the fact that recorded music was what many people wanted. Throughout this forty-year period, however, the Union reinforced its legislative efforts with 'propaganda' about the superiority and authenticity of live music. Where live music used to animate social occasions and cultural events of all kinds, recorded music now often performs the function. As a result, musician performances have declined in number, and appeal to a much smaller segment of the population than they once did.

When sound recording technology was introduced in the late 1870s, Thomas Edison proposed many uses for the new invention, few of which suggested its entertainment value. His recommendations revolved around the notion of a 'talking machine' which could facilitate dictation, record telephone messages, make books for the blind or create family albums for posterity (cf. Read and Welch 1976). Edison mentioned, but did not give much credence to, the phonograph's potential as a 'music box'. Within thirty years, however, music would be the staple noise of recording. Dance crazes, in particular, stimulated the early record business and repeatedly revived it in times of recession. In the 1910s, for example, dance instructors like Vernon and Irene Castle were important advisers to record company Artist and Repertoire departments (known as 'A&R', the division which decides who to sign and what material to record). They supervised records catering to the mania for tangos, one-steps, waltzes and walking dances. Even on the eve of the First World War in 1914, Columbia's and Victor's dance cylinders and discs were selling well (Gelatt 1977: 189).

From its inception, then, one of the main activities of the record industry was the provision of music for dancing, but it was mainly devised for home consumption, for practising dance steps and throwing parties in the private sphere. Throughout the 1920s, sound quality improved, particularly as a result of the introduction of electrical recording. This, combined with the increasing variety of musical material, singers and orchestras offered on record, made the medium more attractive. In the United States, the public performance of records on coin-operated phonographs or 'juke-boxes' kept the industry afloat when domestic sales dried up during the Depression. To 'juke' or 'jook' is an Afro-American vernacular expression meaning 'to dance' (cf. Hazzard-Gordon 1990). That the coin-operated phonograph took this name illustrates the importance of dancing to American out-of-home record-play at this time. In the UK, however, where the Depression took a different form, the juke-box did not significantly penetrate the public sphere until the fifties and sixties, and recordings did not tend to be an attracting feature of out-of-home entertainment.

During the twenties, radio quickly became a dominant source of music, most of which was broadcast live. The most popular programmes featured big dance bands who played for an audience of ballroom dancers at the same time as playing for those at home (cf. Frith 1987a). Record companies saw radio as a problem of competition and so did not send their recordings to stations for promotional purposes. When the first BBC radio programme devoted to records began in July 1927, however, its impact on sales was so obvious that record companies began to actively pursue air-play to the extent of buying plays on commercial continental stations like Radio Luxembourg. By the 1930s, argues Frith, radio was central to the new processes of record-selling and star-making which came with the shift in the commodity status of music:

> The form of that commodity was irrevocably altered from live to recorded performance, from sheet music to disc, from public appearance to public broadcast – and its control passed from one set of institutions (music publishers, music hall and concert promoters, artists and agents) to another (record companies, the BBC, stars and managers). (Frith 1987a: 288)

While it is undeniable that recording took over from publishing as the leading arbiter of musical taste and style, some qualification is required of a historical shift 'from public appearance to public broadcast'. Radio unseated the primacy of the family piano rather than challenging the dance hall; it rearranged domestic consumption (in a way the gramophone had not done) rather than instigating a massive withdrawal into the home.

During the thirties, recorded music was peripheral to out-of-home entertainment with one crucial exception – the cinema. Before the 'talkies', a large portion of Britain's professional musicians were employed to accompany silent films. But within eighteen months of the box-office success of *The Jazz Singer* (1927, the same year as the BBC's first record show), most of these musicians were out of a job and performance had received its first great blow. The development was crucial for the record industry as movies would become a vehicle for the international promotion of records. In the fifties, for example, the cinema would bring rock'n'roll attitudes and music to Britain with the film *Blackboard Jungle* and its closing track 'Rock around the Clock' by Bill Haley and the Comets. By the late fifties, the mutual marketing of movies and discs would be so entrenched that the album charts would be full of film soundtracks. As 45 singles were the format bought by youth in the fifties, the soundtrack albums were not predominantly rock'n'roll. The biggest sellers – *South Pacific* (1948), *Love Me or Leave Me* (1955), *Breakfast at Tiffany's* (1962) and *The Sound of Music* (1960) – still tended towards 'family entertainment'. In the sixties, a fair portion of both Elvis Presley's and the Beatles' albums were marketed as 'original soundtracks' e.g. Elvis's *GI Blues* (1960) and *Blue Hawaii* (1961), the Beatles' *A Hard Day's Night* (1964) and *Help* (1965). By the end of the sixties, the best-selling soundtracks would also be youth-oriented owing to the juvenilization of film audiences (cf. Doherty 1988). and the rising popularity of the album format amongst youth. The success of Simon and Garfunkel's sound track for *The Graduate* in 1968 might be seen as the turning-point here.

Aside from cinemas, recorded music could be heard in pubs, restaurants and coffee bars. As early as the 1930s, the record industry began to take a financial interest in the public performance of its product. The Copyright Act of 1911 was regarded as protecting manufacturers against the unauthorized *copying*, as opposed to *playing*, of their sounds; it established a reproduction, but not a performance, right. Nevertheless, in the early thirties, record companies started to affix labels stating that the record should not be publicly performed and in 1934 they sued Cawardine's Tea Rooms in Bristol for copyright infringement, winning the rights to the sound contained in their recordings, and set up Phonographic Performance Limited (PPL) to license the broadcast and public performance of their records.

Until the Second World War, records tended to provide background accompaniment to leisure activities; they were rarely the main entertainment at large public events. Owing in part to further improvements in technology, but primarily to the devastated condition of the British economy, the public performance of records increased dramatically during and after the War. The Musicians' Union (MU) was particularly concerned about the use of records for dancing as the bulk of its membership worked in dance bands. In 1949, the cover of its in-house journal, *Musicians' Union Report*, bore the watchwords 'Recorded Music or You!' and inside the Secretary General warned:

> Probably the greatest threat from recorded music to the employment opportunities of our members exists in the field of casual dance engagements. There is abundant evidence that in recent years more and more dance promoters have availed themselves of the services of the public address engineer. In almost every town the man who runs the radio shop, or specializes in the provision of public address equipment, will undertake to supply recorded music for dances or other social events at a small proportion of the fee a good band would charge. (*Musicians' Union Report* September–October 1949)

At about this time, the Musicians' Union came to the first of many agreements with Phonographic Performance Limited (PPL) to attempt to combat the public use of records. As musicians were hired *to perform* by dancehall operators and *to record* by record companies, the Union was able to impede the use of records by the former through the exploitation of rights's agreements with the latter. Since its formation, PPL had been authorizing the use of its records simply in exchange for a licence fee. From 1946 on, however, it began licensing establishments on the condition that 'records not be used in substitution of a band or orchestra or in circumstances where it would be reasonable to claim that a band or orchestra should be employed.' (Musicians' Union Conference Report 1949).*

Licensing restrictions were the driving force behind one of the first examples of the production of records specifically for public dancing. In 1950–51, Danceland Records produced ballroom numbers in standard arrangements on 78s. The objective of their records was not to provide continuous music nor fill the dancefloor (which would be the case with later formats) but simply to circumvent existing copyright law. They advertised their records for use in ballrooms, hotels, theatres and skating rinks and urged proprietors of these establishments to join the fight against PPL licensing restrictions. (*Musicians' Union Report* 1951). As their recording sessions were held in Mecca ballrooms, the MU suspected that the dancehall chain financed the project.

In 1956, a new Copyright Act clarified the properties of the recording. It re-enacted the rights given to the record companies, defining the copyright in sound recordings as distinct from the copyright in musical works,† and reiterated the three acts which required a PPL licence: making copies of records, playing them in public and broadcasting them. The Musicians' Union was unhappy with the act for several reasons. First, the record companies maintained exclusive copyright and only volunteered royalties to the MU. Second, although it gave PPL the right to set up musician employment restrictions, it also established a tribunal to which users of copyright material (like broadcasters and dancehall owners) could protest. Third, the new Act permitted the free use of

---

* Differences of intention and interpretation arose between the trade union and the record industry association almost immediately. The Union saw the agreement as part of an ambitious initiative whereby 'the performance of every record [could] be controlled and ultimately used for entertainment in the home' (Musicians' Union Conference Report 1951). PPL, on the other hand, favoured less constraint because increased use of their copyright meant more income for their members. Typical of their compromises was their agreement about the practice of playing records between band sets. The MU wanted no recorded interval. PPL thought this unreasonable. They eventually agreed that future licences would limit recorded intermissions to a total of twenty minutes – a stipulation that would be difficult to enforce (Musicians' Union Conference Report 1954).

† The copyright in sound recording is defined as the 'aggregate of the sounds embodied in, and capable of being reproduced by the means of a record' (Copyright Act 1956).

Plate 3 One of the first instances of records made specifically for the public dancefloor. In 1950 'Danceland Records', allegedly payrolled by Mecca Ballrooms, advertised the sovereignty and savings that their releases afforded dancehall operators.

(Reproduced by kind permission of the Musicians' Union)

records 'at any premises where persons reside or sleep' as long as no special price was charged for admission and at non-profit clubs and societies whose main objectives were charitable, religious or educational (*Musicians' Union Report* October 1956).

Many dance clubs came to exploit these loopholes. For instance, the Whisky-a-Gogo in Wardour Street (which, in the 1980s, abbreviated its name to the WAG) claimed exemption from the licence fee on the grounds that the club was the headquarters of an international students' association. The club's solicitors drew up the charter of the so-called 'Students' United Social Association' which included the following tongue-in-cheek objectives: 'to promote opportunities for recreation, social intercourse and refreshment for foreign and English students . . . to advance . . . good international relations between young persons . . . to assist the promotion of social contacts for foreign students with English-speaking persons . . . ' (*Musicians' Union Report* 1963).

Other small clubs dodged PPL licences or their conditions of use in a variety of ways. For example, the Saddle Room, once described as the 'most fashionable discotheque in London', full of people from the rag trade and 'most noticeably, a great many fashion models' was licensed by PPL on the condition that it hire a trio of musicians, but musicians never actually performed at the club (Melly 1970: 63). But, these individual cases were generally too difficult and expensive to prosecute, so the MU focused its attention on dancehall chains like Mecca and Top Rank where employment and licence fees could be gained *en masse*.

During the fifties, the Musicians' Union started calling for a propaganda campaign against records which would attack their moral and aesthetic inferiority, draw on new notions of live music and strengthen its position with PPL. The term 'live' entered the lexicon of music appreciation only in the fifties. As more and more of the music heard was recorded, however, records become synonymous with music itself. It was only music's marginalized *other* – performance – which had to speak its difference with a qualifying adjective.

At first, the word 'live' was short for 'living' and modified 'musicians' as in the following passage: 'during and since the war, recorded music has been used more and more instead of "live" instrumentalists' (*Musicians' Union Report* 1949). Later it referred to music itself and quickly accumulated connotations which took it beyond the denotative meaning of performance. First, 'live music' affirmed that performance was not obsolete or exhausted, but full of energy and potential. Recorded music, by contrast, was dead, a decapitated 'music without musicians' (*Musicians' Union Report* 1956). Second, the term also asserted that performance was the 'real live thing'. Liveness became the truth of music, the seeds of genuine culture. Records, by contrast, were false prophets of pseudo-culture.

Through a series of condensations, then, the expression 'live music' gave positive valuation to and became generic for performed music. It soaked up the aesthetic and ethical connotations of life-versus-death, human-versus-mechanical, creative-versus-imitative. Furthermore, Union discussions about live music were overlaid with a Cold War rhetoric typical of the time. Records were a 'grave threat', a 'serious danger' and an 'ever-present menace' to the livelihood of the musician. Recording technology was a bomb – a set of inventions which could bring about professional death: 'The musician may well become extinct and music may cease to be written' (*Musicians' Union Report* 1961). The term 'live' suggested that performance was fragile in its vitality and in need of protection.

The ideology of 'liveness' was one of the Union's principal strategies 'to combat the menace' of recorded music. The Union initiated its 'live' music campaign in the fifties, adopted the slogan 'Keep Music Live' in 1963 and appointed a full-time official to oversee the project in 1965. Invoking a difficult combination of aesthetic, environmental and trade union concerns, the campaign was meant 'to convince the community of the essential human value of live performance' and of 'the social good [generated when] the public has more contact with the people who make music' (*The Musician* August 1971; *Music Week* 7 January 1978).

It is tempting to draw parallels between the views of the Musicians' Union and Jean Baudrillard's treatises on hyperreality and the death of culture. For both, culture is dying on the altar of techniques of reproduction. For Baudrillard, images are the 'murderers of their own model' (Baudrillard 1983a: 10). For live music advocates, recording is slowly killing its original, performance: 'technology can destroy music itself' (*The Musician* 1963). Just as

Baudrillard describes the 'precession of simulacra' as the creation of images that no longer reflect the real but engender it, so musicians complained about the ability of recording to make more sounds and styles than were physically possible for a band. Baudrillard and the Musicians' Union held similar notions of *real culture* but, faced with its death, the French theorist chose to write its obituary, while the British Union lobbied for protective legislation and disseminated propaganda.

The Union's promotion of live music was tangibly hampered by the musical taste (and anti-mass culture discourses) that predominated among its members. For a long time, many members refused to pander to 'gimmick-ridden rock'n'roll rubbish' and couldn't understand why teenagers didn't appreciate 'good jazz' (*Musicians' Union Report* 1959). The exigencies of Union taste even allowed for musicians in 'beat groups' to receive lower rates of pay, as their agreements with Mecca and Rank referred only to 'musicians employed by dance band leaders' until well into the 1960s (*Musicians' Union Report* January 1965). The American Federation of Musicians (AFM), which conducted a similar 'Live Music' campaign, seemed to be less caught up in a canon of good music. AFM local branches, for example, offered workshops to keep musicians up-to-date with latest dance music fads (like the Frug) and experimented with event formats (like 'Live-o-theques') (*Billboard* 24 April 1965). The British Union, however, did not just champion performance over recording, it tended to promote certain kinds of music over others. Their discourses and contractual agreements actually reinforced the 'natural' association of certain music genres, like rock'n'roll and later soul, with records.*

The ideology of live music was eventually adopted by rock culture (cf. Frith 1981a), becoming most strident in reaction to the attention disco music brought to discotheques in the mid-seventies, when tensions erupted into what was effectively a taste war. Discos were attacked for epitomizing the death of music culture. They were said to be artificial environments offering superficial and manufactured experiences: 'a slick moving conveyor belt of the best

* In Britain, the music outside PPL copyright control was for many years that of foreign producers and included 'large quantities of soul records which presented particular problems in some types of discotheque use' (MU Conference Report 1971: 46).

product from the world's rock factories, relayed by the finest amplification, with a deejay and lights to inject further doses of adrenalin' (*Melody Maker* 30 August 1975). While the American 'disco sucks' discourse had evident homophobic and racist motivation (cf. Marsh 1985; Smucker 1980), British anti-disco sentiments are more directly derived from classist convictions about mindless masses and generational conflict about the poor taste of the young. This has to do with the disparate audiences with which the same music was affiliated in the two countries. In Britain, discotheques and disco music had a huge straight white working-class following and were not, as they were in the USA, strongly identified with gay, black and Hispanic minorities.

It is difficult to evaluate the effects of the 'Keep Music Live' campaign because, until well into the 1970s, musicians were preferred to records by most people anyway. In 1962, Kevin Donovan opened a discotheque called The Place in Hanley near Stoke-on-Trent. Although it had a capacity of five hundred, it received between ten and fifty patrons a night until Donovan started booking live bands. As the owner explains:

> The good people of Stoke-on-Trent had decided there was no point in paying to hear records which were played on the wireless for nothing . . . We were taught our first major lesson in promotion – give the public what THEY want. If you want to advance your own ideas, these must be solidly hooked to an established and accepted aspect in order to attract any audience . . . The format was decided, we would become a Discotheque which also provided Live music. (Donovan 1981: 14)

In general, records infiltrated the public sphere from the least profitable to the most lucrative hours of the week. In the 1940s, it became standard for records to be played between the main band's sets (replacing the second support band) at all but the most affluent or 'muso' of dance gatherings. In the early 1950s, the public use of records was facilitated by the introduction of vinyl 33 and 45 rpm records which were lighter, more portable, less breakable and had superior sound quality to 78s. This did not cause, but probably aided the proliferation of lunchtime rock'n'roll record hops. In the 1960s, most disc sessions, whether in live venues or discotheques, took place early in the week. For example, in 1963, The Scene, a well-known Mod discotheque, had exclusively recorded entertainment ('Guy Stevens' R&B Record Night' and 'Off the Record with Sandra') only on Monday, Tuesday and Wednesday nights, while they featured live bands at the weekends (*New Record Mirror* 2 November 1963).

In the 1970s, records began to dominate the 'prime time' of out-of-home entertainment on Friday and Saturday nights. Moreover, in certain circumstances, live music effectively became the interval between record sets. For example, musicians on the Northern Soul disco circuit tell of being hired to play very early or very late in the evening (when the venue was empty) to fulfil PPL licence agreements. When they did play at the height of the evening, however, patrons used the performance as an opportunity to take a break from dancing (Alan Durant in conversation, 1989). By the mid-1980s, the temporal organization of performance and recorded entertainment had been reversed: live music was relegated to the beginning of the week when profit margins were not expected to be as high, while DJs and discs were the main attraction at the weekends.

Just as dancing to discs progressed through the structure of weekly leisure time, so records were selectively assimilated by diverse premises at different rates. Records first gained a foothold in schools, community centres, youth clubs, town halls and other locations with low budgets. From non-profit premises, records moved to commercial ones – starting out small in basements, as extensions of coffee bars and as additional rooms to established venues. Only in the 1970s and 1980s, did the leisure chains start converting their ballrooms into large-scale discotheques.

By substantially cutting costs, records improved the profit margins and turnover of dance establishments internationally. Through the 1960s and 1970s, this was regular 'news' in relevant trade magazines: for example, when Gabriel's Lounge in Detroit installed a discotheque, the club was able to 'sell drinks at only a nickel above other neighbourhood tavern prices, but fifteen and twenty cents below prices charged by clubs with live entertainment' (*Billboard* 20 March 1965). In fact, one juke-box manufacturer ran a hard-sell advertising campaign stating that they 'pre-programmed profits into their records' (Seeburg ads in *Billboard* 1965). In the United States, this was not much of an exaggeration. In 1965, *Billboard* reported that juke-box collections amounted to $500 million, half the total of television billings but substantially more than the $275 million motion picture receipts and the $237 million in radio billings (*Billboard* 15 May 1965). However, PPL licensing restrictions delayed investment in technology in Britain, hence, fewer juke-boxes and house sound-systems were installed and 'mobile discotheques' were heavily relied on until the late 1970s. But the expense of live music was not only one of musician labour, it was also one of the investment in the technologies of 'liveness', of instruments, amplification, MIDI and sound engineer controls, and in the crews of roadies and technicians needed to move and operate it. From this point of view, discotheques, even lavish ones, are a rational capital investment.

The big boom in investment in permanent discotheque facilities followed the top forty chart achievements of disco – a music made specifically for discotheques which signalled the extensive and durable presence of the institution. In March 1978, London's main listing magazine, *Time Out*, began publishing a weekly listing of discotheques, 'evaluating the music, the ambience, the prices and people' (*Time Out* 24–30 March 1978). Much of this activity took place in the wake of the phenomenal sales of the *Saturday Night Fever* soundtrack album, which was the biggest selling album of all time (until 1983 when it was superseded by Michael Jackson's *Thriller*). It is telling that the film premiered in Cannes, not at the film festival in May but at MIDEM, the annual international record industry convention, in January 1978. This was a music-led media package. After the non-specialist media exposure the genre received on the coat-tails of the film, discotheques were hailed as a 'revolution' rather than a 'fad' in entertainment for the first time. As Britain's main trade paper, *Music Week*, wrote in 1978:

> the disco revolution in America has not been equalled since rock exploded in the fifties – and it will happen here too . . . the rock takeover, the disco takeover . . . We're in the midst of a British club boom. More discos have opened their doors in the past month, it seems, than during the rest of the year. Many are following an All-American format. (*Music Week* 16 December 1978)

Leisure chains (like Rank, Mecca and First Leisure) and breweries (like Whitbread) adopted rolling programmes of refitting and refurbishing (cf. *Disco International* 1976–84). When disco music went out of fashion, pubs and dancehalls continued to be converted and discotheques purpose-built. As the first discotheque trade magazine, which began publication in 1976, wrote: 'It's comforting to predict that as America's disco dinosaur becomes extinct, the social bedrock of the British disco is as firm as ever' (*Disco International* December 1979). Throughout the 1980s, the size and number of disc-dance venues continued to increase.

Developing alongside the permanent sites with their own alternative ancestries were extended versions of the mobile discotheque. With them, records became the source of music for increasingly big events, to the extent that they eventually entertained arena-size crowds of ten and fifteen thousand people at 'raves' in unconventional locations. 'Raves' grew out of the semi-legal warehouse parties organized by young entrepreneurs in reaction to the expansion of the leisure industry and perceived 'commercialization' of night-life in the 1980s. The warehouse events, in their turn, drew their inspiration from the Afro-Caribbean 'sound-systems' which had been a feature of black entertainment since the 1970s. All three incarnations of the discotheque took advantage of its flexibility and mobility, exploring new kinds of environment which contributed to novel 'atmospheres'.

The development and spread of permanent and mobile discotheques is part of a general re-location and re-positioning of live music. Before the Second World War, the majority of Musicians' Union members were employed to play at dances of one sort or another. Today, few British musicians make a living from dance engagements. Live dancehalls dwindled in number and deteriorated in condition; some were restored for the use of devoted ballroom dancers; many were transformed into discotheques, converted into bingo halls or less commonly into cinema multiplexes and concert halls. The economics of music is such that live music is only profitable under certain conditions – and dance venues are no longer one of them.

Despite the resilience of live ideology, the professional performance of popular music has receded. The slow transition has gone relatively unnoticed. Periodically, the threatened closure of premier venues has provoked concern about a general decline of live music. In the seventies, for example, the Rainbow Club was on the brink of closure for several years and became a symbol of the threat discos posed to live music in London (cf. *Melody Maker* and *New Musical Express* 1973–5). In the 1990s, the possible closure of the Town and Country Club spurred similar outcries: 'Live music in London is in crisis: audiences are down, venues are changing hands at an alarming rate and many promoters are being forced to rely on club DJs instead of bands . . . the decline of live music is a national phenomenon . . . there is a whole generation out there which isn't being encouraged to go to gigs' (*Time Out* 3–10 April 1991).

That live music has been marginalized is perhaps best demonstrated by the fact that in many British towns, the principal live venues have been owned, operated or subsidized by local governments and student unions. In the 1990s, venues in York, Sheffield, Cambridge, Norwich and London opened and closed their doors at the expense of local taxpayers. The largest share of middle-sized gigs, however, are hosted by university student unions who support around eight hundred venues around Britain. When the national government threatened to pass legislation preventing student unions from funding 'non-essential' campus activities, the importance of this subsidy became clear; if events had to be self-supporting, roughly seventy-five per cent of their gigs would have to be cut because ticket prices would be forced up beyond the reach of most students (*Music Week* 19 February 1994). Needless to say, college students now make up the bulk of the audience for live popular music and the live circuit is heavily dominated by a few subgenres, like alternative rock and indie music (cf. Central Statistical Office, General Household Survey 1986; EMAP Metro, Youth Surveys 1988). Another subsidizer of this scene is the record industry who give 'tour support' to emerging acts because they see gigs as a means of building fan bases, establishing markets and promoting records.

One live circuit which can be lucrative (but often incurs huge losses) is the arena and stadium concerts of the established pop and rock act. This sector would not exist if it were not for the massive audiences generated by records and other media. Here, tours are again sponsored by record companies, but also by advertisers of soft and alcoholic drinks, youth-oriented clothes and the like. While promoters of this sector (and there are not many in this league) make money from ticket prices, the bulk of revenue for the band often comes from the sale of merchandise such as T-shirts, posters and tour booklets. Although merchandising had been around since the 1960s, it was not until the 1980s that it became integral to the economics of touring (and part and parcel of developing an artist) to the extent that acts now often sign merchandising agreements at the same time as they sign recording contracts. The landmark legal action through which artists gained the copyright to their image was against a company producing unofficial Adam and the Ants merchandise in the early 1980s. Some indie bands like James or the Inspiral Carpets (famous for their 'Cool as Fuck' T-shirts) allegedly became wealthy by 'self merchandising' (*Applause* May 1991).

All this is not to argue that live music is dead, but that it no longer appeals to the broad base of the population that it once did and is no longer economical in many of the circumstances it once was. Much live music is made by unpaid amateurs and semi-professionals. Performance is an enjoyable hobby for many pub musicians, buskers, church choirs and brass bands (cf. Finnegan 1989). However, some bands in this category, who aspire to a recording contract but need to be heard in the appropriate venue first, may find themselves paying the venue for the privilege of performing. These 'pay for play' situations usually take the shape of 'ticket deals' where the band buys fifty tickets then sells them to friends.

In 1988, the Monopolies and Mergers Commission recommended that PPL completely withdraw its musician employment requirements. The Commission agreed with dance operators who argued that the live music requirements were 'not only expensive but pointless' for two reasons. First, they argued that the dance sound conveyed by the records 'cannot be reproduced by instrumentalists playing direct to an audience'. Second, they maintained that 'audiences prefer recorded sound' (Monopolies and Mergers 1988: 41). As a result, live music (or rather the requirement to hire musicians) was not found to be in the public interest. The ruling against the Musicians' Union is typical of the fate of much union-related legislation under the Thatcher government. However, in few countries other than Britain, did musicians enjoy such protective arrangements in the first place. Later, Musicians' Union representatives would admit that live music 'has ceased to be "hip". Clubs with name DJs and the latest remixes are what appeals to people today' (Mark Melton, IASPM conference, 19–21 April 1990).

For over forty years, the Musicians' Union and the dancehall/ discotheque operators negotiated their conflicting interests through the mediation of the record company collective body, PPL. Given their disparate financial stakes in 'phonographic performance', the relatively congenial relationship between the Musicians' Union and the record companies requires some explanation. The benefits to the MU are more apparent. Because all copyrights were those of the record company, the Union's rights' revenue was entirely dependent on its donation by PPL. Between 1947 and 1989, PPL gave 12.5 per cent of its net royalty revenue to the MU in respect of 'the services of unidentified session musicians'. In 1987, that percentage amounted to £1.3 million. The reasons why PPL agreed to restrictions on the use of its product are less obvious but perhaps more numerous. First, the Union helped PPL maintain its control on repertoire in so far as it forbade its members to record with non-PPL record companies. Although PPL administered the rights of ninety per cent of all commercial sound recordings in the late 1980s, its monopoly was much less secure in the 1950s and 1960s (cf. *Musicians' Union Report* 1961). Second, Union members monitored record performances and copyright infringement at a local level – something PPL, with a staff of less than sixty, had never been equipped to do. It was Union members who wrote letters to local newspapers, knocked on venue doors, censured club managers and effectively enforced copyright legislation on the ground. Third, the Musicians' Union helped legitimate the record companies' claims to copyright as a reward and incentive for creative production. As a 1989 PPL press release explained: 'The British recording industry is dependent upon the services of musicians for the continued uninterrupted production of excellent sound recordings. This requires a healthy broad based musical profession covering the whole spectrum of performance.' Finally, despite the fact that the record industry does not profit directly from live performance, but rather spends substantial sums on tour support, record company executives have tended to believe that the most artistically and commercially successful music comes from live 'working' acts (cf. Negus 1992: 52–4). The ability of a band to perform live is seen as insurance for a strong image and long career. Since disco, the global successes of non-live dance music have led to a proliferation of in-house and satellite dance labels and to 'club promotions' departments (whose aim is to nurture fan bases by plugging records to key DJs). Nevertheless, the ideal of the traditional performing rock group still prevails in many record companies who see the live version of authenticity as a key selling point.

Since the 1950s, records have supplanted musicians as the source of sounds for most social dancing and contributed to the re-location and re-definition of live music in general. This section has explored the technological, economic and legal determinants of the shifting public presences of recording and performance. Musician resistance to the enculturation of records was only effective in so far as it could be seen to coincide with the 'public interest'. When the Union eventually lost the ideological battle, it was only a matter of time before it lost the legislative one. Changes in the ideological status of recorded entertainment were dependent on several key factors which are the subject of three of the next four sections. First, records increased their allure as a result of being affiliated with the new types of occasion, new social spaces and 'new' social groups – all of which contributed to the increasing subcultural authenticity of records. Second, records adapted to their public use, changed their format to suit discotheques and to satisfy the exigencies of a new profession, the club disc jockey. And, third, as the studio rather than the stage became the key site for the origination of music, so recordings in certain genres began to acquire aura.

'Real' Events and Altered Spaces

The authentication of discs for dancing was dependent on the development of new kinds of event and environment, which recast recorded entertainment as something uniquely its own, rather than a poor substitute for a 'real' musical event. These new time-frames and spatial orders exploited the strengths and compensated for the weaknesses of the recorded medium. By using new labels, rubrics, interior designs and distracting spectacles, disc dances were rendered distinctive. They were effectively transformed from an occurrence into an occasion, from a migrant practice into a unique place, from a diverting novelty into an entertainment institution.

Before record hops, dancing to discs was not a cultural event in itself. The use of records was not highlighted in flyers, listings or advertisements. The Musicians' Union protested that dances using records were advertised in such a way as to create the impression that a live band would be playing. More peculiarly, Union members often reported that audiences didn't notice the absence of performers. In 1953, one member contended that one young dance crowd had no idea they were dancing to records: 'Amplification was so good as to be indistinguishable from an actual band heard outside the hall; and inside, soft lights, and a quick-change of records made the absence of a band unnoticeable. [There were] about 300 teenagers jiving like mad entirely oblivious of no band being present' (*Musicians' Union Report* 1954). Similarly, another MU member claimed that he had attended a musical play in which records had been so perfectly synchronized with voice and action that the audience thought an orchestra was playing. When he told people sitting on either side of him, they allegedly refused to believe him. He concluded his report with the lesson: 'Members will therefore appreciate that the public, unless they are properly informed, will not know whether the music they are hearing is recorded or an actual live performance' (*Musicians' Union Report* 1956).

Although these reports are undoubtedly exaggerated in the direction of stereotypes about mass culture and false consciousness, it does appear that many people didn't note the absence of musicians during this period. When asked today whether they danced to records at their local dance halls and youth clubs *before* rock'n'roll, people tend to remember if they were dancing to a band but not if they weren't. This may be evidence of the ability of records to 'simulate' in Baudrillard's sense of the word; they do not so much *imitate* as '*mask the absence*' of performance (Baudrillard 1983a: 11). However, it is also testimony to the more mundane fact that, in the reports, the music was subordinate to, first, a social event and, second, a theatrical spectacle. Given these conditions of consumption, the audience didn't give the music the attention musicians expect and appreciate. In Benjamin's terms, these audiences were 'distracted': they absorbed the music but the music did not absorb them (Benjamin 1970: 239).

Rock'n'roll record hops, however, focused favourable attention on the entertainment format. In the US, the record 'hop' was endorsed by the new and still glamorous medium of television with the after-school show, *American Bandstand*. In Britain, the American import with a distinct name brought dancing to discs into vogue for the first time. 'Hops' gave the activity a distinct identity, transforming it into a noteworthy event rather than simply an intermission or occurrence. Significantly, record hops were identified with youth and youth alone. Like the spate of Hollywood 'teenpics', they capitalized on the emergence of youth as a consumer category and cultural identity. Conveniently, youth were the group with the least prejudice about the inferiority of recorded entertainment and the one with the most interest in finding a cultural space they could call their own. More than any other cultural phenomenon of the fifties, record hops came to symbolize the new youth culture. Along with labels like 'teenager', they contributed to a heightened consciousness of generation and, with their large-scale collective gathering, fuelled the first fantasies of a movement of youth. Records had become integral to a public culture; they were the symbolic axis around which whirled the new community of youth.

Later incarnations of disc dances did not target only youth, but smaller demographic segments and shades of taste. In 1966 in *New Society*, Reyner Banham argued that the cultural formations that grew up around records were characterized by what he playfully called *'vinyl deviationa'*. One of the main social functions of records – their distribution of culture – had been superseded by radio. As a result, the gramophone became 'a system for distributing deviant sound to the disaffected cultural minorities whose peculiar tastes are not satisfied by the continuous wallpaper provided by radio [like the] BBC' (*New Society* 1 December 1966). Of course, dance clubs are not only significant for minority taste cultures, but also for class, ethnic and sexual ones (cf. chapter 3).

The enculturation of records for dancing was first fostered by the development of new kinds of event and, only second, promoted by new kinds of environment. The initial 1950s disc hops did little to transform the dancehalls and youth clubs in which they took place. The following description of a record session at the Lyceum Ballroom in the Strand, for example, contrasts the traditional architecture with the new cultural form:

The Lyceum was originally a theatre, and Mecca Dance Halls Ltd have left most of its Edwardian-baroque opulence untouched. Above, all is crimson and gold, cherubs and swags of fruit. On the band stand, a sharp young man in horn rimmed spectacles fades the records in and out on the two turntables of the enormous record player. On the floor over a thousand teenagers jive . . . the atmosphere is solemn and dedicated . . . All the dancers without exception wear the fashionable cut-off expression. (Melly 1970/1989: 68–9)

In the early 1960s, the 'discotheque' rendered dancing to discs fashionable in the way the record hop had done a few years before. This time, however, the institution was conceived as a French import and extended its influence to its architectural surroundings. Changes in environment were crucial to the definition of the new institution; they were meant to complement the culture of contemporary youth. La Discothèque in Wardour Street, for instance, was very dimly lit, gloomy by some accounts, with a number of double beds in and around the dancefloor. Invoking the new permissive sexual mores, the outlandish interior was an attraction in itself. The Place in Hanley near Stoke-on-Trent provides another example. It was lit by red light and decorated entirely in black with the exception of a few rooms: the entrance hall was sprayed gold, the toilets sported imitation leopard-skin wallpaper and a small sitting-room was painted white, lit by blue light and called 'the fridge' (cf. Donovan 1981).

The spaces of 1960s' discotheques defined themselves against the architecture of the dancehalls whose interiors stayed the same for years and whose models of elegance were royal (hence the 'Palais' and 'Empires') or relics of nineteenth-century bids for respectability (which referenced the classical world of 'Lyceums' and 'Hippodromes'). Either way, the ideologies of ballrooms did not speak to the youth of the day. Discotheques were emphatically different and self-consciously unconventional. They were *lounges*, *rooms* or simply *spots*; they were *places* with presence rather than palaces, hence names like the Saddle Room, the Ad-Lib, the Place and the Scene. The suffix 'a-Gogo' was also used internationally to make their existence as young urbane dancing establishments absolutely clear: London and Los Angeles had Whisky-a-Gogos, named after the Parisian club. Chicago not only had a Whisky-a-Gogo, but a

Bistro-a-Gogo, Gigi-a-Gogo and a Buccaneer-a-Gogo (*Billboard* 6 March 1965).

But transformations in name and interior design did not stop here. The institution continually renovated and effectively *rejuvenated* itself in order to appeal to an ever-shifting market of youth. Late-sixties' discotheques would embrace psychedelic and strobe lighting, slide projectors and hanging beads. Seventies 'discos' would become a maze of shiny futuristic surfaces, chrome party palaces of mirrors and glitter balls. Eighties 'clubs' abandoned mirrors: walls in black or grey were particular favourites early in the decade, while painterly postmodern or tribal styles made their appearance in the second half of the decade. Late eighties 'raves' took dance events outside what had become 'traditional' venues to unorthodox locations in industrial districts and remote rural areas. Each new version of the institution was meant to be an advance on the old – an adventurous departure into a realm which seemed to have fewer rules and regulations.

The fresh names and renovated interiors were not simply a means of *rejuvenation*: the discotheque's constant search for liberation from tradition extends to the legacy of British class cultures. The early-sixties discotheque not only rejected the aristocratic fantasies of the ballroom but also effaced the hierarchical distinction between the elite nightclub and the common dancehall. The discotheque, like youth culture generally, was positioned as classless. In 1965, George Melly described discotheques as 'those wombs of swinging London' which were 'virtually classless' where 'success in a given field is the criterion and, in the case of girls, physical beauty' (Melly 1970/1989: 104). A few years later, Tom Wolfe took a more critical view, suggesting that these youngsters seemed to be classless because they had dropped out of the conventional job system: 'It is the style of life that makes them unique, not money, power, position, talent, intelligence ... The clothes have come to symbolize their independence from the idea of a life based on a succession of jobs' (Wolfe 1968b: 104).

Each change in institutional identity positioned the new disc dance as significantly different from what went before. Generally, the 'revolution' in leisure was seen as both democratic and *avant-garde*. 'Discotheques', 'discos' and 'clubs' were all meant to be both exclusive and egalitarian, classless but superior to the mass-market institution that preceded them. Raves, in their turn, were enveloped in discourses of utopian egalitarianism: they were events without door policies where everybody was welcome and people from all walks of life became one under the hypnotic beat. But the discourse could hardly be tested, for only those 'in the know' could hear of and locate the party. Moreover black and gay youth tended to see rave culture as a straight, white affair.

It is a classic paradox that an institution so adept at segregation, at the nightly accommodation of different crowds, should be repeatedly steeped in an ideology of social mixing. The discotheque/ disco/club/rave regularly re-invented itself to maintain an eternal youth and to obfuscate dated relations to class cultures. As Barbara Bradby argues, this kind of utopianism ignores the subordinate position that women occupy at most levels of rave culture (cf. Bradby 1993). The dance acts, music producers, DJs, club organizers and bouncers who structure the events are predominately male and require that women prove themselves twice over if they want to do more than sing, check coats or tend the bar. Moreover, although raves are supposed to be 'sexless' affairs – that is, clothing is unisex and participants are not there to get laid – it does not follow that they are necessarily sexually progressive.

The regular redecoration of the discotheque also addressed the main deficiency of recorded entertainment. Eye-catching interiors were meant to compensate for the loss of the spectacle of performing musicians. In the 1960s, the biggest global juke-box manufacturer, Seeburg, publicly lamented the machine's 'negative image' (*Billboard* 27 February 1965). The key to improving its status, they argued, was their new high volume, minimum distortion, stereo juke-box called 'DISCOTHEQUE', which they hoped would be accepted 'as a form of entertainment in much the same way as [the public] accepts films, radio or television' (*Billboard* 15 May 1965). Crucially, the machine was accompanied by an 'INSTANT NIGHT CLUB' package of wall panels, modular dancefloor, napkins, coasters and other decorations 'needed to transform a location into a discotheque' (Ad in *Billboard* 23 January 1965). Equally significantly, the wall panels portrayed life-size white jazz musicians in the midst of a spirited jam session. Intended for the wall behind the juke-box, these panels offered a literal solution to the phonograph's problem of having no visual focus or, as Dave Laing writes, 'a voice without a face' (cf. Laing 1990).

Although this sort of literalism was relatively rare, one trajectory in the changing shape of discotheques has been the proliferation of visuals. Lighting, in particular, has become an elaborate accompaniment to the music, emphasizing its rhythms, illustrating its chords. Sometimes, the roving coloured beams and flashing strobes decorate the dancers, making a better spectacle of the crowd. At other times, swishing lasers and figurative patterns of light are an optical phenomenon in their own right. Computer-generated fractals and other abstract designs of coloured light can act as visual equivalents of the instrumental sounds of house and techno music, while film loops, slide projectors and music videos punctuate the space with figurative entertainment. The discotheque bears witness to the symbolic possibilities of electric light which, since the nineteenth century, has been used to signal the consequence and difference of night-time social gatherings (cf. Marvin 1988).

In contrast to the record sessions held in old-style dancehalls, discotheques attempted to offer complete sensory experiences – ones often intensified by the use of alcohol and/or drugs, which have been mainstays of youthful dance experience since disc sessions took on their own premises. Only with the discotheque of the 1960s did the institution develop into a total environment where 'dream and reality are interchangeable and indistinguishable' (Melly 1970: 9). In what must be the first study of discotheques, Lucille Hollander Blum argues that their appeal results from the way they offer ritual catharsis. Discotheque dancers, she asserts, experience a 'delirious sense of freedom', enter a 'state of complete thoughtlessness' and escape from 'present day reality' (cf. Blum 1966). Since then, discotheques have evolved further into multimedia installations whose worlds are contiguous with the recorded fantasies of music video and the virtual realities of computer games, but are still a site of tangible human interaction. 'Club worlds' are markedly divorced from the work world outside. Door restrictions sharply divide inside from outside, while long corridors, inner doors and stairways create transitional labyrinths. Raves add the pilgrimage, the quest for the location, to extend the ritualistic passage. Like Alice's rabbit hole, both convey the participant from the mundane world to Wonderland.

Disc Jockeys and Social Sounds

Discotheques have carved out distinctive times and places for recorded music. With their different senses of place and occasion,
they have, as their name suggests, effectively accommodated discs.
But records have also adapted to the social and cultural requirements of the evolving dance establishment, modifying their formats
and formalizing the manner in which they are played. Disc jockeys
have had a decisive role in conducting the energies and rearranging
the authenticities of the dancefloor.

Essential to the altered space of discotheques is the enhanced
acoustic atmosphere which results from high volume, continuous
music. The initial popularity of juke-box-fitted coffee bars and
purpose-built discotheques over the record sessions in dancehalls
related not only to architectural style but also to improved sound-
systems. According to one music weekly of the early sixties, La
Discothèque in Streatham was 'more than a dance hall' because of
the 'quality and the volume' of the records they played (*New Record
Mirror* 19 January 1963). In the 1950s, record playback technology
was not able to fill a large ballroom with high fidelity sound. Even
in the early 1960s, few discotheques could provide all-around
sound, highs or lows, or thumping bass.

In the mid-1960s, many juke-box manufacturers, including the
three largest, Seeburg, Wurlitzer and Rowe, started to manufacture
extended-play records for their dance-oriented juke-boxes – a decade before record companies extended the length of the single with
the twelve-inch format. Seeburg argued that the discotheque would
prevail as a form of entertainment only if it offered 'uninterrupted
music'. As a result, they issued dance music in the format of the
'Little LP', a recording with three titles per side, with music in the
lead-in and lead-out grooves, amounting to seven and a half minutes of continuous music (*Billboard* 6 February 1965 and 1 May
1965). So, the practice of dancing to discs began to affect the design
of the record itself.

Record companies were slow to react. At around this time, *Billboard* introduced a discotheque chart because they said that the
discotheque was having 'a major effect on the entire music and
entertainment industry. A look at *Billboard*'s Hot 100 shows disco-

theque industry material all over the chart' (*Billboard* 27 February 1965). But it was not until a decade later, with disco music, that the industry really opened its eyes to the 'concept of transforming a routine nightclub into a catalyst for breaking records' (Wardlow in Joe 1980: 8–9). In his extensive analysis of the introduction of the twelve-inch single in America, Will Straw argues that record company interest in dance clubs coincided with shrinking radio playlists; promotions departments were looking for alternative means of plugging their music (cf. Straw 1990).

In the 1970s, extended twelve-inch singles became a standard product amongst American, then British, record companies. The idea came from American DJs who had been mixing seven-inch copies of the same record for prolonged play. Some began recording their mixes, editing them on reel-to-reel tapes, then playing them in clubs. When these recordings were transferred to vinyl, the extended remix was born. Record labels became involved when they realized that discotheques were sufficiently widespread to make catering to them with special vinyl product a promotional necessity.*

The new record format was better suited for playing at high volume over club sound-systems and its extended versions had instrumental breaks where the song was stripped down to the drums and bass with very little vocal in order to facilitate seamless mixing of one track into another. (Interestingly, dance bands of the 1920s and 1930s constructed dance numbers in a way not unlike twelve-inches, with extended instrumental introductions and finales and short segments of lyrics in which the vocal acted as if it were merely another instrument. *Simon Frith in conversation.*) These

---

* Although twelve-inches were originally made for public performance only, within a few years, they became retail products. In Britain, the first two retailed twelve-inch disco singles were Undisputed Truth's 'You Plus Me' (issued in a limited edition of three thousand) and Goodie Goodie's 'No 1 DJ' in 1978. The first twelve-inch-only release to make it into the top ten was Abba's 1981 single 'Lay Your Love on Me'. This honour is usually assumed to be held by New Order's 'Blue Monday', which was released on twelve-inch-only but, despite high sales and many weeks in the chart, it peaked at number nine. Although roughly forty-five per cent of singles sold in the early 1990s were twelve-inches, major record labels still see the format as primarily promotional. Profits on twelve-inches are such that they are usually only relevant to small companies with low overheads and low turnover.

extended dance 'tracks' (rather than 'songs') helped sustain the momentum of the dancefloor and contributed to the other-worldly atmosphere of the discotheque. The constant pulse of the bass blocks thoughts, affects emotions and enters the body. Like a drug, rhythms can lull one into another state. With rave culture, this potentiality was ritualized as the 'trance dance' by dancers actively seeking an altered state of consciousness through movement to the music.

Pre-eminently, twelve-inch records were made specifically for DJs. The recorded entertainment at the heart of disc cultures is not automated. DJs incorporate degrees of human touch, intervention and improvisation. They play a key role in the enculturation of records for dancing, sometimes as an artist but always as a representative and respondent to the crowd. By orchestrating the event and anchoring the music in a particular place, the DJ became a guarantor of subcultural authenticity. As Daniel Hadley writes, although DJs lack absolute control over the proceedings, they are 'still responsible for the creation of a musical space, a space which is formed according to the expectations of the crowd and the specific kinds of DJ practices in place' (Hadley 1993: 64).

The changes in the DJ's occupational status reflect the progressive enculturation of recorded entertainment. The DJ's job has changed dramatically since the Second World War, moving from unskilled worker through craftsman to artist, but also through a less linear process involving degrees of anonymity and celebrity, collection and connoisseurship, performance and recording (cf. Kealy 1979/ 1990; Langlois 1992). In the forties, the person who played records for public dancing was not seen to possess much technical skill, let alone artistry. Although the Musicians' Union referred to the services of the 'public address engineer', it also suggested that the job was simply a question of unskilled supply. In a passage quoted earlier, for example, it was reported that, 'In almost every town the man who runs the radio shop, or specializes in the provision of public address equipment, will undertake to supply recorded music for dances or other social events at a small proportion of the fee a good band would charge' (Musicians' Union Conference Report 1949). Even in the 1950s, playing records for dancing was considered so unskilled that most thought it best to do it oneself. One didn't hire mobile DJs but their records. The advertisements read:

'Party records for a record party. Hire an evening's recorded music' (*New Musical Express* December 1957). General opinion in the record industry was that the DJ was not endowed with any particularly special skills. As its main trade paper observed: 'The position of the disc jockey is not an easy one. He becomes a public figure by presenting someone else's talent' (*Record Retailer and Music Industry News* 10 March 1960). A decade later, however, DJs came to be acknowledged by the record industry as experts about dance music and its markets. DJs entered a number of new jobs, invading A&R, promotions and marketing departments, sometimes even becoming managing directors of their own labels. DJs were also brought into the studio as remixers, producers and even artists in their own right. In fact, by the mid-nineties, it was a rarity to find a dance musician who had not spent at least some time working as a DJ.

Supplying the records was certainly the first and most vital function of the DJ. Consistently through the years, DJs have been heavy record buyers, product hunters, zealous collectors. For example, *Jocks* (later relaunched as *DJ* magazine) ran a weekly column 'How to be a DJ' which included a section on 'Buying Records'. They argued that the most important investment of a mobile DJ, other than his/her turntables and amplifiers, is a constantly updated record collection. Shopping 'once a fortnight is the absolute minimum ... records can become huge surprisingly quickly and nothing is worse than going to a gig where half your audience wants you to play something new and you've never heard of it' (*Jocks* October 1990).

Certain DJs have built a reputation upon having the most comprehensive collections of particular genres. An ad for a Northern Soul night at Blackpool Mecca in 1974 identifies the night's DJs, Ian Levine and Colin Curtis, and proclaims their main selling point: 'We have records that no one else has' (*Black Music* January 1974). At this time, the status of DJs was partly the status of an exclusive owner with discerning taste. As one journalist commented, 'the disc jockeys are becoming more and more of a cultural elite in their efforts to outdo each other in finding exclusive records' (*Black Music* June 1974).

Beyond the supply of records, the uses, skills and talents of DJs have long been viewed with some suspicion. The origins of the curious term, 'disc jockey', are disputed. Nevertheless, whatever its etymology, the expression suggests that some sportsmanlike dexterity was required to perform the job. The new professional had to 'ride' a record much as a racing jockey might handle his horse at the track. But 'to jockey' also means to gain advantage by skilful manoeuvering, trickery or artifice. The implication might have been that disc jockeys deceived their listeners into thinking that what they heard was a live performance. Well into the 1970s, the DJ had a dubious reputation. S/he was often considered to be 'a parasite, the less successful being a mere spinner of discs, while the ranking DJ is a synthetic rock star with no musical ability' (*Melody Maker* 15 November 1975).

For several decades, the expectations of the DJ's job varied greatly. For example, in the mid-1960s, the American Whisky-a-Gogo chain employed women who acted as both DJs and gogo dancers. Called 'dance-DJs', they changed records and did 'dance routines in glass cages above the crowd' (*Billboard* 1 May 1965). However, this arrangement was anomalous. The master of ceremonies, presenter or 'personality DJ' was a more common role. Most 'personality DJs' with a national profile came from radio. They filled the gaps between records with informative chatter and presided over disc hops, touring the country promoting the product of a sponsoring record company. They also might broadcast a regular weekly show from a particular club. Radios Caroline, London and Luxembourg broadcast disc shows from venues like the Marquee and the 100 Club throughout the 1960s.

Amongst youthful crowds, DJs were developing into leaders and local celebrities. In *New Society* in 1968, Angela Carter wrote about a disc jockey in an unnamed provincial city as the 'prince of cloud-cuckoo land'. She described how, wearing extravagant white suits, he presided over the controls of a monumental record-player and she paraphrased his philosophy: 'A disc jockey is in a position of power. He can mould taste. Maybe he could do more. You've got all these kids looking up to you and you're in a position of authority' (Carter 1968). In this way, DJs started to be perceived as taste-makers or 'moulders of musical opinion in a very similar – and far more direct – way to the music journalist' (*Melody Maker* 15 November 1975).

By the mid-seventies, it was generally understood that the best DJs built up a rapport with their crowd to the degree that the crowd would follow the DJ from one club to another. The 'Tom Cat' mobile discotheque, for example, claimed a 'fan club' of two thousand members. They would hire the venues, promote the show by printing then distributing a thousand handbills in the street, put up posters, advertise in the press and take the money on the door (as it was the only way to earn more than ten pounds a night). The lead DJ explained their strategy: 'We're just like a pop group. We have our own signature tune and a back up jock who plays slow records for ten minutes before I come on' (*Melody Maker* 30 August 1975).

However, it was as mixers, rather than personalities, that DJs entered the hallowed world of musicianship. As 'turntable musicians', they would perform elaborate mixes which required much rehearsal (with names like the running mix, the chop mix, transforming, etc.). DJs created new music in the process of mixing. Records became the raw material of DJ performance just as, with sampling, they had become the raw material of composition. As Tony Langlois argues in his study of British house music DJs, 'house records are not recordings of performances, but are actively performed by the DJ himself, allowing spontaneity, surprise and creativity' (Langlois 1992: 236). This is one reason why tapes of DJ mixes can be bought at raves, outdoor markets and under the table in dance record shops or downloaded from rave bulletin boards and internet sites. In other words, dance fans desire documents of DJ performance.

As the vinyl single had been the raw material of DJ performance since rock'n'roll, it is not surprising that there was moment in the late 1980s when disc jockeys reacted negatively to the rise of the CD in a manner not unlike the way musicians of the 1970s responded to the proliferation of mobile discos. Both involved threats to livelihood and creativity. Just as the dance musicians' repertoire became outmoded so the DJ's vast record collection threatened to become obsolete. And just as the years of practice in mastering an instrument by the musician no longer promised employment, so DJs who had spent hours perfecting their touch, feeling the groove, sighting the track, were faced with a technology whose operations they could not see or touch. As one journalist wrote: 'In the age of digital reproduction ... the DJ may be the last musician ... records represent the last technology you can

Plate 4 In the late eighties DJs worried about the death of vinyl as a threat to the value of their record collections, mixing skills and livelihood. By the mid-nineties most DJs had come to use CDs, although the twelve-inch record was still their preferred medium.

grasp – now with CDs it's all digital' (*Jocks* September 1990). The analogy between musicianship and DJ-ing extended to the properties attributed to vinyl. According to mixing DJs the sound of vinyl was 'real', 'warm', 'imperfect' but full of integrity, while CDs were 'cold', 'clinical', 'inhuman' and 'unreal'. Their language resembled the way live music was polarized from recorded music only a few years before. By the early 1990s, however, many clubs were fitted with CD mixers, and DJs were adjusting to the new format, seeing the possibilities of its 'purer' sound.

Though DJs may be musicians, they are rarely performers in the pop sense of the word. In purpose-built clubs, mixing booths tend to be tucked away and DJs unseen. As cultural figures, DJs are known by name rather than face. Although in the mid-nineties in a minority of London clubs, the 'cult of the DJ' led to the practice of facing the DJ booth whilst dancing, this has not been a widespread activity. The enduring spectacle afforded by discotheques has been the dancing crowd. In the absence of visually commanding performers, the gaze of the audience has turned back on itself. Watching and being seen are key pleasures of discotheques. Angela McRobbie extends an analogy between the gazes involved in the cinema and those of the discotheque: both offer 'a darkened space where the [individual] can retain a degree of anonymity and absorption . . . but where the cinema offers a one-way fantasy which is directed solely through the gaze of the spectator at the screen, the fantasy of dancing is more social, more reciprocated' (McRobbie 1984: 146).

What authenticates club cultures is not so much a unique DJ performance, as the 'buzz', 'vibe', 'mood' or 'atmosphere' created in the interaction of DJ and crowd in space. It is as orchestrators of this 'living' communal experience that DJs are most important to music culture. DJs respond to the crowd through their choice and sequence of records, seek to direct their energies and build up the tension until the event 'climaxes'. DJs are supposed to have their finger on the pulse of the event in order to give the dancing crowd 'what [they] need rather than what [they] want' (Graeme Park quoted in *New Musical Express* 27 February 1988). In this way, DJs are artists in the construction of musical experience. As Jon Pareles argues:

> Disc jockeys, improvising with records or electronic gadgets and usually backed by immense sound systems, produce variations on hit records by taking them apart, adding new drum tracks, superimposing tunes or bass-lines – all with a careful attention to the sensuality of sound and the efficacy of rhythm. Not only does the music have the freshness of improvisation – and a function, to keep people dancing – but it has a richness rarely heard in live pop music. In clubs, there's no tension between music, technology and audience. (*New York Times* 22 July 1990)

Records are the pivot around which dance cultures have come to revolve. Contrary to the old rock ideologies, the 'live' does not have an exclusive claim on collective music culture, nor is it the original to which disc culture is a dull and distant echo. Disc culture is a distinct high-tech folk culture and twelve-inch dance records in the hands of a mixing DJ are, quite literally, social sounds.

The Authenticities of Dance Genres

The perceived authenticity of particular records and music genres is a complex issue entangled in several factors which are the subject of this section. First and most obviously, given the discussions of the past two sections, authenticity is dependent on the degree to which records are assimilated and legitimized by a subculture. Authentication is the ultimate end of enculturation. Second, the distance between a record's production and its consumption is relevant to the cultural value bestowed upon it. When original performers are remote in time or place, as is the case with foreign imports and revived rarities, records can acquire prestige and authority. Third, the environment in which a record is produced contributes to its authenticity. Records are more likely to be perceived as the primary medium of musics whose main site of production is the studio. And, finally, the ideological vagaries of music genres like their communication of bodily 'soul' or their revelation of technology play a main role in whether records come across as genuine. In other words, authenticity is ultimately an effect of the discourses which surround popular music.

In the 1930s, the British jazz appreciation societies called 'rhythm clubs' held 'recitals . . . given by records loaned by members' (Godbolt 1984: 138). These gatherings mark a shift in cultural values whereby records became the pivot around which a collective culture developed and revolved. One of the first jazz fans to analyse the rhythm club movement from an academic perspective described its mania for the recorded form:

> To understand the function of this sort of organization in the life of the European jazz fan, his utter dependence on phonographic records will have to be remembered. Cut off from the living music by time as

well as space he submits to a particular shift in values. The record becomes more important than the music; minor musicians who have left recorded examples of their own work behind them become more important than those major musicians who for one reason or another have never got around to a recording studio; and the man who has met the musicians and knows his way through a maze of records becomes more important than the musician himself. (Ernest Borneman 1947 quoted in Godbolt 1984: 142)

The resolute focus on records in jazz connoisseur circles was an anomaly in the thirties which would become the norm much later with the advent of teenage dance cultures. Despite the unlikely pedigree, the genealogy is preserved in the etymology of the word 'discotheque' which literally translated from the French means 'record library' and gained currency in relation to Parisian jazz clubs.

Although jazz fans collected and fetishized records, they valued discs as 'records' in the strict sense of the word, as transcriptions, accounts, replicas, reproductions of a unique jazz performance. Jazz records were enculturated, they had prestige and authority, but they were still a secondary medium for reasons that related both to their process of production (they were relatively straightforward documents of particular performances) and also to the discourses in which they were enveloped (as performance was considered unquestionably superior to recording, even though recording was superior to notation) (cf. Newton 1959).

It was not until rock'n'roll that *records* started to serve as the *original*. With rock'n'roll, spinning discs were no longer a poor imitation of performing musicians; they were music itself. As one 'jiver' remembers it: records brought 'the real sound and real tempo of the mainly American [music that was] taking the charts by storm, rather than the house band's well-meaning but tidied up cover versions' (Nourse with Hudson 1990: 43). In fact, rock'n'roll was so tightly identified with records in Britain that PPL, which was willing to regulate the use of records for any other kind of music during this period, thought it 'unreasonable that musicians should be employed at so called "rock'n'roll" dances' (Musicians' Union Conference Report 1961).

This was mainly due to changes in media environment and studio production. For example, in America as well as Britain, the

development of rock'n'roll depended on records. The cross-fertilization of Hillbilly music and Rhythm & Blues that engendered
rock'n'roll was primarily brought about by records on radio. As
Kloosterman and Quispel write, the black and white music scenes
had few 'live' contacts because the southern states were strictly
segregated. When television took over from radio as a national mass
medium in the 1950s, radio went local and its audience segmented.
One of its new target markets was the black population whose
recently increased affluence meant that they were now attractive to
a handful of advertisers. Black music, therefore, made it on to airwaves which crossed neighbourhood boundaries and diffused
black music among the white youngsters who chose to tune in (cf.
Kloosterman and Quispel 1990).

Elvis Presley, who had little contact with the local black population, gained his knowledge of R&B music from Memphis's black
radio station (cf. Quain 1992, Wark 1989). Moreover, his sound
and image were fashioned from an array of recorded influences,
including radio, records, comic books, movies and television.
Elvis's early records abandoned the attempt to mimic a live performance in the studio; their novel use of echo created a specifically
studio sound (Middleton 1990: 89). Elvis's professional live act followed his first hit on local radio; it was developed to promote his
records. This series of inversions of the 'natural' route from performance to recording was an exception at the time (for example,
Bill Haley and Little Richard were seasoned touring performers
before they entered the studio). However, depending on the genre,
the precedence of recording over performance would gradually
become the rule.

It is worth considering the role played by distinct times and sites
of production and consumption. Records were preferred to performance in circumstances where the qualities specific to records
were exploited. So, the ability of records to travel in space and time
led to disc cultures revolving around imports, new releases or lost
and almost forgotten old records. By these means, records acquired
credibilities independent of performance. And, the onus of authenticity was shifted from a regard for the unique to an interest in the
degrees of exclusivity found in the new, rare and antique. However,
a 'unique recording' or 'only copy' has occasionally figured in disc
cultures. One key to the success of reggae sound-systems, argues

Les Back, is having original music in the strict sense of the word: 'Dub plates, or recorded rhythms, are original acetates and they are usually the only copies ... The records are made by artists especially for the sound-system' (Back 1988: 145–6).

Since the 1950s, one way in which disc sessions have attracted audiences is by playing the 'latest releases'. In a modern world of proliferating communications media where the speed by which information travels and fashions change seems to get progressively faster (just as the music seems to quicken, from the 120 beats per minute standard of disco to 200 bpm with techno and jungle music), discotheques are able to deliver the freshest sounds. With dance music, performance has a difficult time keeping up: musicians must decide to expand their repertoire, rehearse the songs, by which time the sound may have lost its currency. As a result, cover or copy bands are now few and far between. Live acts either play their own material or versions which are truly 'their own'. Today, British dance sounds are distinguished by a quick turnover of records, styles and subgenres to the extent that vanguard audiences often dance to tracks on 'import' or limited edition 'white label' *before* their commercial release. (Pre-release to clubs is, in fact, a standard promotion strategy.) Amongst pop music cultures, novelty and rarity displace uniqueness. This may be an instance of what Benjamin called the 'phoney spell of a commodity' but, in this way, records nevertheless enjoy a kind of attenuated aura (Benjamin 1955/1970: 233).

The time-binding power of records fosters interest not only in the novel, but in the archival. Records expedite cultural revival; they allow for 'dancing to music recorded and forgotten in another world and another time' (*Black Music* June 1974). In London in the early 1990s, one could attend record hops where the boys jived and the girls did 'the Madison' or visit funk (also called 'rare groove') clubs where the crowd would 'get down' in 1970s style. Meanwhile 'Classic Disco' nights had become a feature of almost every British provincial town, particularly in gay clubs.

Perhaps the first fully-fledged *archival* dance culture to draw attention to the distinct potentials of discs over and above performed music was the 'Northern Soul' scene of the early 1970s. Populated by white working-class youth from Northern England who danced to obscure, in fact unpopular and long forgotten, Afro-American soul records from the 1960s, the scene was considered by many to be 'the strangest and most unlikely manifestation of the entire black music experience' (*Black Music* November 1975).

The logic of Northern Soul's appeal was not nostalgia but rarity. Taking the Mod taste in soul music (around 1966) off on a tangent, Northern Soul DJs played increasingly rare records from the period. Not only were these records unavailable to dancers but also few of them knew the names of the artists or record labels to which they danced. Nevertheless, the dancers avowed that they went to the Northern Soul discos to hear sounds they couldn't hear anywhere else (*Black Music* June 1974).

Northern Soul records effectively displayed many of the characteristics of the work of art *before* the age of mechanical reproduction. They functioned as the axis of an elaborate ritual and displayed 'cult value'. Certainly, their scene bordered on the religious. As one commentator wrote at the time, Northern Soul 'has evolved its own temples (Wigan Casino, Blackpool Mecca), high priests (the disc jockeys), false prophets (the bootleggers) and congregation (thousands of working class kids pulled from the heavy industry belt of the North and Midlands)' (*Black Music* January 1975).

The ease with which records travel in space and time has enabled the continual crossover and growing globalization that characterize post-war popular music. While not quite 'a music hall without walls', recording technology does trespass on the borders of neighbourhood and nation (McLuhan 1964: 248). Significantly, it also traverses time: records are more readily available *and* longer-lasting than live music; they efficiently distribute *and* preserve sound. It was in exploiting the time and space-binding characteristics of recording that disc cultures acquired distinction.

The ideologies of music genres also played a crucial role in the authentication of recorded music and discotheques. Contemporary pop music has seldom been anathema to discotheques and has rarely tried to deny its recorded form. Rock, however, has pivoted ideologically around the ideal of the live music event despite the fact that it is known by most listeners primarily in its recorded form and has often been played in discotheques. This idea took root with late-sixties rock. In the mid-sixties, *Billboard*'s list of top discotheque records not only included the Beatles' 'Eight Days a Week' and the Beach Boys' 'Do You Wanna Dance?', but also Bob

Dylan's 'Subterranean Homesick Blues' (*Billboard* 1 April 1965). Only a few years later, Dylan would not be considered optimum discotheque music.

The meta-genre, 'dance music', does not have an exclusive claim on dancing. For instance, rock audiences do not sit in quiet, contemplative appreciation. Headbanging, fist-raising, air-guitar solos and other movements which mimic the performers are all 'dancing' in the broad sense of the word. Many live rock gigs involve degrees of toe-tapping, finger-snapping, rhythmic clapping, pogoing, slamming and moshing. Even though the audience tends to face forward, eyes fixed on the stage, these crowds are physically responsive; they do dance and their musics do inspire it.

The repertoire of body movements associated with rock music often fails to be categorized as 'dancing'. This may be because the gaze of the dancers is focused elsewhere, but it may also relate to issues of cultural hierarchy. In the late 1960s, when rock'n'roll became rock, the music abandoned its *overt* function for dancing. (This is not to say that people didn't dance to rock, but that dancing wasn't considered the optimal response.) If rock was to be taken seriously as an art form, then listening, not dancing, would be the requisite mode of appreciation. Dancing is still frequently stigmatized as being uncritical and mindless to the extent that it can debase the music with which it is associated. (That dance-influenced 'ambient' music distinguishes itself as a cerebral listening, or more accurately 'head', music would seem to reinforce this point. It is part and parcel of the genre's bid to be taken seriously by non-clubbers.)

What contemporary British youth call 'dance music' is more precisely designated as discotheque or club music. Rather than having an exclusive claim on dancing, the many genres and subgenres coined obsessively under the rubric share this institutional home. Genres often announce it in their names: disco music was so called because of discotheques, while 'house' and 'garage' were named after key clubs – the Warehouse in Chicago and Paradise Garage in New York. Discotheques have historically played a wide range of music. Afro-American and Afro-Caribbean genres have been particularly affiliated with the institution: R&B and soul in the 1960s; funk, disco and reggae in the 1970s; hiphop, house and garage in the 1980s; ragga, dancehall and jungle in the 1990s. Nevertheless, one should not reify the relationship and forget about white traditions in 'dance music'. Rock'n'roll, electro pop, varieties of gay and Euro-disco, new wave and the New Romantics, Hi-NRG, British acid house and techno, to name just a few, have had predominantly white performers, audiences and sounds.

The ideological categories of 'black' and 'white' define the main axes of authenticity within dance music. Categories of gender and sexuality are employed with reference to pop, but varieties of dance pop such as Madonna or the Pet Shop Boys actually fall outside the definitions of dance music which circulate in the predominantly straight and white club and rave cultures investigated here. Although issues of gender and sexuality can be read into the music and are clearly important discursive categories in gay club cultures (cf. Dyer 1992; Hughes 1994), they are not a conspicuous feature of the discourses of straight club cultures, for the main reason that the feminine tends to signal the inauthentic, and the authentic is rendered in genderless or generically masculine (rather than macho) terms (cf. chapter 3).

'Black' dance music is said to maintain a rhetoric of body and soul despite its use of sampling and other computer technologies. Whereas 'white' or 'European' dance music is about a futurist celebration and revelation of technology to the extent that it minimizes the human among its sonic signifiers. Of course, these categories often have little to do with the actual colour of the people making the records; rather they are two discourses about the value of dance music. Both have their authenticities. For white youth, 'black' musical authenticity is rooted in the body, whereas Euro-dance authenticity, like white ethnicity, is disembodied, invisible and high-tech. In other words, to be organic to a discotheque, music must ring true to its recorded form.

Both 'black' and 'white' dance traditions have been at the forefront of studio experimentation since the sixties. Free from the constraints of imminent performance, makers of dance music have explored the aesthetics of new musical instruments such as synthesizers, drum and bass-line machines and samplers. Unlike rhetorically 'live' genres, the truth of dance music is often found in the revelation of technology. Genres like house, hiphop and techno have conspicuously featured technologies hidden by other genres. They sampled and blatantly manipulated vocals at a time when most pop producers were using samplers to mimic the high production values usually furnished by numerous studio musicians and to correct the lead singer's odd bad note. They used new equipment, not to imitate 'natural' sounds, but to explore and create new sounds.

The 'black' tradition, however, maintains a key interest in vocals and, in certain subgenres, 'funky' instrumentation. For white youth, black authenticity tends to be anchored in the body of the performer/artist/star – in the grain of the voice, the thumping and grinding bass, the perceived honesty of the performance. In other words, authenticity is rooted in the romance of body and soul and relates to essential, verifiable origins. Whether it be soulful house or rap, musical authenticity resides in a rich, full, emotive and embodied sound.

The 'white' dance tradition exchanges fidelity to the body for the romance of technology. Described as electronic, progressive, industrial and techno, these musics tend towards the instrumental and explore new computer sound possibilities. When they use vocals, they tend to be sampled and heavily manipulated into something which sounds futuristic or 'inhuman'. Moreover, their technophilia is demonstrated in their choice of name: for example, LFO, T99, or 808 State (named after the Roland 808 drum machine). Often, certain technologies will come to define a genre. For instance, the signature sound of acid house was a novel bleep produced by a Roland TB303 bass-line machine. Although the DJs in Chicago who first used this sound, like DJ Pierre (also known as Phuture, producer of 'Acid Tracks') were black (and gay, for that matter), the sound came to be associated with a predominantly white club culture in Britain. By 1989, few black clubbers seemed to perceive acid house as black music, although white clubbers seemed to hear the music as 'black' for almost another year. Interestingly, in America, house and acid house were perceived first and foremost as gay and could be heard only in gay clubs until they were re-exported back to the United States as 'English acid house'. Despite the continual cross-fertilization and hybridization of 'black' and 'white' dance musics, the two are kept remarkably separate in discourse. Genres which mix colours aesthetically are always emerging – hip-house, ethnotechno and jungle – but they often float to one pole or the other depending on their association with different audiences.

Both 'white' and 'black' dance music are primarily producers' rather than performers' media. But a producer is a hypothetical, remote origin. So, in the 'black' music tradition, individual singers or rappers will often stand in as authentic sources, whereas in the 'white' tradition dance groups embrace the 'facelessness' often seen as a problem with dance music. Sometimes this denial of image seems to allude to art discourses which celebrate the autonomy of music and the purity of engaging a single sense with sound. But when the act uses a corporate, logo-style name like DNA, SL2 or the KLF, it becomes clear that they are playing with strategies of *branding* rather than the personas of the *artiste*. To some extent, their credibility is measured by their author's invisibility. Album covers and videos (when they have them) are likely to sport computer-generated animation or heavily manipulated and abstracted photographs. Their lack of figurative human image corresponds with their aural abstraction, for as Robert Christgau has written, techno reduces 'vocals to samples and melodies to ostinatos, the average techno hit doesn't leave the average listener . . . much to grab onto' (*Village Voice* 16 February 1993). Moreover, not only do techno acts adopt brands, they also continually change them, eschewing the brand as soon as it is established. In so doing, they avoid 'selling out' and preserve their niche audience.

Another way in which 'black' and 'white' versions of authenticity differ is in their provenance. Although both bear witness to trans-Atlantic influences, 'black' dance musics are more likely to be rooted in local urban scenes and neighbour-'hoods'. Even gestures to the black diaspora point to local subcultures and city places – New York, Chicago, Detroit, Washington. These specific places anchor and authenticate music, render it tangible and real. 'White' dance musics, by contrast, are more likely to claim to be global, nationless or vaguely pan-European.

The trajectory of the genre 'techno' – which began as a 'black' music and ended as 'white' – is revealing of these cultural logics. 'Techno' was launched in the UK by the Virgin Records compilation, *Techno: The Dance Sound of Detroit*, in June 1988. In the months leading to the release, the company's A&R and marketing departments held discussions with DJs and other consultants to decide what to call the music of the three black Detroit-based DJs whose tracks were featured on the album. The term 'house' was then strongly identified with Chicago and was in dangerously ubiquitous use in the UK. They decided on the name 'techno' because it gave the music a distinct musical identity and made it appear as something substantively new (Stuart Cosgrove: interview, 25 August 1992). Crucially, the press release validated the music by emphasizing its roots in subcultural Detroit: 'Techno is the new music of the motor city, a highly synthesized form of modern dance music made in basement studios by Detroit's new underground producers.' In the subsequent articles in music and style magazines, the city was subject to as much copy as the DJ-artists. Despite the fact that the music was not on the playlist of a single Detroit radio station, nor a regular track in any but a few mostly gay black clubs, the British press hailed 'techno' as the sound of that city. Although the genre was not met with contestation* and a few singles from the album (notably Inner City's 'Big Fun') were hits, the genre *as a category* didn't quite take off. Because it was only a little faster and more melodic than 'Chicago' house, techno was not needed as an explanatory rubric or mark of club identity at this time.

Ironically, the term 'techno' was later appropriated to describe a slightly different descendant of Chicago house. When 'acid house' became unserviceable because of tabloid defamation and general overexposure (cf. chapter 4), the clubs, record companies and media went through a series of nominal shifts (about twenty different adjectives came to modify the word 'house', sometimes in pastiches like 'deep techno house') until they finally settled on 'techno'. The term had at least two advantages: it was free from the overt drug references of acid house and it sounded like what it described – a high-tech predominantly instrumental music. Record companies may coin a genre but they cannot control its circulation. By the time Virgin came to release Inner City's third album *Praise* in 1992, they had to shuffle the band's position, redefining their genre niche rather awkwardly as 'soulful techno' – reasserting the 'blackness' of the sound with reference to 'soul'.†

---

* Newly coined genres are often challenged. For example, in the same period, Balearic Beat was hotly debated and criticized for being 'conjured out of thin air' and 'merely a scam' (*Soul Underground* August 1988, *Melody Maker* 20 August 1988).

† There are advantages to having your genre hijacked. For example, when American *Time* magazine introduced techno music to their readers, they said it was 'born in Detroit during the mid-eighties' and by implication positioned Inner City as the founders of rave (*Time* 17 August 1994).

Importantly, the shift from the first to the second kind of techno, from a 'black' to a 'white' sound, is accompanied by a shift in the discourses about their places of origin. Later techno was said to be a musical Esperanto. It was not considered to be the sound of any particular city or any definite social group but rather as a celebration of rootlessness. As one producer said, 'Electronic music is a kind of world music. It may be a couple of generations yet, but I think that the global village is coming' (Ralf Hutter quoted in Savage 1993: 21).

The authenticities of dance music are complex and contradictory. They waver between an ancestral world of real bodies and city places and the new high-tech order of faceless machines and global dislocation. The categories 'black' and 'white' are often used as shorthand for these different sets of cultural values. In practice, however, it is very difficult to map this terrain in these terms because dance music is characterized by a constant borrowing and hybridization.

Since the 1950s, studios have been editing their wares into 'records of ideal, not real, events' (Frith 1987a: 65). Discotheques are an ideal environment for ideal musical events. They are an appropriate site of consumption of musics for which the studio is the main site of production, for the development of genres of music which are quintessentially recorded and the growth of the values which assert their cultural worth. Whether they draw from older live or newer disc-oriented value systems, discotheque musics have evolved their own auras and authenticities.

The Response of the 'Live' Gig

Record sessions and discotheques gained popularity as sites of youthful leisure because they were set up for socializing to an easily altered soundtrack, they targeted youth and cohered with their subcultural ideologies. Additionally, within the aesthetic frameworks of many music genres, records, rather than performances, were increasingly being perceived as offering the best sound. These factors, combined with the economic conditions described in the first part of this chapter, curtailed engagements for live music.

Confronted with, at worst, being swept out with the tide or, at best, positioned as a simulation of recording, performers reacted in two principal, seemingly contradictory ways: they faced the threat of recording by embracing new technologies *and* they positioned themselves as the opposite of the mechanical and predictable disc, reinventing performance as 'live music'. In other words, technology alone could not save the gig. Performance had to find its essence, its superior values, its *raison d'être*. Its response to recorded entertainment was not unlike the reaction of painting to photography a century earlier.* Painting became impressionist and expressionist, rhetorically more spontaneous and personal. It experimented with colour, light and shade, investigated perception and portrayed layers of inner selves. So music performance would transform itself, by developing spectacle, amplifying personalities and heightening the semblance of spontaneity.

Since the 1960s, records have increasingly dictated the nature of performance for reasons related to changes in both consumption and production. First, people came to know a group's music through its records and their aural expectations shifted accordingly. As early as the mid-fifties, there were complaints about the quality of live music. Letters from fans complained not only of high prices, but of bad sound: 'While promoters continue to bring bands to [Manchester], my friends and I will just buy a record with the money and be more satisfied,' wrote one music weekly reader (*Melody Maker* 29 December 1956). The record moved from being 'a primarily mnemonic form (preserving songs known through performance) into a formative or prescriptive one' (Durant 1984: 111). Moreover, live performances were 'checked' against memories of recordings to the extent that when the band fail to approximate their recordings, the 'audience's collective memory takes over and it "hears" what it cannot hear, in the sketch provided by the band' (Middleton 1990: 88).

Second, records have become paradigms for performance because new production techniques, particularly those derived from the use of magnetic tape, have allowed for multi-track recording as well as corrective and creative editing. These changes in production

---

* Of course, records are not like photos *per se* but 'comparable to a photomontage' (Laing 1990: 188).

were preconditions for the development of the *concept album* and the genre, *album rock*, both of which operated under the assumption that rock records could be musical events in themselves. It is no coincidence that the album, rather than the single, was the format to be elevated and, given the centrality of the single to dance culture, it is worth outlining why. First, the duration of the album was similar to a band's set and allowed for the exploration and development of sounds, themes, even movements. Second, since the fifties, the LP had been the configuration of classical music. Presumably, rock and other genres could ennoble themselves by association. Third, album consumers had the appropriate demographics: the bulk of them were white, male and adult (rather than teenage or pre-teen). Whatever the sociological catalysts behind the formation of 'album rock', its accompanying aesthetic of experimental recording presented further challenges to music performance.

The problems that this inverted relationship of recording and performance posed for artistically ambitious bands of the mid-sixties is perhaps best illustrated by the Beatles, particularly the shape of their American tours and their decision in 1966 to abandon performing. The Beatles were the first band to hold concerts in huge arenas and stadiums normally reserved for sporting events and possibly the last band to get away without dramatically changing their style of performance to accommodate this new environment. At New York's Shea Stadium in 1965, for instance, they played a pub-style set on a small platform perched on the pitcher's mound in the middle of the field. There were no elaborate sets or lights, just the four band members poorly amplified and looking like ants even to those screaming in the front row. Drowned out and effectively overpowered by their fans, it's not surprising that they stopped gigging the following year. In fact, the Beatles said that their main reason for retiring from 'live' music was that it impeded their musical creativity. As George Harrison told their authorized biographer in 1968: 'We were held back in our development by having to go on stage all the time and do it, with the same old guitars, drums and bass' (Davies 1968/1992: 344). Faced with conflicting aesthetic demands, the Beatles decided to align themselves with the new aesthetics of recording.

Other bands, however, negotiated the tensions between performance and recording by bringing the technologies of the studio to the stage. The Grateful Dead, for example, one of the most successful live acts in the history of rock, invested heavily in new sound technologies from their inception in the sixties. As Tom Wolfe recounts:

> The Dead [had] equipment such as no rock'n'roll band ever had before ... all manner of tuners, amplifiers, receivers, loudspeakers, microphones, cartridges, tapes, theater horns, booms, lights, turntables, instruments, mixers, muters, servile mesochronics, whatever was on the market. The sound went down so many microphones and hooked through so many mixers and variable lags and blew up in so many amplifiers and rolled around in so many speakers and fed back down so many microphones, it came on like a chemical refinery. (Wolfe 1968a: 223–4)

The Dead pioneered the development of music performances as mixed-media events. Motivated by a desire to simulate an LSD drug experience 'without the LSD', their gigs used black light, strobes, slide and film projections as well as a machine that projected light through plates of glass containing oil, water and food colouring which later became the visual hallmark of the psychedelic movement.

This mode of spectacular technological display is a main way by which live music meets the expectations and proportions of stadium crowds. In the 1970s, the tradition was advanced particularly by progressive rock groups, like Pink Floyd, whose elaborate sets, giant inflatables and pyrotechnics were stage experiments meant to live up to, or at least properly accompany, their studio experiments in sound. By the 1980s, the stadium concerts of all kinds of pop and rock acts had become so complex that they were planned down to the smallest detail with storyboards by concert designers (such as Fisher Park and Robert LePage) who like film directors had their own recognized *oeuvres* and signature-styles. Needless to say, the financial investments of touring have sky-rocketed in accordance with this form of spiralling visual excess.

Today, the record is not the only medium against which performances are measured. Audiences have come to expect a spectacle akin to or better than the one they have experienced by watching music videos. The 'Baudrillard effect', as Frith jokingly calls it, is when 'a concert feels real only to the extent that it matches its TV reproduction' (Frith 1988b: 124–5). So, Janet Jackson's *Rhythm Nation* tour captured not just the flavour of her videos but sometimes re-enacted them in what seemed like a step-for-step duplication of their choreography. Moreover, the concert dance routines were then projected on to an enormous video screen to the side of the stage, so that the audience could then receive the routine through the same medium as it had originally.

Large-screen high-definition video has become a standard feature of many stadium gigs. Sometimes these screens depict segments of the artist's music video; at other times they display newly chosen imagery. Mostly, however, they offer 'live' close-ups of the performers, so the audience can enjoy intimacies of the kind they are accustomed to seeing on television. But, at the show, they see the performer sweat, grin and grimace in *real* time, something they can verify by comparing the positions of the cameramen on stage with the video image above or to its side. On his *Secret World* tour, Peter Gabriel ironically played up to the desires of fans to get close to the star – and be familiar with the famous – by strapping a tiny pivoting video camera to his head which allowed his audience to watch his pupils dilate and to peer into his mouth.

One of the main objectives of concert technologies, then, is not only to enlarge the spectacle, but also to intensify the presence of its personalities. Beatles' fans may have been satisfied by being in the physical presence of the stars – basking in the aura of the band – but subsequent acts needed to dramatize their appearance to maintain an audience for repeated stadium shows. The ways and means of magnifying aura are manifold. The glam images of David Bowie and Roxy Music in the 1970s, for example, meant that although these musics sounded good in discotheques, their fans still wanted to be in the presence of these characters. With flamboyant dress and make-up, these artists gave striking features to what could have been faceless records. With the help of light, smoke and sets, lead singers are often portrayed as the conductors of the show, sometimes they are even positioned as an orchestrating deity. On his *Dangerous* tour, for example, Michael Jackson waved his arms as if to gesture 'let there be light' and there was. He opened the show by emerging 'mysteriously' from clouds of smoke and ended the spectacle without an encore by seeming to ascend to heaven in an astronaut suit.

No matter how dazzling the technological revelation of the artists, the band are still expected to personify the music. At smaller gigs, in particular, they should *appear* to be the inspired source of the sound. The audience expects to appreciate aura. For example, when Madness played a few reunion gigs in late 1992, they were panned. As one reviewer explained:

> Rarely have I seen such a bored bunch of people at a gig. Not the crowd . . . But [the band who] look as bored as a plank full of drill holes. It was like being at a show by the Australian Madness – Mad Again or somesuch; as if a crew of clones had donned the clothes, got the hits down pat, and dragged themselves out onto the stage. (*Melody Maker* 2 January 1993)

Here the missing ingredient is not so much presence as that other principle of 'live' music, spontaneity, which is crucial to performances in so far as it elevates them into unique events. Sometimes, the enactment of spontaneity is as limited as the well-rehearsed deviation from the record track in the form of the guitar or drum solo. At other times, the deviation is more dramatic, involving special guest stars ('my good friend, Eric Clapton, on the guitar') or what has become a perennial crowd-pleaser, smashing one's instruments on stage. More than anything else, it is perhaps this act of destruction which signals that, since the late sixties, music performance has moved into territories well beyond its usual preserve. The Who, the first well-known band to wreck their instruments during a gig, borrowed ideas from artworld 'happenings' which fetishized the impermanence of performance. Later, punk groups, then grunge bands, would turn guitar-smashing into a semi-regular rite.

Spontaneity is one way to make an event seem unique, but musical improvisation in the strict sense of the word is a specialist taste. Regular gig and concert-goers are likely to enjoy behavioural, as much as musical, spontaneity. If one analyses gig reviews published in the music weeklies which keep live music in high regard, musicianship is rarely mentioned. Many of the most celebrated rock musicians are not known as expert players of their musical instruments. Although their particular styles may come to admired, it is as much for their revelation of distinctive personality as for any absolute measure of their musical mastery. Janis Joplin, Jimi Hendrix and Jim Morrison have legendary status as live performers, not only because they were innovative musicians who died young, but because their abuse of drugs and alcohol made them appear out of control on stage. Their dramatic, reckless, involuntary, even unconscious, behaviour was something special for an audience to witness. With punk, good performance actually came to be defined against good musicianship. Punk bands found the essence of performance in all the 'mistakes' that would have been edited out of recorded versions, like flat singing full of wrong notes and brazen displays of musical incompetence.

While there are few allusions to musicianship in gig reviews, references to records abound. Singles and albums and their place in the charts are repeatedly referred to by critics as if they were signposts to the meaning and structure of a performance. No matter how much musicians attempt to distinguish their performances from their recordings, it would seem that the latter reign supreme. So much so that, during the 1980s, a high proportion of shows began using recorded music and sound effects to bring the performed music closer to the clarity and richness of its 'original' recording. According to *Rolling Stone*, 'anywhere from 75% to 100% of touring rock acts use technology to reproduce sounds achieved in the studio and 25% or more of what the audience hears in an arena show is pre-recorded' (*Rolling Stone* 6 September 1990). Only a minority of fans seemed to notice or care that much of the music was recorded: synthesizers replaced horn sections and stringed instruments; drum machines were used instead of drummers and other percussionists; digital samples supplemented on-stage session musicians. Amazingly, none of this extensive use of recorded music seemed to threaten the 'liveness' of these large-scale performances, at least not until it was suggested that the star might be lip-synching.

The meaning and value of 'liveness' in most pop and rock genres cannot be attenuated to the degree that it includes recorded *lead* vocals. (Back-up vocals do not pose the same problem.) Live lead vocals act as a guarantee of star presence and sincerity and, as such, are part of the perceived essence of pop music performance. For this reason, a 'PA' (or 'public appearance') by Sister Sledge at the Odyssey discotheque in Bristol received a improbably favourable review in that outpost of indie rock values, *New Musical Express* (*NME*), at least in part because, despite the fact that all instrumentation was supplied on backing tapes, they had a 'live' vocal presence which was the convincing origin of the sound: 'The atmosphere in this cavernous glitzerama niterie borders on volcanic, but Sister Sledge . . . soak up this scary mass hysteria with seasoned assurance . . . such is the euphoria three feisty divas and a karaoke machine can inspire for half an hour . . . great disco, like fine wine, clearly matures with age' (*NME* 30 January 1993).*

While many concerts are covertly part-record/part-performance, PAs or 'track dates' are an explicit hybrid of the two forms. On one level, then, their difference from gigs is a matter of degree, involving the ratio of high tech to old tech, recorded to 'live' music. On another level, the aesthetic ramifications of the two kinds of show could not be farther apart. For example, the following dance fanzine writer prefers PAs in part because of their less 'macho' gender connotations:

> Gigs are out – PAs are in. A gig was originally a musician's term for a live show or concert . . . Very often it's a complete mess with feedback, bum notes, inaudible vocals, broken guitar strings, vomit and punch ups. A 'PA' or 'Public Appearance' on the other hand is designed to bring a little order to the proceedings. The band (or more often solo artists) perform their songs to a backing tape or CD. Some will 'mime' totally with not one note actually being sung or played. Others will prefer to sing and play part of the music live whilst using CDs to enhance the backing . . .
>
> So where does this leave the 'Sweat & Blood' attitude of the good ol' rock'n'rollers? In reality they're in a different league, where classic poses, endless guitar solos and the 'macho man' image still rules. (*Tab Bumper Techno* Issue 1991)

Dance acts, however, have felt pressure to live up to 'live' aesthetics for several decades – if only because their record labels see touring as a main means of building the artist identity essential for big sales. In the 1990s with the popularity of raves, PAs have developed into more elaborate quasi-live affairs. Acts like Adamski, The

* However, Wendy Fonarow, who has conducted extensive ethnographic research of the British indie scene, argues that another reason why the PA would receive a positive review in *NME* is because, in liking something inappropriate, the reviewer could assert his distinctively individual taste (Fonarow in conversation 1994).

Orb, 808 State and The Prodigy have toured clubs playing sets with computers, samplers and 'improvised' keyboard parts, vocalists and other guest instrumentalists (not to mention turntables). These artists create events that have been hailed as 'live' and have generated stars in ways previously not considered possible by these kinds of club dates.

The key to the success of these new kinds of performance was their delivery of recorded music different from that already available on released records. Much like the 'live' rock show, they found it necessary to deviate from the album to underline the status of the event as a happening. Many dance acts re-enact the procedures involved in making the music in the first place. The Orb, for example, explain: 'What we're trying to do is take the studio out in front of 2,000 people and mix it live . . . For previous [tour] excursions . . . we mixed all the tracks completely differently in the studio, then re-recorded them and ran samples and weird effects over the top live' (*Future Music* June 1993).

The lines which previously demarcated the gig, the PA and the club have been blurred. One group that has actively tried to bring this about is the Shamen. They started out as an indie band, then they got involved with the rave scene and progressively began playing more dance-orientated music. They came up with a cross-breed show they called 'Synergy' where their own set was integrated into a night's entertainment which included DJs, MCs, rappers, 'live keyboards' and creative visual and lighting effects. To the Shamen, the logic was simple: the traditional rock gig 'is outmoded . . . They're no fun to do and no fun to go to: you stand around listening to crappy tapes played through a [public address system], the band comes on and then you go home' (*Face* April 1990). Their Synergy events, by contrast, were said to keep interest and momentum going all night long. According to participants, the party was seamless; people danced to DJ-spun discs, then continued to dance when 'the band' came on.

Since the fifties, the ascendancy of recording as the primary means of communicating music has led both to the divergence and convergence of 'live' and recorded aesthetic values. On the one hand, the 'live' was defined against the supposedly lifeless, banal predictability of the record. It pursued new forms of performance – accentuating its status as spectacle and happening and emphasizing both the proximity and transcendence of the star. On the other hand, recorded events from hops to raves have increasingly integrated the human touch, particularly in the figure of the DJ with his finger on the pulse of the crowd, as well as generating new forms of public appearance which enliven the presence of dance acts. Although once a value assigned exclusively to performance, since the mid-eighties, 'live' qualities have been increasingly attributed to recorded events. At the same time, music performances have become more and more reliant on recording and other mediating technologies which question the integrity of the 'live'. Undoubtedly, the permutations of this history are not over. What is clear, however, is that accounts of the aesthetics of post-war popular music have not, for the most part, addressed this important axis of meaning.

Conclusion

Authenticity in popular music and its primary medium, recording, appears at first to be an idiosyncratic value. Upon sustained consideration, however, one can discern material foundations and ideological logics. The vagaries of the value can be related to concrete practices of production and consumption. With respect to production, I have tried to explore some of the ramifications of 'original' records, the changes in value that occur when the studio is the main site of music production and records precede and prescribe performance. First, records found artistic credibility by exploiting properties specific to them rather than qualities which imitated performance. Second, under certain circumstances, rare and exclusive recordings acquired aura.

This chapter, however, has concentrated on processes of consumption and has found that enculturation is key. The enculturation of records for dancing was not automatic but slow enough to be the subject of 'gaps' between several generations. It was (and still is) an uneven process dependent on diverse influences. Its history involves big businesses, trade unions and copyright law, the semantics of interior design, the social requirements of distinct crowds, the evolution of new professions, the production processes and travel patterns of particular genres, and discourses about the honesty and integrity of music.

Records were no mere substitute for performance, they were a different form altogether – one which fostered new types of event and social space. To accommodate such sounds harmoniously, dances had to change their appearance and structure. So the discotheque eventually became a site of consumption appropriate to music whose site of production is the studio.

Since rock'n'roll, records have become increasingly indispensable, integral and organic to music cultures. They have become the musical axis around which club and rave crowds gather and scenes revolve. But what exactly are the configurations of these crowds? What hierarchies define and divide clubbers? What social demographics and cultural values distinguish them? These are the issues investigated in the next chapter.

3

Exploring the Meaning of the Mainstream (or why Sharon and Tracy Dance around their Handbags)

A Night of Research

Saturday, 22 September 1990. Wonderworld, London W8, 11 p.m. It's exactly eleven and I'm waiting for Kate.* We've never met before, but she knows I'm researching clubs and has promised to show me 'how to have fun'. The 'hardcore techno-house' of the dancefloor is just audible from here. Two women police officers patrol on foot. Mostly same-sex groups wear casual clothes and casual expressions; they walk slowly and deliberately until they've got past the door staff, then plunge down the stairs into the club. I feign uninterest because clubbing is the kind of activity that shuns official, parental, constabulary or even 'square' observation. Clubbers often voice antipathy towards the presence of people who don't belong and come to gawk.

A few minutes later, Kate jumps out of a black cab. She's energetic

* The names of people and clubs have been changed. 'Kate' and I made contact through the letters page of *The Face* magazine. In the summer of 1990, I received thirty-five letters in response to ones I'd published in the monthly style magazines, *i-D* and *The Face*, and the London listings magazines, *City Limits* and *Time Out*. I used these letters from clubbers and ravers (some of which are quoted) as a source of information about the values of club culture and as a means of making contact with possible guides and informants.

and her immaculately made up eyes gleam. Her brother runs this club, so she asks the doorwoman to 'sort us out'. The woman takes a pack of cards and hands me a three of diamonds, smiling: 'This will get you all the way.' We descend a flight of steps where a bouncer inspects my card, then ushers us in. The doorwoman insisted that this club, run by ex-rave organizers in rave style, has no door policy – absolutely anyone could come in. Nevertheless, the crowd looks pretty homogeneous. They are mostly dressed in a late version of the acid house uniform of T-shirts, baggy jeans and kickers boots; they're white and working-class. There is also a handful of Afro-Caribbean men hanging-out near the door who look as if they might be friends of the entirely black crew of bouncers.

We walk around the club. The venue is early-eighties plush, but it's transformed for tonight's club by large unstretched glow-in-the-dark canvases of surreal landscapes with rising suns and psychedelic snakes. A white boy, wired and talking a mile a minute, stops me in my tracks: 'Want some "E"?' He's referring to 'Ecstasy' and he's eating his words. The volume of the music is such that I can only catch bits of his sales pitch: 'I got burgers and double burgers . . . fifteen quid.' He is a poor advertisement for the effects of his wares. From his aggressive and jumpy delivery, I assume that he is really on some speed concoction or perhaps this is his first night on the job.

We descend more stairs to the VIP room where another bouncer gestures for my card, then waves us in. No door policy upstairs, but an exacting one down here. This room is so restricted that, at this hour, there is no one here except the barmaid. But it's still early. We get a Coke and a mineral water and sit down. It feels private. Kate is very much at home. 'Tell me about your research then.' She's genuinely interested in my work, but also probing into whether I can be trusted. Her brother is one of the original rave organizers, who began by putting on parties in barns and aircraft hangars, then went legit, organizing weekly clubs for ravers in venues around London. As Kate tells it, the police monitored all their parties from the beginning, but as soon as the 'gutter press' were hard up for a front-page story the scene got out of hand: 'Kids, who shouldn't even have known about drugs, read about the raves in the *Sun* and thought, "Cor – Acid. That sounds good. Let's get some", and loads of horrible people started trying to sell "swag" drugs.'

During our conversation, the VIP room has filled up. Kate suggests I meet her brother who is sitting at the bar with a long blonde and a bottle of Moët et Chandon on ice. He is in his early twenties and wears a thick navy-and-white jumper, something which immediately distinguishes him from those here to dance. Kate tells him that I've never taken Ecstasy ('Can you believe it?') and that we are going to do some tonight. He's not pleased. 'How do you know she won't sell this to the *Daily Mirror*?' he asks. Kate assures him that she's checked me out, that I'm all right. Later, they explain that they want someone to tell the 'true story' of acid house and that they'll help me do it as long as I don't use their names.

Kate pours me a champagne and takes me aside. A friend has given her an MDMA (the pharmaceutical name for Ecstasy) saved from the days of Shoom (the mythic club 'where it all began' in early 1988). We go to the toilets, cram into a cubicle where Kate opens the capsule and divides the contents. I put my share in my glass and drink. I'm not a personal fan of drugs – I worry about my brain cells. But they're a fact of this youth culture, so I submit myself to the experiment in the name of thorough research (thereby confirming every stereotype of the subcultural sociologist). Notably, there's 'Pure MDMA' for the VIPs and 'double burgers' for the punters. The distinctions of Ecstasy use are not unlike the class connotations of McDonald's and 'no additives' health food.

Millennium, London W1, 1 a.m. Millennium is the kind of club that pretends it's not mentioned in listings magazines but is. It imagines itself as entirely VIP chiefly because it's heavily into cocaine. At first, they won't let us in, but Kate uses her brother's name, and we're admitted free. The crowd is older than average (mid-to-late twenties), dressed in designer-labels (lots of Jean-Paul Gaultier and Paul Smith), and obviously concerned about who's who. There is a contingent of gay men by the bar and a scattering of women with handbags and high heels on the dancefloor. The music is familiar, dance-oriented pop.

The club's organizer is famous for his early-eighties New Romantic clubs. He looks worn out. His face is pale and dry. Later, when I tell people I went to his club, they ask 'Is he still going?' The question seems to be written on his face. He's a has-been in a world whose fashions last six months and old in a world that fetishizes youth. As we shake hands, he introduces me to a journalist who covers the club scene.

Mick writes regularly for a weekly music magazine and a daily newspaper. After a chat about sociology and some people we know in common, he pulls out a flyer for a rave in a church, suggesting I come along. The flyer is in the form of an elaborate card: its front cover displays a crest of a chicken dressed as a vicar holding a bible; inside are an odd mixture of quotations from the New Testament, DJs and clothing designers. It's a charity benefit – 'strictly invitation only'.

Cloud Nine, London EC1, 2:30 a.m. Cabs are scarce, but we're finally in one, driving around looking at churches as the invite gives only a vague address. The driver stops and asks two police on their beat for directions. The policewoman peers into the back seat and asks, 'Are you going to see Boy George?' She's heard about this event and there is trace of envy in her voice. But her partner dutifully points the way – 'take your first left, then second right.' This club scene sees itself as an outlaw culture, but its main antagonist is not the police (who arrest and imprison) but the media who continually threaten to *release* its cultural knowledge to other social groups.

St George's is an eighteenth-century, neoclassical church on a side street. Nothing announces the club except for a few lights and a lone black doorman who, although he's a giant, looks dwarfed between the temple's columns. The DJ console is on the altar. The congregation dances, leans and lounges on pews. The all-male line-up of DJs are known to be trend-setters; they play records before their commercial release and influence the sound of the national club scene. Some have their own radio shows or act as record company A&R men. Others are full-fledged 'artists' who have produced 'underground' dance hits and even number-one singles.

The dancers are aged eighteen to twenty-two, mostly white and 'beautiful'. Typically, the girls have dressed with more attention and elaboration than the guys. A handful sport this week's fifteen-minute fashion, sixties-style bouffants. Thick black eyeliner and pale lipstick stare at you with studied blankness from every direction. I believe this is the straight hairdressers and fashion retail crowd, with a few models and art school students mixed in for good measure. But it is often difficult to tell. Questions about work are taboo in this leisure environment. You could have a long conversation in the toilets with a woman who tells you she's taken two 'E's, just been jilted by her boyfriend and is sleeping with his best friend for revenge, but ask her what she does for a living and she may well stop in mid-sentence at this insulting breach of etiquette. It is rude to puncture the bubble of an institution where fantasies of identity are a key pleasure.

Determining social background can be just as tricky. Obviously, one can*not* inquire about parental occupation. Accents can offer some indication, but it is relatively common for upper-middle-class Londoners to adopt working-class accents during their youth and vice versa. However, in their pursuit of classlessness, they are still interested in being a step ahead and a cloud above the rest. Like disco before it, acid-house-cum-rave supposedly democratized youth culture. Now, the 'everybody welcome' discourse lingers at some clubs and is emphatically out at others. But whether they are 'no door policy' or 'invitation only' events, the composition of their crowds generally has some coherence. The seemingly chaotic paths along which people move through the city are really remarkably routine.

Sometime after 4 a.m. – time seems to be standing still – we venture into the VIP room in the minister's office behind the altar. It is white-walled and spartan, with a desk, fireplace and bookshelves. The room is full of men who know each other – mostly DJs and club organizers – who are talking about the quality of recent releases and club events. Around another corner, I'm introduced to the operator of a Soho venue with a long-standing reputation for the hippest DJs, music and crowd. He tells me he's been running clubs since 1979, then snorts some coke off the corner of a friend's Visa card. His blue eyes actually dart about like whirling disco spotlights and his conversation is a chaotic compilation of *non sequiturs*. Ecstasy turns banal thoughts into epiphanies. I see how club organizers, DJs and journalists – the professional clubbers – get lost within the excesses and irresponsibilities of youth. With no dividing line between work and leisure, those in the business of creating night-time fantasy worlds often become their own worst victims.

The lights come on. All of a sudden, it's 6 a.m. The party's over. The remaining dancers mill about, saucer-eyed, confused about what to do with themselves. We bump into the 'official photographer' of the event who tells us that Boy George never turned up and the church has to be cleaned for mass at ten o'clock. The press weren't allowed in, but the church wanted some documentation on the fund-raiser, so they hired him. 'Hilarious,' says Mick, 'what religion will suffer to stay in business.' The photographer tells us he has a few shots the *Sun* would pay dearly for, but he won't yield to temptation – it would be 'bad faith'.

Academic Accounts of the Cultural Organization of Youth

> Sociology has to include a sociology of the social world, that is a sociology of the construction of world views, which themselves contribute to the construction of the world.
>
> Bourdieu 1990: 130

One of the prices paid by subculturalists and sociologists of youth for neglecting issues of cultural value and hierarchy is that they have become inadvertently ensnared in the problem. When investigating social structures, it is impossible to avoid entanglement in a web of ideologies and value judgements. Nevertheless, it is important to maintain *analytical* distinctions between: empirical social groups, representations of these people and estimations of their cultural worth. Academic writers on youth culture and subculture have tended to underestimate these problems. They have relied on binary oppositions typically generated by *us-versus-them* social maps and combined a loaded colloquialism like the 'mainstream' with academic arguments, ultimately depicting 'mainstream' youth culture as an outpost of either 'mass' or 'dominant' culture. In this chapter, I explore the organization of club culture by comparing the social worlds portrayed in clubber discourses with the social worlds I observed as an ethnographer. This reflexive methodological approach enables a double interrogation the meaning of the 'mainstream' and the social logic of youth's subcultural capitals. In this way, I attempt to offer a fuller representation of the complex stratifications and mobilities of contemporary youth culture.

Before this, however, it is worth considering the ways in which the cultural world of youth has been previously constructed by British academics. Dick Hebdige's *Subculture: The Meaning of Style* (1979), one of the most influential texts in the field, is heavily dependent on the mainstream as the yardstick against which youth's 'resistance through rituals' and subversion through style is measured. But Hebdige's mainstream is abstract and ahistorical. For example, he compares punk apparel, not to disco attire or other contemporary clothing, but to 'the conventional outfits of the man and woman in the street' (Hebdige 1979: 101). He contrasts punk 'anti-dancing' with the 'conventional courtship patterns of the dancefloor' (Hebdige 1979: 108). One could point out, however, that the influence of 'conventional courtship patterns' has been decreasing since the Twist. Although end-of-night 'slow dances' linger at school discos and are occasionally subject to ironic revival, they have been marginal to club culture for almost thirty years.

Each reference to the 'mainstream' in *Subculture* points in a different direction, but if one added them up, the resultant group would be some version of the 'bourgeoisie' whose function within Hebdige's history is, of course, to be shocked. While this framework complements his repeated characterization of subcultural youth as 'predominantly working-class', it hardly does justice to the bulk of young people who are left out of the picture. Hebdige's multiple opposition of avant-garde-versus-bourgeois, subordinate-versus-dominant, subculture-versus-mainstream is an orderly ideal which crumbles when applied to historically specific groups of youth.

Inconsistent fantasies of the mainstream are rampant in subcultural studies. They are probably the single most important reason why subsequent cultural studies find pockets of symbolic resistance wherever they look (cf. Morris 1988). Rather than making a clear comparison, weighing the social and economic factors, and confronting the ethical and political problems involved in celebrating the culture of one social group over another, they invoke the chimera of a negative mainstream.

When academics turn their full attention to the mainstream (and don't just infer it from their discussion of subcultures), the results may also turn out to be reductive. Geoff Mungham's article 'Youth in pursuit of itself' is based on research done at a Mecca dancehall in an unnamed town. Despite the singular site of his research,

Mungham contends that his study is not about any particular dancehall, but about the 'scenario of the mass dance' which is the 'forum for what might be called mainstream working-class youth' (Mungham 1976: 82). In order to make this dancehall stand in for the mainstream, Mungham doesn't rationalize its representativeness but, rather, strips it of its differences and specificities by refusing to mention details of occupation and location and by avoiding cultural references altogether. In fact, according to Mungham, the cultural aspects of the 'mass dance' are insignificant to its real meanings:

> While the music may change, while shifting fashions and tastes may chase after new stars and performers, social relationships inside the dance hall stay unchanged. There is an order and youth partakes of it gladly. Respectable working-class youth, on its nights out, is largely quiescent and conforming. (Mungham 1976: 92)

Mungham searches for the normal, the average, the routine and the mundane. He positions his study as a counterbalance to sociology's orientation toward the conspicuous and bizarre, repeatedly straining to emphasize the conformity, conservatism and 'sheer ordinariness of this corner of youth culture' (Mungham 1976: 101). In the end, Mungham describes the dance as a 'mechanical configuration' and as a '*Mecca*nization of the sexual impulse' (Mungham 1976: 92). Despite his ethnographic observation, he projects a 'Mass Society' style vision on to the Mecca dancers, portraying them in a way not unlike Adorno depicted jitterbug dancers of the 1940s as 'rhythmically obedient . . . battalions of mechanical collectivity' (Adorno 1941/1990: 40).

Both Hebdige and Mungham define subcultures and mainstreams against each other. Their antithesis partly derives from the high cultural ideologies in which both formulations are entangled. Hebdige perceives his mainstream as bourgeois and his subcultural youth as an artistic vanguard. Mungham sees his mainstream as a stagnant 'mass', only their deviant *others* are, by implication, creative and changing. Although assigned different class characteristics, both 'mainstreams' are devalued as normal, conventional majorities.

In her article 'Dance and social fantasy', Angela McRobbie questions the basis of these value judgements but still preserves their

binary structure (cf. McRobbie 1984). McRobbie maintains the opposition between mainstream 'respectable city discos' and 'subcultural alternatives', but instead of exclusively celebrating the latter,
she suggests that dancing offers possibilities of creative expression,
control and resistance for girls and women in either place. In several
essays, McRobbie has explored the substantial complications that
gender poses to these distinctions, but she stops short of disputing
the dualistic paradigm (cf. McRobbie 1991).

The mainstream–subculture divide is not the only dichotomy to
which the musical worlds of youth have been subject. Other sociologists contrast the culture of middle-class students with that of
working-class early school-leavers. For example, Simon Frith outlines a split between a mostly middle-class 'sixth-form culture' of
individualists who buy albums, listen to progressive rock and go to
concerts and a working-class 'lower-fifth-form culture' of cult fol-
lowers who buy singles, listen to 'commercial' music and go to
discos (cf. Frith 1981a). He links these research findings to a broader
distinction between rock culture and pop culture:

> the division of musical tastes seemed to reflect class differences: on the
> one hand, there was the culture of middle-class rock – pretentious and
> genteel, obsessed with bourgeois notions of art; on the other hand,
> there was the culture of working-class pop – banal, simple-minded,
> based on the formulas of a tightly knit body of business men. (Frith
> 1981a: 213–14)

Frith admits that this conception of two worlds is a simplification in
so far as 'pop culture' is both younger and predominantly female in
addition to being working-class. But a further problem arises. The
sixth-formers of his study do espouse this us – them binarism; they
'differentiated themselves from the masses as a self-conscious elite
by displaying exclusive musical tastes' (Frith 1981a: 208). His lower-
fifth-formers, however, seem to embrace a more plural vision of
music audiences – one in which the sixth-form 'hippies' become just
one among many youth cultures. As one fifth-former says, 'I don't
know what youth culture means. I think it means what you are –
Skin, Greaser, or Hairy. I am none of these' (Frith 1981a: 207). Frith
seems to view the terrain of music crowds through the eyes of his
middle-class student interviewees – the result of a 'natural' and,
perhaps, not quite conscious identification.

In his paper 'Nightclubbing: An exploration after dark', Stephen Evans similarly universalizes the outlook of the students who now frequent dance clubs and distinguish themselves from a mainstream of working-class Mecca disco attenders (cf. Evans 1989). Accordingly, Evans finds two distinct nightclub cultures in Sheffield: one 'commercial', the other 'alternative'. The commercial culture takes place in 'glitzy palaces' which play top forty chart music and are populated by white, early school-leavers of working-class origin. The 'alternative' culture, by contrast, is situated in darkly lit 'dives' which focus on the newest developments in dance music and are attended primarily by students.

There are certainly differences between the leisure cultures of early school-leavers and higher education students, but this is only one measure of difference – and not the one privileged by the working-class 'glitzy palace' crowd. Even in a small city like Sheffield, this schema necessarily omits specialist music club nights as well as the city's gay and rocker clubs. It could certainly not cope with the highly differentiated activities of a metropolitan centre like London or the complex cultural axes of the national club scene.

Dichotomies like mainstream/subculture and commercial/alternative do not relate to the way dance crowds are objectively organized as much as to the means by which many youth cultures imagine their social world, measure their cultural worth and claim their subcultural capital. Hebdige, Mungham, McRobbie, Frith and Evans uncritically relayed these beliefs and, with the exception of Frith, got caught up in denigrating or, in the case of McRobbie, celebrating the 'mainstream'.

Interestingly, the main strands of thought on the social structure of youth amongst these British scholars contradict one another. One positions the mainstream as a middle-class, 'dominant' culture, while the other describes it as a working-class, 'mass' culture. Some, then, see the alternative as (middle-class) student culture, others as (working-class) subculture. (In figure 3, Hebdige and the Birmingham tradition espouse axis *A*; Mungham and McRobbie embrace *B*; Frith and Evans advocate *C*.) Moreover, each tradition has tended to subsume, rather than properly deal with, the contradictions raised by the other. For example, the subculturalists address the complications posed by student culture by arguing that it is not really a 'subculture' but a diffuse 'milieu' within the dominant culture (cf.

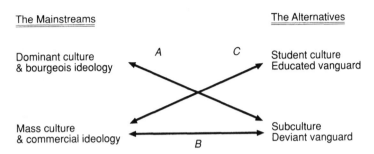

Figure 3 The academic divides of youth culture

Clarke et al. 1976). While sociologists, like Frith, have pointed to the student origins of many 'working-class' subcultures (cf. Frith and Horne 1987). These discrepancies might equally have been used to prise open the dichotomies themselves.

In the 1970s and early 1980s, when the study of popular culture was just beginning, these formulations represented important forays into mapping the social organization of music culture. In the 1990s, however, one needs to draw a more complicated picture which takes account of both subjective and objective social structures as well as the implications of cultural plurality. North American exponents of cultural studies have begun to take up the latter task. In his 'The politics of music: American images and British articulations', Lawrence Grossberg begins by asserting that subcultures and the mainstream have 'fluid boundaries' which are a 'matter of degrees and situated judgements' (Grossberg 1987: 147–8). Later, he goes further, contending that subculture and mainstream are indistinguishable: 'the mass audience of pop, the mainstream of style, is the postmodern subculture' (Grossberg 1987: 151). Grossberg does so by imploding polar opposites. For him, the centre is 'a floating configuration of marginality', and homogeneity is 'a social pastiche'; conformity is the pursuit of individualism and authenticity is really co-optation (Grossberg 1987: 147–8).

In 1990s Britain, many have opted for a similar vision of plural subcultures. For example, a detailed commercial report on youth culture researched by the British Market Research Bureau and compiled by Mintel claimed that a mass of teenage consumers no longer exists: 'Marketers and advertisers should be constantly aware that the young are not a broadly homogeneous group taking part in a mass event called the late 1980s (as was to some extent the case in the 1960s or early 1970s). In the UK, youth culture, if it exists at all, is made up of a highly diverse mixture of subcultures' (Mintel 1988c).

Although Grossberg's argument is in many ways appealing, two problems arise for those concerned with understanding the distinctions of youth (in both Britain and North America). First, Grossberg shuns notions of social *structure* in favour of plurality without pattern or design. He ultimately pictures youth as an undifferentiated mass – homogeneous in their heterogeneity and indifferent to distinction. Second, Grossberg ignores the social significance of the concept of the 'mainstream' to youthful maps of the cultural world – which are arguably stronger in Britain, but still influential and active in the States (cf. Christenson and Peterson 1988).

Rather than painting an omniscient picture of the social organization – or disorganization – of youth culture, I investigate the mainstream as an important feature of the 'embodied social structure' of youth. Popular discourses about dance crowds have the crucial function of anchoring and orienting their beholders in the social world, but they do not offer a value-free account of that world. So, while it is important to take up youth's perspectives and grant credibility to their views (cf. Becker 1967), it is also vital to contextualize, compare and contrast their outlooks. In the following sections, I shall explore some of the ideological functions and social ramifications of the mainstream. I'll then consider some of the methodological and epistemological problems involved in researching and representing the social organization of club culture.

The Social Logic of Subcultural Capital

'Clubland', as many call it, is difficult terrain to map. Club nights continually modify their style, change their name and move their location. Individual clubbers and ravers are part of one crowd, then another, then grow out of going out dancing altogether. The musics with which club crowds affiliate themselves are characterized by a fast turnover of singles, artists and genres. Club culture is faddish and fragmented. Even if the music and the clothes are globally marketed, the crowds are local, segregated and subject to distinctions dependent on the smallest of cultural minutiae.

For these reasons, many clubbers would say it is impossible to chart the patterns of national club cultures. Nevertheless, they constantly catalogue and classify youth cultures according to taste in music, forms of dance, kinds of ritual and styles of clothing. They carry around images of the social worlds that make up club culture. These mental maps, rich in cultural detail and value judgement, offer them a distinct 'sense of [their] place but also a sense of the other's place' (Bourdieu 1990: 131). So, although most clubbers and ravers characterize their own crowd as mixed or difficult to classify, they are generally happy to identify a homogeneous crowd to which they don't belong. And while there are many *other* scenes, most clubbers and ravers see themselves as outside and in opposition to the 'mainstream'.

When I began research in 1988, hardcore clubbers of all kinds located the mainstream in the 'chartpop disco', specifically the Mecca disco. 'Chartpop' did not refer to the many different genres that make it on to the top forty singles sales chart as much as to a particular kind of dance music which included bands like Erasure and the Pet Shop Boys but was identified most strongly with the music of Stock, Aitken and Waterman (the producers of Kylie Minogue, Jason Donovan, Bananarama, Kim Appleby and other dance-oriented acts). Although one is most likely to hear this playlist at a provincial gay club, the oft-repeated, almost universally accepted stereotype of the chartpop disco was that it was a place where 'Sharon and Tracy dance around their handbags'. This crowd was considered unhip and unsophisticated. They were denigrated for having indiscriminate music tastes, lacking individuality and being amateurs in the art of clubbing. Who else would turn up with that uncool feminine appendage, that burdensome adult baggage – the handbag? 'Sharon and Tracy' were put down for being part of a homogeneous herd overwhelmingly interested in the sexual and social rather than musical aspects of clubs. Many clubbers spoke of 'drunken cattle markets', while one envisioned a scene where 'tacky men drinking pints of best bitter pull girls in white high heels and Miss Selfridge's miniskirts.'

Towards the middle of 1989, in the wake of extensive newspaper coverage of acid house culture, clubbers began to talk of a new mainstream – or rather, at first, it was described as a second-wave of media-inspired, sheep-like acid house fans. This culture was populated by 'mindless ravers' or 'Acid Teds'. Teds were understood to travel in same-sex mobs, support football teams, wear kickers boots and be 'out of their heads'. Like Sharon and Tracy, they were white, heterosexual and working-class. But unlike the girls, the ravers espoused the subterranean values proper to a youth culture (like their laddish namesakes, the Teds or Teddy Boys of the fifties) at least in their predilection for drugs, particularly Ecstasy or 'E'.

However, when the culture came to be positioned as truly 'mainstream' rather than just behind the times, it was feminized. This shift coincided with the dominance of house and techno (with titles like *Hardcore Ecstasy, Awesome 2* and *Steamin! – Hardcore '92*) in the compilation album top twenty throughout 1990, 1991 and 1992. By the end of this period, talk of 'Acid Teds' was superseded by disparagement of raving Sharons and 'Techno Tracys'. The music genre had even come to be called 'handbag house.' As one clubber explained to me, 'The rave scene is dead and buried. There is no fun in going to a legal rave when Sharons and Tracys know where it is as soon as you buy a ticket.' Consumer magazines ran spoof columns, 'Six of the best ways to be a Techno Tracy', which advised readers to 'discard your 25-carat gold chains in favour of a crystal pendant' and 'laugh at the girls you've left behind at the local disco, because "they just don't understand good music" ' (*Face* November 1991).

Some clubbers and ravers might want to defend these attitudes by arguing that the music of Stock/Aitken/Waterman, then acid house-cum-techno, respectively dominated the charts in 1987–8, and then in 1989–91. But there are a couple of problems with this reasoning. First, the singles' sales chart is mostly a pastiche of niche sounds which reflect the buying patterns of many taste cultures rather than a monolithic mainstream (cf. Crane 1986). Moreover, buyers of the same records do not necessarily form a coherent social group. Their purchase of a given record may be contextualised within a very different range of consumer choices; they may never occupy the same social space; they may not even be clubbers.

Second, whether these 'mainstreams' reflect empirical social groups or not, they exhibit the burlesque exaggerations of an imagined *other*. *Teds* and *Tracys*, like *lager louts, sloanes, preppies* and *yuppies*, are more than euphemisms of social class and status, they demonstrate 'how we create groups with words' (Bourdieu 1990: 139). So, the activities attributed to 'Sharon and Tracy' should by no means be confused with the actual dance culture of working-class girls. The distinction reveals more about the cultural values and social world of hardcore clubbers because, to quote Bourdieu again, 'nothing classifies somebody more than the way he or she classifies' (Bourdieu 1990: 132).

It is precisely because the social connotations of the mainstream are rarely examined that the term is so useful; clubbers can denigrate it without self-consciousness or guilt. However, even a cursory analysis reveals the relatively straightforward demographics of these personifications of the mainstream. Firstly, the clichés have class connotations. Sharon and Tracy, rather than, say, Camilla and Imogen, are what sociologists have tended to call 'respectable working-class'. They are not imagined as poor or unemployed, but as working and aspiring. Still, they are not envisaged as *beneath* 'hip' clubbers as much as being *classed* full stop. In other words, they are trapped in their class. They do not enjoy the classless autonomy of 'hip' youth.

Age, the dependence of childhood and the accountabilities of adulthood are also signalled by the mainstreams. The recurrent trope of the handbag is something associated with mature womanhood or with pretending to be grown-up. It is definitely *not* a sartorial sign of youth culture, nor a form of objectified subcultural capital, but rather a symbol of the social and financial shackles of the housewife. The distinction between the authentic original and the hanger-on is also partly about age – the connoisseur deplores the naive and belated enthusiasm of the younger raver or, conversely, the younger participant castigates the tired passions of the older one for holding on to a passé culture.

Young people, irrespective of class, often refuse the responsibilities and identities of the work world, choosing to invest their attention, time and money in leisure. In his classic article 'Age and sex in the social structure of the United States', Talcott Parsons argues that young people espouse a different 'order of prestige symbols' because they cannot compete with adults for occupational status (Parsons 1964: 94). They focus less on the rewards of work and derive their self-esteem from leisure – a sphere which is more conducive to the fantasies of classlessness which are central to club and rave culture. In *Distinction*, Bourdieu identifies an analogous pattern solely for French middle-class youth. 'Bourgeois adolescents,' he writes, 'who are economically privileged and (temporarily) excluded from the reality of economic power, sometimes express their distance from the bourgeois world which they cannot really appropriate by a refusal of complicity whose most refined expression is a propensity towards aesthetics and aestheticism' (Bourdieu 1984: 55).

A refusal of complicity might be said to characterize British youth culture in general. Having loosened ties with family but not settled with a partner nor established themselves in an occupation, youth are not as anchored in their social place as those younger and older than themselves. By investing in leisure, youth can further reject being fixed socially. They can procrastinate what Bourdieu calls 'social ageing', that 'slow renunciation or disinvestment' which leads people to 'adjust their aspirations to their objective chances, to espouse their condition, become what they are and make do with what they have' (Bourdieu 1984: 110–11). This is one reason why youth culture is often attractive to people well beyond their youth. It acts as a buffer against social ageing – not against the dread of getting older, but of resigning oneself to one's position in a highly stratified society.

The material conditions of youth's investment in subcultural capital (which is part of the aestheticized resistance to social ageing) results from the fact that youth, from many class backgrounds, enjoy a momentary reprieve from necessity. According to Bourdieu, economic power is primarily the power to keep economic necessity at bay. This is why it 'universally asserts itself by the destruction of riches, conspicuous consumption, squandering and every form of gratuitous luxury' (Bourdieu 1984: 55). But 'conspicuous', 'gratuitous' and 'squandering' might also describe the spending patterns of the young. Since the 1950s, the 'teenage market' has been characterized by researchers as displaying 'economic indiscipline'. Without adult overheads like mortgages and insurance policies, youth are free to spend on goods like clothes, music, drink and drugs which form 'the nexus of teenage gregariousness outside the home' (Abrams 1959: 1).

Freedom from necessity, therefore, does not mean that youth have wealth so much as that they are exempt from adult commitments to the accumulation of economic capital. In this way, youth can be seen as momentarily enjoying what Bourdieu argues is reserved for the bourgeoisie, that is the 'taste of liberty or luxury'. British youth cultures exhibit that 'stylization of life' or 'systemic commitment which orients and organizes the most diverse practices' that develops as the objective distance from necessity grows (Bourdieu 1984: 55–6).

This is true of youth from all but the poorest sections of the population, perhaps the top seventy-five per cent. While youth unemployment, homelessness and poverty are widespread, there is still considerable discretionary income amongst the bulk of people aged 16–24. The 'teenage market', however, has long been dominated by the boys. In the 1950s, 55 per cent of teenagers were male because girls married earlier, and 67 per cent of teenage spending was in male hands because girls earned less (cf. Abrams 1959). In the 1990s, the differential earnings of young men and women have little changed – a fact which no doubt contributes to the masculine bias of subcultural capital.

Although clubbers and ravers loathe to admit it, the femininity of these representations of the mainstream is hard to deny. In fact, consistently over the past two decades, more girls have gone out dancing than boys. This is particularly marked amongst the sixteen-to-nineteen age-group because girls start clubbing at a younger age. Dancing is, in fact, the only out-of-home leisure activity that women engage in more frequently than men. Men are ten times more likely to attend a sporting event, twice as likely to attend live music concerts and marginally more inclined to visit the cinema (Central Statistical Office General Household Surveys 1972–86). When it comes to preferences rather than the practices, gender is again decisive; the first choice for an evening out for women between fifteen and twenty-four is a dance club whereas the most popular choice of men the same age is a pub (Mintel 1988b).

Girls and women are also more likely to identify their taste in music with pop. Over a third of women (of all ages), compared to about a quarter of men, say it is their favourite type of music. Women spend less time and money on music, the music press and going out, and more on clothes and cosmetics (Mintel 1988c; Euromonitor 1989). One might assume, therefore, that they are less sectarian and specialist in relation to music because they literally and symbolically invest less in their taste in music and participation in music culture.

In their American study, Christenson and Peterson found marked gender differences in attitudes to the 'mainstream' amongst American youth. Their research suggested that men regarded the label *mainstream* as 'essentially negative, a synonym for *unhip*' whereas women understood it as 'another way of saying *popular* music' (Christenson and Peterson 1988: 298). Their women respondents were more likely to say that they used music 'in the service of secondary gratifications (e.g. to improve mood, feel less alone) and as a general background activity'. They conclude by describing the male use of music as 'central and personal' and the female orientation to music as 'instrumental and social' (Christenson and Peterson 1988: 299). These American findings about women's use of music correlate with British clubbers' assumptions about the mainstream.

The objectification of young women, entailed in the 'Sharon and Tracy' image, is significantly different from the 'sluts' or 'prudes', 'mother' or 'pretty waif' frameworks typically identified by feminist sociologists (cf. Cowie and Lees 1981; McRobbie 1991). It is not primarily a vilification or veneration of girls' sexuality (although that gets brought in), but a position statement made by youth of both genders about girls who are not culturally 'one of the boys'. Subcultural capital would seem to be a currency which correlates with and legitimizes unequal statuses.

These mainstreams also point to the relevance of Andreas Huyssen's arguments about how mass culture has long been positioned as feminine by high cultural theorists, but here the traditional divide between virile high art and feminized low entertainment is replayed within popular culture itself (cf. also Modleski 1986a and Morris 1988). Even among youth cultures, there is a double articulation of the lowly and the feminine: disparaged *other* cultures are characterized as feminine *and* girls' cultures are devalued as imitative and passive. Authentic culture is, by contrast, depicted in gender-free or masculine terms *and* remains the prerogative of boys.

The refusal of parental class and work culture goes some way towards explaining why young people seem to borrow tastes and fashions from gay and black cultures. Jon Savage has argued that the camp and kitsch sensibilities of gay male culture have been repeatedly taken up by British youth (cf. Savage 1988). Stephen Lee has argued that, in an American context, the trendy club scene often maintains its esotericism by hiding in gay clubs and drawing from gay cultures which threaten the college 'jocks'. More often noted (and arguably more relevant to club cultures in this period) is British youth's habit of borrowing from African-American and Afro-Caribbean culture – often with a romantic, 'orientalist' appropriation of black cultural tropes (cf. Hebdige 1979; Said 1985). Even the word 'hip' is said to have its origins in black 'jive talk' where the phrase 'to be on the hip' initially meant that one was an opium smoker but was later generalized to mean simply being 'in the know' (Polsky 1967).

Subcultural capital is the linchpin of an alternative hierarchy in which the axes of age, gender, sexuality and race are all employed in order to keep the determinations of class, income and occupation at bay. Interestingly, the social logic of subcultural capital reveals itself most clearly by what it dislikes and by what it emphatically isn't. The vast majority of clubbers and ravers distinguish themselves against the mainstream. In the final section of this chapter, I discuss some of the methodological problems involved in mapping the cultural organization of clubs, given the specific social agendas to which clubber representations of the clubworld are put.

Participation versus Observation of Dance Crowds

One complication of my fieldwork resulted from the fact that the two methods that make up ethnography – participation and observation – are not necessarily complementary. In fact, they often conflict. As a participating insider, one adopts the group's views of its social world by privileging what it *says*. As an observing outsider, one gives credence to what one *sees*. In this case, the results of the two methods contrasted dramatically. The 'mainstream' was a perennial point of discursive reference, perpetually absent from view.

This methodological contradiction between participation and observation is best understood within the larger epistemological conflict which Bourdieu discusses in terms of subjectivism and objectivism. As John Thompson aptly summarizes, subjectivism is an 'intellectual orientation to the social world which seeks to grasp the way the world appears to individuals within it'; it explores people's beliefs and ignores the unreliability of their conceptions. Objectivism, by contrast, is an approach to the social world which 'seeks to construct the objective relations which structure practices and representations'; it explains life in terms of material conditions and ignores the experience individuals have of it (Thompson 1991: 11). According to Bourdieu, both modes of thought are too one-sided to describe adequately the social world. On their own, neither approach can come to grips with the double nature of social reality. On the one hand, social life is determined by material conditions but, on the other, these conditions affect behaviour through the intercession of beliefs and tastes. In the previous section, I investigated the subjective social worlds of clubbers and ravers; in this one, I pursue a more objectivist line of inquiry.

Between 1988 and 1992, I acted as a participant observer at over two hundred discos, clubs and raves and attended at least thirty live gigs for comparative purposes. In the course of these four years' ethnographic research, I was unable to find a crowd I could comfortably identify as typical, average, ordinary, majority or mainstream. Not that I didn't witness people dancing to 'chartpop' or to techno music at raves. On the contrary, I observed all sorts of different configurations of these crowds. Several times, I even observed the old and the new mainstreams together in the same room. At a Glasgow club in the spring of 1989, for example, the music alternated between Stock/Aitken/Waterman and what had just ceased to be called 'acid house' (because of mass media overexposure). The population and practices of the dancefloor fluctuated according to the shift of genres, going from being almost entirely female to mostly male, from soulful free-form dancing in pairs to ecstatic trance-dancing in groups of six and eight. But I also observed a multitude of other cultural configurations. To apply the label 'mainstream' to any of these would have run the risk of denigrating or normalizing the crowd in question. I could always find something that distinguished them – if not local differences, then shades of class, education and occupation, gradations of gender and sexuality, hues of race, ethnicity or religion.

Ethnography is a qualitative method that is best suited to emphasizing the diverse and the particular. The mainstream, by contrast, is an abstraction that assumes a look of generality and a quantitative sweep. Participant observation is not equipped to establish whether a particular dance crowd is nationally dominant unless, of course, it is mass-observation proposing to collect and quantify the work of many researchers. (For this reason, as mentioned above, it is rather incredible that Mungham (1976) professes to offer an ethnography of mainstream dancing by doing research in a single dancehall.) My method was one of ethnographic survey, rather than the more common ethnographic case study, which meant that representativeness was a particular concern. I consulted government statistics and market research but because their data on dancing tends to be either incomplete or very general, I was unable to construct a convincing random sample of clubs. Nevertheless, I did discover material that helped me to assemble a more objectivist picture of club culture, particularly with regard to the site that has been consistently identified as the location of the mainstream by dance crowds and academics alike – the Mecca disco.

In 1990, Mecca owned fifty-eight out of an estimated four thousand nightclubs in Britain. Publicly listed leisure corporations own just five per cent of British clubs – a situation dramatically different from that of, say, the record industry where the five majors are generally responsible for seventy per cent of annual sales. Unlike other nightclub operators, Mecca (which has since been taken over by Rank Leisure) promoted its clubs under four hierarchically ranked brands: their two main chains, Ritzy and 5th Avenue, their so-called 'smaller, more intimate and exclusive brand', Cinderella Rockerfellas, and their flagship venue, The Palais in Hammersmith. In 1992, however, they came to realize that their branding policy was backfiring. Marketers in other kinds of business are usually keen to be perceived as 'mainstream'; they are particularly intent for their brand name to become generic for all products of the same kind – in the manner of, say, Biro, Hoover or Kleenex. However, as Mecca–Rank discovered rather belatedly, generics are anathema to club culture. Their active branding had actually facilitated their negative positioning as the mainstream. As Mintel reported it, 'Rank does not see any advantages of nationwide branding in this market', so the company abandoned the unifying brands' concept and renamed each of their venues individually (Mintel 1992).

Although big business is often aligned with mass culture, the empirical grounds for the association in this case are slim. Mecca 'chartpop' disco culture would seem to be yet another niche culture – one positioned as the norm, partly because of Mecca's long history and its misguided business strategies. Moreover, the youth cultures housed by Mecca clubs are not, and have never been, homogeneous. Despite their centralized operations, Mecca dancehalls have long been the home of traditional spectacular subcultures. For example, Tottenham Mecca was a key Teddy Boy hang-out in the 1950s and Blackpool Mecca was one of the main hubs of the Northern Soul scene in the 1970s. In the late eighties, the Hammersmith Palais frequently played host to Banghra events.

In distributing my participant observation, I was certain to attend Mecca venues and mixed-genre 'chartpop' clubs, but I also did my best to explore a balance of black and white, gay and straight, student and non-student clubs and raves. I was concerned to investigate a broad range of musical styles: from rock'n'roll revival through classic disco to new age cyberpunk clubs; from clubs with reggae, rare groove and hiphop playlists to ones featuring indie, industrial and rock music. Nevertheless, the balance of my research was tipped in favour of the house–techno–rave continuum which did seem to eclipse other club sounds during the period in question. My study also had a distinct urban bias. Most of my research was carried out in London, with substantial preliminary research conducted in Glasgow. Although I visited clubs around the country, from the Haçienda in Manchester to Bobby Brown's in Birmingham, this work was complementary rather than core.

As I mentioned in the Introduction, being foreign had some research advantages. It was easier to approach and to obtain information from strangers, particularly in as much as they were more likely to explain the obvious. Moreover, British ideologies about the mainstream baffled me where they might have been taken for granted by a British researcher. They were a puzzle that I was determined to resolve. After much questioning, it turned out that many clubbers who disparaged the mainstream confessed that they had never attended such a dance club. Moreover, their use of a limited repertoire of cultural details, metaphors and metonyms suggested that their knowledge of these other crowds was mostly second-hand, either heard along grapevines or gathered from media sources. Both mainstreams were, in fact, closely associated with specific media texts. The 'dancing around handbags' crowd was imagined principally as an enthusiastic audience of *Top of the Pops* (for over twenty-five years, the key point of television exposure for the singles sales chart); as one clubber put it, these clubs were full of people who 'think *Top of the Pops* is trend-setting'. This crowd was also identified with a late-night programme called *The Hitman and Her* presented by Pete Waterman of the production trio, Stock/ Aitken/Waterman; as another clubber explained, 'chartpop' discos were 'full of the *Hitman and Her* elements'. (It is worth noting that many of Pete Waterman's *Hitman and Her* television shows were shot on location in Mecca venues and that Waterman-produced artists, Kylie Minogue and Jason Donovan, did their initial national 'public appearance' tours in Mecca discos.) Acid Teds and Techno Tracys, by contrast, were often characterized as *Sun* readers (the widest-read daily paper in the world, with a circulation which hovers around four million).

In contemporary Britain, the media are bound to be an important source of information about other social groups and, consequently, a means of orientating oneself in the social world. Like its ancestor the 'mass', it would seem that the mainstream is, to a large extent, read off media texts. Theodor Adorno associated the worst tendencies of mass culture with the 'radio generation' much as David Riesman defined his indiscriminate majority as 'the audience for the larger radio stations and the hit parade'; so club crowds conceive their mainstreams with the aid of national television and tabloids (Adorno 1941/1990: 40; Riesman 1950/1990: 8). This process may be common to other interest groups, but it is inflected by the youthful commonsense that club culture is the inverse of broadcasting's domestic accessibility and that it is the antithesis of widely disseminated tabloid talk.

The concept of the mainstream grows out of the inextricability of the media and lived culture. For this reason, it is no wonder that the consensus in North America is that the mainstream is a cluster of subcultures (cf. Crane 1986; Grossberg 1987; Straw 1991). The size, ethnic diversity and proliferation of local, regional and niche media in the United States weaken the myth of the 'mainstream'. Whereas, in the United Kingdom, the 'mainstream' is a more powerful idea to youth and academics alike not only because of a predominately white and Anglo-Saxon population, but also due to the primacy of national mass media centralized in London. (This is explored in depth in the next chapter.)

So how are club crowds objectively organized? First, it is worth emphasizing that 'crowd' is the word used by clubbers and ravers to describe the collections of people who go out dancing. It is an appropriate term for it implies a congregation of limited time and unity, but leaves the exact structure open to further definition; crowds may contain a nucleus of regulars, degrees of integration and clusters of cliques. Unlike the 'mass', they are local and splintered. Crowds are the building-blocks of club cultures and, until the day when communications media offer multi-sensory interaction in the form of a fully *virtual reality* nightclub, it is likely that such congregations will be important to many kinds of music scene, community and culture.

Pre-eminently, crowds act as a concrete reminder that any analysis of the cultural organization of youth needs to take into account the social groups to which they belong. In subcultural studies, the spatial and social existence of youth cultures have often been lost under the symbolic weight of their clothes and their consumer habits. Despite scholars' claims that subcultures are 'not simply ideological constructs', empirical social groups have often been elided. (Clarke et al. 1976: 46) This is true not just of 1970s subcultural studies, but of recent work in the field. In his otherwise compelling article, 'Systems of articulation, logics of change: Communities and scenes in popular music', for example, Will Straw maps out two communities – the North American dance music and heavy metal scenes – with little reference to the people who inhabit or imagine them. Whether the people actually gather is irrelevant. Despite use of the term 'community', the communal is all but ignored. Even the nature of the differences between the communities as subjectively imagined and objectively practised is eclipsed by an implicit notion that it is all discourse.

One function of a disparaged *other* like the mainstream is to contribute to the feeling of community and sense of shared identity that many people report to be the primary appeal of clubs and raves. As clubbers and ravers explain:

> It is so wicked to go somewhere and be surrounded by loads of people your own age and into the same stuff – the last time you had that it was at school, but that wasn't through choice!

> The appeal of clubs comes down to people who you would like to surround yourself with. Being with people who are similar to yourself creates a feeling of belonging . . .

> The thrill (and it really is a thrill) of going to clubs is the communal experience, the feeling of sharing something with other like-minded people.

The feeling of belonging can override obvious social differences. A straight woman who goes dancing only in gay men's clubs writes:

> I tell my [boyfriend] that this is my private – among two thousand people – freak out session . . . I do not want him to come with me when I go out dancing . . . this is one place that is my place . . . I love to wander around the club and feel unthreatened by being female.

Many clubbers talk about the rightness and naturalness of the crowds in which they have had good experiences. They feel that they fit in, that they are integral to the group. The experience is not of conformity, but of spontaneous affinity. 'Good' clubs are full of familiar strangers who complement that 'well developed leisure activity, the discovery of self' (Dorn and South 1989: 179).

Despite being 'similar' and 'like-minded', when asked to describe the social character of the crowd at the clubs they attend, clubbers are inclined to say they are 'mixed'. Just as *other* crowds are assumed to be homogeneous, so their *own* crowds are perceived as heterogeneous. Nevertheless, most clubs have observable 'master statuses'. In his article, 'The dilemmas and contradictions of status', Everett Hughes argues that race, sexuality, class and professional standing take on different precedence in different contexts (cf. Hughes 1945). So, different clubs contextualize social differences in different ways: in one sexual identity is primary; in another racial or occupational identity unify the crowd.

Although no one social difference is paramount in all clubs, the axis along which crowds are most strictly segregated is sexuality – a fact which betrays the importance of clubs as a place for people to meet prospective sexual partners whether they are gay or straight. This separation was perhaps more extreme between 1988 and 1992 than in other periods. The New Romantic, 'gender-bending' clubs of the early 1980s were reported to be sexually mixed. The late 1980s saw a decline in clubs where gay, bisexual and straight people socialized perhaps because of the rise of AIDS and anti-gay legislation like Clause 28 and 29 which led to both increased separatism on the part of the gay community and also to intensified homophobia on the part of young heterosexuals. However, a vogue for cross-dressing clubs like Kinky Gerlinky in 1991–2 and a mildly sexually experimental mod revival in 1993–4 were signs that this was again shifting. Nevertheless, sexuality is a perennial divider. Most listing magazines catalogue dance clubs together in a single section, except for gay and lesbian clubs which are put in a completely different part of the magazine under rubrics like 'Gay' or 'Out in the City'.

After sexuality, the second most important factor determining who congregates where is taste in music. Clubbers and ravers generally explain their attendance at particular events in terms of their love of the music played. The centrality of music is further indicated by the fact that amongst the information on flyers promoting clubs, music is the only cultural attribute that is almost always mentioned. Usually the music is specified by a short generic list: for example, 'techno, hardcore, alternative, trance' or 'ragga-hiphop-jungle'. The music is also invoked by naming DJs who are associated with certain sounds and crowds. (In the case of indie clubs, which experience their apogee elsewhere at gigs and revolve around bands, the music is often specified by an exhaustive catalogue of the artists played, e.g. 'The Charlatans, Happy Mondays, Farm, Stone Roses . . .' or 'Blur, Pulp, Suede, Oasis' etc.) By whichever means the music is conjured, it relates directly to the promised crowd because taste is not, of course, an individual matter.

Musical preference has a complicated and contingent but unmistakable relation to the social structure. As George Lewis succinctly explains, 'we pretty much listen to, and enjoy, the same music that is listened to by other people we like or with whom we identify' (Lewis 1992: 137). Bourdieu argues that next to taste in food, taste in music is the most ingrained. Aesthetic appreciation is passionate (people *love* their music) and aesthetic intolerance violent (they *hate* that noise) perhaps because aural experiences take firmer root in the body than, say, visual ones. Although socially conditioned, musical taste is experienced as second nature. It is *felt* to be involuntary, instinctive, visceral. As a deep-seated taste dependent on background, music preference is therefore a reasonably reliable indicator of social affinity.*

Although taste usually ensures that the appropriate crowd turns up at the right venue on a given night, door policies also regulate the crowd. Here, the first set of differences crucial to admission relate to the body. Policies that involve age, gender and sexuality are often explicitly administered. Door staff will tell people waiting outside a club that three men and a woman are more likely to get into a straight club than an all-male group and that women in general are favoured. The staff will also inform punters that they are too old or occasionally too young for the place, while doormen at gay clubs will warn or question men whose body language appears too heterosexual. Refusing entry to a gay man at a straight club, however, is likely to employ the excuse of dress, just as discrimination against youth of African or Asian descent is never openly acknowledged. Ratios of black to white patrons are often carefully managed, frequently by black bouncers. (For an analysis of the way clubs employ black bouncers to implement racist door policies, cf. Mungham 1976.) Usually the alibi here is clothes. For example, in the summer of 1989, a trendy house music club in a black neighbourhood conducted a strict ban on trainers (running shoes) which had the effect of admitting the *Doc-Martens*-wearing white kids and excluding the *Nike*-wearing Afro-Caribbean kids at a moment when white youth were less likely to sport a hiphop-influenced wardrobe.

Self-selection is the first principle in the organization of club

* This might offer a clue to the resilience of the categories of 'black' music and 'white' music despite their conspicuous aesthetic cross-fertilization discussed in chapter 2. The aesthetic distinctions are held on to because the social distinctions remain.

crowds; routes of communication (discussed in the next chapter) is the second; door policy is the third. Door people put the finishing touches to the composition of the crowd. They style the club's internal image and contribute to its cohesive total environment. As such, they are key readers and makers of the 'meaning of style'. Most analysts of subcultural style have de-contextualised clothes and overlooked the role of the situated viewer (cf. Hebdige 1979; Wilson 1985). Rather than privileging their own free-wheeling interpretations, these critics could keep the clothes *in situ* and anchor their discussions of sartorial meaning in key social interactions like those of the club .

Some clubbers liken getting through the door to passing an exam: one needs to study the look, prepare the body and stay cool under pressure. This does not mean that club crowds are stylistically or superficially similar rather than substantially alike. Clothing is a potent indicator of social aspiration and position; as Tom Wolfe once put it, 'fashion is the code language of status' (Wolfe 1974: 23). As forms of objectified subcultural and economic capital, clothes frequently act as metonyms for larger social strata. 'Blue collar' and 'white collar' are euphemisms for class, just as references to stilettos and handbags are roundabout ways of saying that a social group lacks subcultural capital.

Conclusion

Whatever its exact status, the mainstream is an inadequate concept for the sociology of culture. References to the mainstream are often a way of deflecting issues related to the definition and representation of empirical social groups. Sometimes, it signals an unquestioning acceptance of youth's point of view or rather the universalization of the embodied social structure of a particular group. On other occasions, the binary thinking which accompanies references to the mainstream is entangled in a series of value judgements, political associations and journalistic clichés which hardly do justice to the youth cultures in question. Their schemas (like the youthful ideologies they reproduce) mix and match oppositions such as the following:

US	THEM
Alternative	Mainstream
Hip/cool	Straight/square/naff
Independent	Commercial
Authentic	False/phoney
Rebellious/radical	Conformist/conservative
Specialist genres	Pop
Insider knowledge	Easily accessible information
Minority	Majority
Heterogeneous	Homogeneous
Youth	Family
Classless	Classed
Masculine culture	Feminine culture

Popular ideologies about dance crowds are riddled with implied statuses, refined echelons and subcultural capitals. Rather than subverting dominant cultural patterns in the manner attributed to classic subcultures, these clubber and raver ideologies offer 'alternatives' in the strict sense of the word, namely other social and cultural hierarchies to put in their stead. They may magically resolve certain socio-economic contradictions, but they also maintain them, even use them to their advantage. For many youthful imaginations, the mainstream is a powerful way to put themselves in the big picture, imagine their social world, assert their cultural worth, claim their subcultural capital. As such, the mainstream is a trope which betrays how beliefs and tastes which ensue from a complex social structure, in turn, determine the shape of social life. This is the 'double nature' of social reality.

4

The Media Development of 'Subcultures' (or the Sensational Story of 'Acid House')

The Underground versus the Overexposed

The idea that authentic culture is somehow outside media and commerce is a resilient one. In its full-blown romantic form, the belief suggests that grassroots cultures resist and struggle with a colonizing mass-mediated corporate world. At other times, the perspective lurks between the lines, inconspicuously informing parameters of research, definitions of culture and judgements of value. Either way, theorists and researchers of music and youth culture are among the most tenacious holders of the idea. This chapter, however, contends that the distinctions of youth subcultures are, in many cases, phenomena of the media.

Every music scene has its own distinct set of media relations. 'Acid house', a dance club culture which mutated into 'rave' after sensational media coverage about drug use, is particularly revealing of the cultural logics involved. In considering this case, I argue that there is, in fact, no opposition between subcultures and the media, except for a dogged ideological one. I do not uncover pure origins or organic homologies of sound, style and ritual, nor vilify a vague monolith called 'the media'. Instead, I examine how various media are integral to youth's social and ideological formations. Local micro-media like flyers and listings are means by which club organizers bring the crowd together. Niche media like the music press construct subcultures as much as they document them. National mass media, such as the tabloids, develop youth movements as much as they distort them. Contrary to youth subcultural ideologies, 'subcultures' do not germinate from a seed and grow by force of their own energy into mysterious 'movements' only to be belatedly digested by the media. Rather, media and other culture industries are there and effective right from the start. They are central to the process of subcultural formation, integral to the way we 'create groups with words' (Bourdieu 1990: 139).

The term 'underground' is the expression by which clubbers refer to things subcultural. More than fashionable or trendy, 'underground' sounds and styles are 'authentic' and pitted against the mass-produced and mass-consumed. Undergrounds denote exclusive worlds whose main point may not be elitism but whose parameters often relate to particular crowds. They delight in parental incomprehension, negative newspaper coverage and that best blessing in disguise, the BBC ban. More than anything else, then, undergrounds define themselves against the mass media. Their main antagonist is not the law which might suppress but the media who continually threaten to release their knowledges to others.

Like 'subcultures', undergrounds are nebulous constructions. They can refer to a place, a style, an ethos, and their crowds usually shun definitive social categorization. Mostly they are said to be 'mixed' but, although the subcultural discourses I describe do cross lines of class, race and sexuality, their holders are less likely to physically cross the relevant thresholds (see previous chapter). Generally, underground crowds are attached to sounds. As one label manager put it: 'There are records out there that are more radical and, at this moment, have a more radical audience – a smaller, more selective audience – but the sounds in that area will be the next generation of sounds we're all used to . . . That's what I mean by underground' (*Select* July 1990: 57).

The logic of the underground is aptly symbolized by its attitude to two product types. Its distinctive format is the 'white label' – a twelve-inch single produced in a limited edition without the colourful graphics that accompany most retailed music, distributed to leading disc jockeys for club play and to specialist dance record shops for commercial sale. The rarity of white labels guarantees their underground status, while accumulating them can contribute to their owner's distinction. (The size of a *man's* record collection has long been a measure of his subcultural capital!) At the other end of the spectrum, the format with the least credibility is the television-advertised compilation album of already charted dance hits. One fanzine writer ranted against amateur ravers who buy such albums: 'Wise up sucker, get hip to musical freedom, stop investing in K-Tel compilations with titles like *Nonstop Mental Mega Chart Busting Ravey Rip Off Hits Vol 234516'* (*Herb Garden* December 1991). While these hit compilations may contain music that was on a white label only six months earlier, the sounds are corrupted by being accumulated and packaged.

The underground espouses a fashion system that is highly relative; it is all about position, context and timing. Its subcultural capitals have built-in obsolescence so that it can maintain its status not only as the prerogative of the young, but the 'hip'. This is why the media are crucial; they are the main disseminators of these fleeting capitals. They are not simply another symbolic good or indicator of distinction, but a series of institutional networks essential to the creation, classification and distribution of cultural knowledge.

Before going on to survey relations between the dance 'underground' or subculture and various media, I should explain that this part of my work is based on several different methods of research. First, it derives from my ethnographic research in clubs; I was careful to pay heed to passing comments, and to question clubbers, about their use of and attitudes towards diverse media. So, rather than a study of reception *per se*, this chapter offers an analysis of the larger site of media consumption. Second, it draws on interviews with professionals in the field – particularly club organizers, journalists and record company PR and promotions people. Finally, it is based on a extensive textual analysis of the media under consideration. This unorthodox combination of methods was necessary to give a fuller picture of the myriad relations between club cultures and the media.

I should also clarify how my approach is indebted to and critical of four existing accounts of the relationship between youth, music and media. First, it diverges on several key points from the cultural studies associated with the Birmingham tradition. In the Introduction to *Resistance through Rituals,* Clarke et al. suggest that their consideration of post-war youth subcultures will 'penetrate beneath [the] popular constructions' of the mass media (Hall and Jefferson 1976: 9). When they come to define 'subculture', they position the media and its associated processes outside, in opposition to and after the fact of subculture. In so doing, they omit precisely that which clearly delineates a 'subculture', for labelling is crucial to the insiders' and outsiders' views of themselves as different. By discarding this key symbolic interactionist insight, their classification of subculture is indeterminate (cf. Becker 1963). Subcultures are said to have a 'distinctive enough shape and structure to make them identifiably different'; they are 'focused around certain activities, values ... territorial spaces' and can be either 'loosely or tightly bounded' (Hall and Jefferson 1976: 13–14). This definition could be applied to many cultural groups.

The Birmingham tradition tended to study previously labelled social types – 'Mods', 'Rockers', 'Skinheads', 'Punks' – but gave no systematic attention to the effects of various media's labelling processes. Instead, they described the rich and resistant meanings of youth music, clothing, rituals and argot in a miraculously media-free moment when an uncontaminated homology could be safely identified. Moreover, the Birmingham tradition frequently positioned subcultures as transparent niches in an opaque world as if subcultural life spoke an unmediated truth. They were insufficiently critical of subcultural ideologies, first, because their attention was concentrated on the task of puncturing and contesting dominant ideology and, second, because their theories agreed with the anti-mass media discourses of youth music cultures. While youth celebrated the 'underground', the academics venerated 'subcultures'; where one group denounced the 'commercial', the other criticized 'hegemony'; where one lamented 'selling out', the other theorized 'incorporation'.

Sociologies of 'moral panic', a second academic tradition that addresses the subject of youth cultures and the media, contrast with the cultural studies on several key points (cf. Cohen 1972/1980; Young 1971; Cohen and Young 1973). While the subculturalists depict full-blown subcultures without any media intervention, scholars of 'moral panic' assume that little or nothing existed prior to *mass* media labelling. So, in his classic *Folk Devils and Moral Panics,*

Stanley Cohen suggests that there were few antagonisms between Mods and Rockers, nor even thoroughly articulated stylistic differences, before reports of their seaside scuffles (cf. Cohen 1972/1980). Also, while the subculturalists are implicitly indebted to the youth-oriented music and style press, the 'moral panic' scholars often seem unaware of their existence. In Cohen's book, for instance, the media is synonymous with local and national newspapers, while magazines which might have been read by his subcultural subjects are ignored (i.e. the Mod girl's *Honey* or the Mod boy's *Record Mirror*).*

Sociologies of 'moral panic' offer important theories of deviance amplification, self-fulfilling prophecies and composite stereotypes called 'folk devils', but they do not take a sufficiently sweeping look at associated processes of cultural production and consumption. According to Cohen, 'folk devils' are 'unambiguously unfavourable symbols' but a devil in the tabloids is often a hero or, more commonly, an idiot in the youth press (cf. Cohen 1972/1980). The negative tabloid coverage of acid house, for example, was subject to extensive analysis by the music and style magazines. The writers were fascinated by their own representation and, however much they condemned the tabloids, they revelled in the attention and boasted about sensational excess. What could be a better badge of rebellion? Mass media misunderstanding is often a goal, not just an effect, of youth's cultural pursuits. As a result, 'moral panic' has become a routine way of marketing popular music to youth.

Ethnographies of music scenes, like subcultural studies, tend to see the media as outside authentic culture (cf. Finnegan 1989; Cohen 1991). They depict internally generated culture, disclose local creativity and give positive valuation to the 'culture of the people' but only at the cost of removing the media from their pictures of the cultural process. When media are theorized by traditional ethnographies, they are generally seen as akin to the ethnographer's own representational practice, as depicting and disseminating the cul-

---

* Features such as *Queen*'s 1964 'Tickets and other Labels' offer empirical evidence which substantially complicates, perhaps even confounds, Cohen's version of 'moral panic'. It describes a 'Ticket' as a 'sub-Mod, imitating the Mods but always three months behind' who nevertheless knows that 'nothing happened' at Brighton or Margate and that 'the whole incident was simply a Press invention' (see *Queen* 26 August 1964).

ture in question (cf. Clifford and Marcus 1986). But media sights, sounds and words are more than just representations; they are mediations, integral participants in music culture. Needless to say, there are no primordial pre-media cultures in Britain today. Even when a youth culture defines itself against the overexposed entertainments of the *Sun* or the prime-time pleasures of *Top of the Pops*, its identity and activities are conditioned by the desire to be part of something that is not widely distributed or televised.

This is not to posit the reverse, postmodern 'ecstasy of communication' proposition, in either its euphoric or mournful incantation. Visions of endless mediascapes are as wilfully one-sided as the anthropologist's dream of pure culture. Iain Chambers's cruise through 'the communication membrane of the metropolis', for instance, does little to clarify the concrete relations between youth and music cultures and their various media. When we are said to have screens for eyes and headphones for ears, then communication is automatic, indiscriminate and total (cf. Chambers 1986). But access to information is restricted at every turn. We are not all plugged in, so to speak, and certainly not into some central bank of sight and sound. In fact, being 'hip' or 'in the know' is testimony to the very selective nature of contemporary communications; 'subcultural capital' is defined against the supposedly obscene accessibility of mass culture (cf. Baudrillard 1982).

To understand the relations between youth subcultures and the media, one needs to pose and differentiate two questions. On the one hand, how do youth's subcultural ideologies position the media? On the other, how are the media instrumental in the congregation of youth and the formation of subcultures? The two questions are entwined but distinct. Youth's 'underground' ideologies imply a lot but understand little about cultural production. Their views of the media have other agendas to fill. Like other anti-mass culture discourses, they are not always what they purport to be, i.e. politically correct, moral or vanguard. As discussed in the previous chapter, subcultural ideologies are a means by which youth imagine their own and other social groups, affirm their distinction and confirm that they are not just 'attention spans' to be bought and sold by advertisers.

Similarly, the second question about how the media do not just represent but mediate within youth culture can only be fully understood in relation to club cultural ideologies. For the positioning of various media outlets – prime-time television chart shows versus late-night narrowcasts, BBC versus pirate radio, the music press versus the tabloids, flyers versus fanzines – as well as discourses about 'hipness', 'selling out', 'moral panic' and 'banning' are essential to the ways young people receive these media and, consequently, to the ways in which media shape subcultures.

Mass Media: 'Selling Out' and 'Moral Panic'

Scholars all too often make generalizations about the media based on an analysis of television alone. In the mid-nineties, however, mass media are in decline and the dominance of television – or at least *broad*casting – is in question. We are in an age of proliferating media, of global narrowcasting and computer networks where anyone on-line is 'nearby'. To make sense of the complexity of contemporary communications, it is necessary to divide the media into at least three layers. From the point of view of clubbers and ravers, in particular, micro, niche and mass media have markedly different cultural connotations. Moreover, their diverse audience sizes and compositions and their distinct processes of circulation have different consequences for club cultures. With mass media, for instance, affirmative coverage of the culture is the kiss of death, while disapproving coverage can breathe longevity into what would have been the most ephemeral of fads. In this section, I examine these dynamics of 'selling out' and 'moral panic' in relation to three national media: prime-time television, national public service radio and mass circulation tabloid newspapers.

Although the situation is changing, most British homes still receive only four television channels; cable and satellite TV's audience share hovers just under eight per cent (in 1995): MTV Europe has so few British viewers that it generally refuses to release figures, saying only that the number of homes connected is three and a half million (and sixty-one million for all of Europe). Of the terrestrial stations, the public service BBC1 and commercial ITV account for almost seventy per cent of all television viewed. Television in

Britain is therefore, for the time being, a mass medium in the old sense of word: there is relatively little regional or local programming and niche targeting is a recent entreprise which tends to operate well only outside prime-time. As a result, the only regular prime-time music show occupies a key position within the symbology of the underground.

Having been on the air for over twenty-five years, *Top of the Pops* has close to universal brand recognition; it is seen as the unrivalled nemesis of the underground and the main gateway to mass culture. This half-hour programme combines 'live vocal' performances attended by a free-standing studio audience with video clips – both of which are introduced according to their current position in that week's top forty. The show is considered so domestic, familial and accessible that the ultimate put-down is to say a club event was 'more *Top of the Pops* on E than a warehouse rave' (*i-D* June 1990). Moreover, it is assumed that 'for dance music to stay vital, to mean more than the media crap we're fed from all angles, it has to keep *Top of the Pops* running scared' (*Mixmag* December 1991).

This disdain for *Top of the Pops* is tied up with a measure of contempt for the singles sales chart. Clubbers have a general antipathy to what they call 'chartpop' (or occasionally 'chartpap'), which does not include everything in the top forty but rather the 'teenybop' material identified with girls between eight and fourteen (who are most likely to buy seven-inch singles).* However, when it comes to dance music, clubbers and ravers seem concerned less with actual sales figures than with concomitant media exposure – the ancillary effects of chart placement on television programming, radio playlists and magazine editorial policies. This is perhaps best demonstrated by the fact that clubbers and ravers tend to have deep admiration for tracks that got into the top ten without any radio or video play – simply on the strength of being heard in clubs, covered in the specialist press and bought on twelve-inch by clubbers alone.

Top of the Pops, rather than the singles chart *per se*, is seen as a key point of so-called 'selling out'. For instance, a member of a techno dance act (called LFO) with a single in the charts warns, 'don't

---

* The top forty singles sales chart has long been a symbol of trash in music (see Riesman 1950 on the Hit Parade). The first British singles chart was published in *New Musical Express* in 1952, and the first album chart was published in *Melody Maker* in 1958.

expect to see us on *Top of the Pops*. We might let them show the video, but we [won't] have people pointing at us, regarding us as sell-outs. LFO is purely underground stuff... We hate all those false and fake people in the charts. We only like the hard stuff' (*NME* 28 July 1990). If one were to take this discourse about 'selling out' at face value, one might see it as anti-commerce or resistant.

Dick Hebdige theorizes 'selling out' as a process of 'incorporation' into the hegemony. He describes this recuperative 'commercialization' as an aesthetic metamorphosis, an ideological rather than a material process whereby previously subversive subcultural signs (such as music and clothing) are 'converted' or 'translated' into mass-produced commodities (Hebdige 1979: 97). But as the popular rhetoric of 'selling out' assumes that records with low sales aren't 'commercial' (even though they are obviously products of commerce) and validates the proliferating distinctions of consumer capitalism, this fusion of populist and Marxist discourses is wistful.

Within club undergrounds, it seems to me that 'to sell' means 'to betray' and 'selling out' refers to the process by which artists or songs sell beyond their initial market which, in turn, loses its sense of possession, exclusive ownership and familiar belonging. In other words, 'selling out' means *selling* to *out*siders, which in the case of *Top of the Pops* means those younger and older than the club-going sixteen-to-twenty-four-year olds who do not form the bulk of the programme's audience, partly because they watch less television than any other age-group. (The ratings of *Top of the Pops* are generally highest amongst twelve-to-fifteen-year-olds, followed by those between twenty-five and thirty-four, then the thirty-five to forty-four age-group.)

Despite several academic arguments about the opposition of youth subcultures and television culture (implicit in the Birmingham work, explicitly argued by Attallah 1986 and Frith 1988a). British youth subcultures aren't 'anti-television' as much as they are against a few key segments of TV that expose youth subcultural materials to everybody else. The general accessibility of broadcasting, in the strict sense of the word, is at odds with the esotericism and exclusivity of club and rave cultures; it too widely distributes the raw material of youth's subcultural capitals. Other music-oriented television programmes which tie into club culture like MTV Europe or ITV's *Chart Show* have not accrued the connotations of *Top of the Pops*. First, these programmes are sufficiently narrow-cast to escape negative symbolization as the overground. Second, they have high video content – a form which is somehow seen to maintain the autonomy of music culture and has credibility amongst clubbers.

The techno artist quoted above differentiates between appearing on *Top of the Pops* in person (which amounts to 'selling out') and appearing in video (which is considered a legitimate promotion). This is a common distinction of the underground.* Frith argues that 'the rise of pop video has been dependent on and accelerated the decline of the ideology of youth-as-opposition' (Frith 1988a: 213). But many dance acts seem to think that videos help them resist 'selling out'. A couple of factors might contribute to this attitude. First, videos allow the band to present themselves (with the help of the marketing and promotions departments of their record company) in a controlled manner closer to their own terms. Videos enable them to avoid being tainted by the 'naff' context of *Top of the Pops*. The artists protect their authentic aura by refusing to make a physical appearance (see above, pp. 27, 80–4). Second, the practice of lip-synching and acting out songs which have no 'live' existence undermines the creative credibility of these artists. With few lyrics and few performers *per se*, much contemporary dance music (particularly house and techno) is still in the process of developing an effective style of 'live' presentation. As discussed earlier in the book, much of this elaboration does not centre on the performer as much as on technology (like bringing the studio and new visual forms to the audience) so it tends not to make the most gripping television.

Videos are considered by many to be an appropriate visual accompaniment to a music which is quintessentially recorded. This is particularly the case with dance videos that use animated or computer-generated graphics and abstract visuals which forego depicting the artist. It is now often forgotten that the music video had its debut in discos in the seventies and is still a feature of many clubs.

* To give another example, Lime of the DJ duo SL2 who had a ragga-techno track go to number one believes: 'Bizarre Inc definitely sold out by actually appearing on *Top of the Pops*. You don't have to go that far to promote your record. The Prodigy got to number two and they only had their video shown' (quoted in *Touch* November 1991).

In fact, in 1977, ninety per cent of the video cassette sales were to discos (*Music Week* 24 September 1977).

Dance acts must nevertheless occasionally negotiate 'live' *Top of the Pops* appearances. For, as one television promotions manager put it, 'underground or not, major labels encourage their dance acts to appear because *Top of the Pops* shows hardly any videos, unless you're U2 or a breaker and then you only get twenty seconds' (Loraine McDonald, EMI: Interview, 2 September 1992). Two basic strategies for maintaining an underground sensibility and immunizing oneself against the domesticity of *Top of the Pops* are disguise and parody; dance acts frequently hide their faces with sunglasses, hoods and hats and/or go 'over the top' in their performance. Nothing is less 'cool' than taking *Top of the Pops* seriously.

The other TV programme crucial to youthful conceptions of the national club scene during the 1988–92 period was *The Hitman and Her*. When house music became too popular for its early *aficionados*, it was deplored as being '*Hitman and Her* fodder' (letter to *Herb Garden* April 1992). Though similarly denigrated, this late-night low-budget show was caught in a different cultural logic from *Top of the Pops*. The show was shot on location in dance clubs, rather than television studios, featured a local club crowd rather than a studio audience and revolved around a DJ-presenter (the Hitman) and his assistant (Her). The closest American equivalent to *The Hitman and Her* might have been a programme like *Club MTV* which was shot at the Palladium in New York City. But the MTV show was hosted by a black British woman with a young 'hip' image ('Downtown Julie Brown'), the dancers were vetted and video clips were used to relieve the viewer from the monotony and embarrassment of watching non-professionals dance.

The *Hitman and Her* offended underground sensibilities in at least three ways. First, the show's reception was entangled with the cultural positioning of its DJ-presenter, Pete Waterman, who was also a producer with Stock and Aitken of many chart hits. After many consecutive pop hits, but particularly after the success of Kylie Minogue, a soap opera actress-cum-singer with a large female teenybop audience, Stock/Aitken/Waterman came to be considered as manufacturers of sentimental 'chartpap' to the extent that their music was frequently cited as evidence of the cultural bankruptcy of the major record companies even though they put out

much of their work on Waterman's independent label, *PWL*. Stock/
Aitken/Waterman signified the low end of popular music even
more than *Top of the Pops*.

Worse still, as a DJ, Waterman was seen as someone who preferred to 'fill a club to the rafters with 2,000 of the biggest wallies
than have it half empty with the coolest trendies' (*Clubland* March
1992). This was the second reason for clubber difficulties with *The
Hitman and Her* – the crowds in these televised clubs were not
remotely underground. They were as close to the imagined
'Sharons and Tracys' as television could provide. The following
statement amends the stereotype to include the men depicted on
screen and damns the show with faint praise:

> Despite coming from the *No Jeans, No trainers, Soul in a Basket* optional
> end of clubland, there is something perversely enticing about this
> programme...Pleasure can be gleaned from the sight of 2,000
> Herberts and Tracys dancing around their beer and handbags at La
> Discothèque...The appeal of *The Hitman and Her* lies in its honest
> approach, its admittance of the 'so bad, it's good' theory. (*Soul Under-
> ground* April 1989)

Even with a new presenter and a different crowd, *The Hitman and
Her* would not win subcultural capital, not that it didn't try. In 1992,
Pete Waterman set up a techno label called *PWL Continental* featuring acts like 2 Unlimited, Capella and Opus III, and the television
programme was transformed into a 'mental rave night' called *Not
the Hitman and Her* (*DJ* April 1992). However, the act of putting
bright lights on the crowd as opposed to the dance acts – the process
of illuminating a culture that is supposed to take place in the dark –
usually destroys the atmosphere that is the linchpin of club
authenticity.

Documentarists of club and rave culture repeatedly use techniques like slow motion, rapid and rhythmic editing, extremely
high and low camera angles, continuously moving cameras, computer-generated blurs and high grain celluloid stocks in their attempt to capture the *frissons* of a 'hip' night out. (See, for example,
the following hour-long documentaries: *Club Culture* 1988, *Ibiza: A
Short Film About Chilling* 1990 and *Madchester* 1990.) Borrowing from
promotional video rather than documentary traditions, these
televisual techniques protect the dancers from the harshest of the

camera's demystifying glares. They create a new televisual atmosphere rather than trying to capture a club one.

Research repeatedly finds that young people have more respect for adult-orientated programming than for shows made specifically for their age-group. The 'so bad, it's good' index of appreciation is often the best that non-video youth programming can hope for. Channel 4's *The Word* and BBC2's *DEF II* programmes often fall into this category. According to some market researchers, 'TV programmes made for a young audience are not always the most effective way for youth advertisers to reach their market . . . Fashion advertisers are better off avoiding *The Word* if they want to target trend setters who think the show is naff' (*Music Week* 15 April 1993).

As a medium of image, print and sound which fills more leisure hours than any other form of communication, television is in a unique position to violate the esotericism and semi-privacies of club culture. Nevertheless, clubber and raver discourses about television programmes are intricate and full of discrepancies. They relate to the audience at home because undiscriminating exposure to outsiders is a betrayal. They concern the people depicted who can become objects of ridicule rather than points of identification, seeming incarnations of an ideological *other*. Underground discourses also involve issues of format and aesthetics in so far as music video and its stylistic practices are valued as means by which music culture can be televised but somehow preserve its rhetorical autonomy and authenticity.

Though these are the prevailing ideologies of club culture, they are not all determining nor without loopholes. For example, a *Top of the Pops* appearance is often seen by the dance act's original fans as an affirmation of their taste as well as something to be viewed with suspicions of 'selling out'. Ironically, nothing proves the originality and inventiveness of subcultural music and style more than its eventual 'mainstreaming'. Similarly, subcultures that never go beyond their initial base market are ultimately considered failures. Moreover, programmes like *Top of the Pops* are important for the recruitment of fifteen- and sixteen-year-olds to youth subcultures as its eclectic playlists frequently offer glimpses of other-worldly cult music cultures.

The betrayals of broadcasting and the aesthetics of atmosphere are but two cultural logics of club undergrounds. Negative cover-

age in the form of either well-publicized omissions from programmes like *Top of the Pops* (sometimes characterized as censorship) or television news features on club and rave culture as a
serious social problem (often framed as 'moral panic') are also important to the relationship between media and youth subcultures.
Even though they are relevant to television, I will discuss these
issues in relation to radio and tabloids where they constitute a more
commanding dynamic.

Youth resent approving mass mediation of their culture but relish
the attention conferred by media condemnation. How else might
one turn difference into defiance, lifestyle into social upheaval,
leisure into revolt? 'Moral panics' can be seen as a culmination and
fulfilment of youth cultural agendas in so far as negative newspaper
and broadcast news coverage baptize transgression. Whether the
underground espouses an overt politics or not, it is set on being
culturally radical. In Britain, the best guarantee of radicalism is
rejection by one or both of the disparate institutions seen to represent the cultural *status quo*: the tempered, state-sponsored BBC
(particularly pop music Radio One) and the sensational, sales-
dependent tabloids (particularly the Tory-supporting *Sun*).

Although their audience share has declined markedly due to
increased competition from newly licensed local stations, during
the period in which I did the bulk of my research, Radio One was
listened to by over thirty per cent of the British population every
week – and notably more women than men. Unlike *Top of the Pops*
(and contrary to common perception), the radio station did not limit
its output to the top forty, but played an average of 1100 different
titles a week, including dance catalogue, particularly from the more
melodic end of the genre. Although it had specialist dance shows
(like Pete Tong's Friday night 'Essential Selection'), the dance-
oriented press tended to alternate between complaining that the
station gave short shrift to dance music, and admiring genres like
acid house and techno for not being radio musics. Either way, Radio
One represented the accessible and safe mainstream.

Being 'banned' from Radio One was therefore a desirable pros-
pect. It acted as expert testimony to the music's violation of national
sensibilities and as circumstantial evidence of its transgression. Being banned was consequently the most reliable way to gain what is

in theory a contradiction in terms, but in practice a relatively common occurrence – namely an underground smash hit. The Beatles' 'A Day in the Life' (1967), Donna Summer's 'Love to Love You Baby' (1976), The Sex Pistols' 'God Save The Queen' (1977), Frankie Goes to Hollywood's 'Relax' (1984), George Michael's 'I Want Your Sex' (1987) and The Shamen's 'Ebeneezer Goode' (1992) were all banned because of their references to sex, drugs or politics. All of them either became hit singles or were hit singles which went on to spearhead hit albums. In the case of tracks featuring the word 'acid', several climbed from the bottom forty to the top forty as a result of rumours alone.

For example, in October 1988, the first explicitly acid track to enter the top twenty, D-Mob's 'We call it Acieeed', caused some commotion. Radio One denied allegations, which emerged from the D-Mob's record company, of having banned the record, explaining that the single was not on the playlist because 'it wasn't right for the mood of some programmes such as the breakfast show'. However, as the Radio One playlist functioned only at peak times, the single had received fourteen plays from individual producers outside the playlist system, more times, in fact, than the Whitney Houston track that was number one that week. In other words, Radio One insisted that they had imposed no ban on acid house in the strict sense of the word, that is, they were *not censoring* acid house. However, the record company kept suggesting that the music was 'banned' in the conveniently loose sense of the word, namely that acid house was *not playlisted*. The subcultural consumer press favoured the more sensational record company line – it made better copy and kept things friendly with a main advertiser – and few clubbers took note of the story's sources or distinguished between the two kinds of 'banning'.

The BBC is conscious of the curiosity generated by anything alleged to be censored. As the executive producer of the station at the time explained, 'Radio One, as part of the BBC, is seen as the establishment ... and anything considered anti-establishment has a head start as far as teenagers are concerned' (Stuart Grundy, Interview: 26 August 1992). As a result, the BBC tries to keep their gatekeeping low profile and if that fails it attempts to play down the offending issues. With reference to the 'acieeed' lyrics of the D-Mob single, a BBC spokesman stated that the radio service understood the song to be anti-drugs: 'it expresses the ideal sentiments for our forthcoming Drug Alert campaign' (*NME* 29 October 1988). Meanwhile the then Radio One DJ Simon Bates gave interviews asserting that 'Acid is all about bass-line in the music and nothing to do with drugs' (*Daily Mirror* quoted by *NME* 12 November 1988).

Back in January 1988, however, London Records (a subsidiary of Polygram) had successfully launched acid house as a genre on the coat-tails of its drug-oriented potential for scandal. The sleeve-notes to *The House Sound of Chicago Volume III: Acid Tracks* described the new music as 'drug induced', 'psychedelic', 'sky high' and 'ecstatic' and even concluded with a prediction of 'moral panic': 'The sound of acid tracking will undoubtedly become one of the most controversial sounds of 1988, provoking a split between those who adhere to its underground creed and those who decry the glamorization of drug culture.' In retrospect, this seems remarkably prescient, but the statement is best understood as hopeful. 'Moral panics' are one of the few marketing strategies open to relatively anonymous instrumental dance music.

While the BBC conducts its 'bans', the logic of 'moral panic' operates most conspicuously within the purview of the tabloids. Britons have a choice of eleven national daily newspapers which range between 'quality' broadsheets and 'popular' tabloids. Unlike papers like *National Enquirer* or *USA Today*, the British tabloids are read by over half the British population every day. They cover political issues in dramatic, personal and often sexual terms (hence the biggest selling Sunday paper, *News of the World*, is nicknamed *News of the Screws*). They take a regular interest in youth culture which they tend to treat as either a moral outrage or a sensational entertainment, often both. In fact, in line with their interest in gaining and maintaining young readers, the *Sun*'s favourite 'moral panics' would seem to be of the 'sex, drugs and rock'n'roll' variety – stories about other people having far *too much* fun – which allow their readers to vicariously enjoy the transgression one moment, and then to be shocked and offended the next. As Mark Pursehouse writes, one of the key pleasures in reading the *Sun* is the process of making a judgement about which parts of a story are true, which parts invented (Pursehouse 1991: 108). Despite questions of credibility, the tabloids have a swift domino effect: their 'shock! horror!' headlines frequently make the news themselves, are relayed by television, radio and the quality newspapers and generate much word-of-mouth, so that one often knows what's going on in the tabloids without having read them.

Mods, rockers, hippies, punks and New Romantics have all had their tabloid front pages, so there is always the anticipation – the mixed dread and hope – that a youthful scene will be the subject of media outrage. Disapproving tabloid stories legitimize and authenticate youth cultures. In fact, without tabloid intervention, it is hard to imagine a British youth *movement*. For, in turning youth into news, the tabloids both frame subcultures as major events and also disseminate them. A tabloid front page, however distorted, is frequently a self-fulfilling prophecy; it can turn the most ephemeral fad into a lasting development.

Following London Records' sleeve-notes, the subcultural press repeatedly predicted that a 'moral panic' about acid house was 'inevitable'. In February 1988, a good six months before a daily paper ran a story and a few weeks after the compilation's release, the three main music weeklies ran stories about a new genre called 'acid house' that was liable to cause 'moral panic.' As one of them put it: 'I wonder how long it will be before our moral guardians start claiming that promoting the music is helping to promote drug-taking among the young?' (*Record Mirror* 20 February 1988).

Some months later, innuendo about drug use in British clubs started to appear in the style and music press, but it was left to two music weeklies experiencing flagging sales (and with little feeling of responsibility to this particular club scene) to expose domestic drug-taking. In July 1988, *New Musical Express* (*NME*) ran several stories under the Timothy Leary slogan 'Tune in, Turn on, Drop Out' which exposed and investigated Ecstasy use in British clubs. Although they admitted that it was 'hardly a matter for public broadcast', they explained the appeal of the drug (it gave one the energy to dance all night and reduced inhibitions). They also offered proof of its prevalence (the names of London's house clubs signalled the chemical nature of their attraction, while the packed dancefloors and deserted bars suggested that alcohol was not the preferred substance) and they listed the possible negative effects like nausea and recurring nightmares, emphasizing however that the worst effect was 'making a complete

Plate 5 Front-page coverage of the rave scene, June 1989. The caption read: 'Night of Ecstasy . . . thrill-seeking youngsters in a dance frenzy at the secret party attended by more than 11,000' (Reproduced by kind permission of the *Sun*)

and utter embarrassment of yourself by babbling E-talk and intimate confessions to whoever happens to be in earshot' (*NME* 16 July 1988). *Melody Maker* followed with stories like 'Ecstasy: a Consumer's Guide' which rated batches of MDMA. The legendary 'yellow capsules', they said, induced 'feelings of having being ripped off and a buzz akin to trapping your toe in the door', while the 'New York tablets' were the 'most . . . reliable Ecstasy . . . the lasting sensation being one of unbruisability and general bliss' (*Melody Maker* 20 August 1988).

By the end of August, many music and style magazines were wondering why the tabloids were ignoring the issue. Ecstasy, some complained, had 'received little of the gutter press scare treatment afforded Crack yet the latter drug has yet to make any real inroads into British drug culture' (*NME* 13 August 1988). Others seemed amazed that the acid house scene was 'in many ways . . . still an underground movement' but, confident of eventual 'moral panic', went so far as to project possible headlines:

It's not hard to imagine the angle the tabloid press will choose if they 'report' on the acid house scene. Its supposedly symbiotic relationship with psychedelic drugs will make banner headlines of shock-horror proportions, along the lines of 'London Gripped by Ecstasy!', 'Drug Crazed New Hippies in Street Riot' or 'Yuppies On Acid!' The clubs will be portrayed as drug dens, the music will be 'mind-numbing' and the clubbers 'hooligans'. It could be the ideal Silly Season story once Fergie's little Princess has left the front page. (*Time Out* 17–24 August 1988)

When the 'inevitable' 'moral panic' ensued, the subcultural press were ready. They tracked the tabloids' every move, reproduced whole front pages, re-printed and analysed their copy and decried the misrepresentation of acid house by what they variously called 'moral panic', 'media hysteria', a 'gutter press hate campaign' and a 'moral crusade'. However much they condemned the tabloids, clubbers and club writers were fascinated by their representation and gloried in the sensational excess. As one journalist admitted, 'The irony is that whilst [the *Sun*] runs acid stories, I buy the paper everyday, just to see what they dream up next' (*Soul Underground* July 1989).

Even well after the waves of tabloid coverage, dance magazines and fanzines compiled top ten charts of 'ridiculous platitudes' used by the popular press – 'Killer Cult', 'In the grip of E', 'Rave to the Grave' (*Herb Garden* June 1992). Others ran spoof scandals about millions of kids 'hooked on a mind bending drug called A' (for alcohol) or stories about the designer drug 'T' which was 'openly on sale in supermarkets and supplied in a small perforated bag' (*Herb Garden* June 1992; *Touch* February 1992). Impressed but not surprised, the club press had their explanations. As *i-D*, a magazine whose reader-profile brags that it is, according to the *Economist*, 'painfully hip', wrote:

Every sub-culture breeds its own moral panic, every moral panic is stereotyped by its own devil drug. Think of all those headlines from the past which have screamed themselves hoarse: mods on speed, freaks dropping LSD, punks sniffing glue, blacks smoking dope, even cocaine-crazed yuppies. Gay bikers on acid just about sums it up. (*i-D* June 1990)

In 1991, however, when the negative stories had lost their news value, the tabloids started publishing positive articles with headlines like 'Bop to Burn: Raving is the Perfect Way to Lose Weight', 'High on Life' and 'Raves are all the Rage'. Needless to say, clubbers and their niche press were outraged. How could the tabloids about-face and ignore the abundant use of drugs? How did they think ravers stay up till 6 a.m., if it weren't for the numerous amphetamines inside them? The music press attacked these affirmative tabloid stories with unprecedented virulence. For example, *Touch* magazine wrote:

> '10,000 DRUG CRAZED YOUTHS' This was the headline carried by the *Sun* newspaper during the summer of 1988. It was part of an uncompromising effort to bring disrepute and destruction upon the rave scene that was growing at a rapid rate across the country . . . Now three years after that headline was printed, the *Sun* has launched 'Answers' – its so called comprehensive guide to weekend raving . . . What audacity! How dare they? On approaching the *Sun* about their change in attitude we were informed by some clueless dimwit that the rave scene is now, in their opinion, a respectable, clean and drug-free zone. Anyone who has been to the major clubs recently knows that drugs are still very much a part of the club rave culture. We're not saying this is a good thing, but it does prove that the *Sun* knows absolutely fuck all about what's happening on the Rave scene, just as they knew fuck all in 1988 and 1989. The truth is that the *Sun* is run and staffed by a bunch of hypocritical, no good, Tory, band-wagon jumping wankers. (*Touch* December 1991)

Although negative reporting is disparaged, it is subject to anticipation, even aspiration. Positive tabloid coverage, on the other hand, is the subcultural kiss of death. In 1988, the *Sun* briefly celebrated acid house, advising their readers to wear T-shirts emblazoned with Smiley faces, the music's coat of arms, in order to 'dazzle your mates with the latest trendy club wear', before they began running hostile exposés. Had the tabloid continued with this happy endorsement of acid house, it is likely the scene would have been aborted and a movement would not have ensued. Similarly, rave culture would probably have lost its force with this second wave of positive reports had it not been followed by further disapproving coverage (about ravers converging on free festivals with 'travellers', namely, nomadic 'hippies' and 'crusties' who travel the countryside in convoys of 'vehicles').

Cultural studies and sociologies of 'moral panic' tend to position youth cultures as innocent victims of negative stigmatization. But mass media 'misunderstanding' is often an objective of certain sub-cultural industries, rather than an accident of youth's cultural pursuits. 'Moral panic' can therefore be seen as a form of hype orchestrated by culture industries that target the youth market. The music press seemed to understand the acid house phenomenon in this way, arguing that forbidden fruit is most desirable and that prohibition never works. The hysterical reports of the popular press, they argued, amounted to a 'priceless PR campaign' (*Q* January 1989). Perhaps the first publicist to court moral outrage intentionally was Andrew Loog Oldman who, back the mid-1960s, promoted the Rolling Stones as dirty, irascible, rebellious and threatening (cf. Norman 1993). Rather than some fundamental innovation, Malcolm McLaren's management of the image of the Sex Pistols in the 1970s followed an already well-trodden promotional path. In the 1980s and 1990s, acts as disparate as Madonna, Ice-T and Oasis have played with these marketing strategies, for 'moral panic' fosters widespread exposure at the same time as mitigating accusations of 'selling out'. (Hence, the usefulness of 'Parental Advisory' stickers in marketing certain kinds of acts in the US.)

'Moral panic' is a metaphor which depicts a complex society as a single person who experiences sudden groundless fear about its virtue. Although the term serves the purposes of the record industry and the music press well by inflating the threat posed by subcultures, as an academic concept, its anthropomorphism and totalization mystify more than they reveal. It fails to acknowledge competing media, let alone their reception by diverse audiences. And, its concept of morals overlooks the youthful ethics of abandon.

Popular music is in perpetual search of significance. Associations with sex, death and drugs imbue it with a 'real life' gravity that moves it beyond lightweight entertainment into the realm of, at the very least, serious hedonism. Acid house came to be hailed as a movement bigger than punk and akin to the hippie revolution precisely because its drug connections made it newsworthy beyond the confines of youth culture. While subcultural studies have tended to argue that youth subcultures are subversive until the very moment they are represented by the mass media (Hebdige 1979 and 1987), here it is argued that these kinds of taste cultures (not to be confused with activist organizations) become politically relevant only when they are framed as such. In other words, derogatory media coverage is not the verdict but the essence of their resistance.

So far the discussion has focused on mass media such as prime-time television, national radio and tabloid newspapers whose audiences, aesthetics and agendas are generally contrary to underground ideology. But, what about those micro and niche media which are more directly involved in the congregation of dance crowds and the formation of subcultures? What kind of reputation do they have amongst clubbers and ravers? How do they circulate and control the flow of the crowd?

Micro-Media: Flyers, Listings, Fanzines, Pirates

Flyers, fanzines, flyposters, listings, telephone information lines, pirate radio, e-mailing lists and internet archive sites may not at first seem to have much in common. An array of media, from the most rudimentary of print forms to the latest in digital interactive technologies, are the low circulating, narrowly targeted micro-media which have the most credibility amongst clubbers and are most instrumental to their congregating on a nightly basis. Club crowds are not organic formations which respond mysteriously to some collective unconscious, but people grouped together by intricate networks of communications. Clubbers elect to come together by making decisions based on the information they have at hand *at the same time as* they are actively assembled by club organizers.

The media venerated for epitomizing the authenticity of dance subcultures are first and foremost word-of-mouth, word-on-the-street and fanzines. Although these media are romanticized as pure and autonomous, they are generally tainted by and contingent upon other media and other business. While they are assumed to be in the vanguard, they are just as likely to be belated and behind. Though these media are said to be closest to subcultures, various social and economic factors limit and complicate their intimate relations.

Word-of-mouth is considered the consummate medium of the underground. But conversations between friends about clubs often involve flyers seen, radio heard and features read. Rather than an unadulterated grassroots medium, word-of-mouth is often extended by or is an extension of other communications' media. For this reason, club organizers, like other marketers and advertisers, actively seek to generate word-of-mouth with their promotions. Likewise, romantic notions of the 'street' forget that it is a space of advertising and communication, subject to market research and given ratings called 'OTS' or 'opportunities to see'. The 'OTS' rating considers the details of people who pass particular poster and billboard sites in cars or on foot, adjusting figures to take into account distractions such as rival sites or poor visibility. Although they do not survey illegal communications like flyposting or spray painting, we can infer a similar demographic bias of young, male and up-market viewers. This is one reason why record companies allot marketing pounds to what they call 'street marketing' and why flyposting and spray-painting are effective means for rave organizations to gain a higher profile and draw a crowd. Word-of-mouth and word-on-the-street are rarely as pure and autonomous as clubbers (and academics) would like to believe.

More than any other medium, perhaps, fanzines have been celebrated as grassroots – as the active voice of the consumer and as the quintessence of subcultural communications. While the former is undoubtedly true, the latter is open to question. Rave fanzines give vent to unruly voices, local slang, scatological juvenilia, moaning, ranting and swearing. First person narratives are common, particularly ones about drug experiences which recount stories of brilliant or nightmarish times on Ecstasy, tales of having one's 'gear' stolen by bouncers who then sell it back to you in the club, anecdotes about experiencing 'aggro' from 'charlie casuals' and 'lager louts' (namely, aggravation from abusers of cocaine and beer).

Having small print runs and little money to lose, the fanzines often flout libel and copyright laws, if only in hope of a bit of publicity. Some make allegations about the sexual exploits of 'high profile, coke snorting' record company bosses (*Gear* 2 1991). Others

ask outright: 'Do you know a cause worth fighting or more importantly any chance of some free publicity? Write and let us know. We
pay five pounds' (*Herb Garden* April 1992).

Fanzines are the only place to find writing about clubbing from
an explicitly female (though not always feminist) point of view.
Several were edited by women (for example, *Duck Call* and *Gear*),
while even the laddish *Boy's Own* has the occasional 'Girl's Own
Nightmare' feature which discusses such problems as 'death by
sisterhood on eight tabs', surviving the loo queue and the handbag
problem. Similarly, *Herb Garden* ran a spoof of a woman's magazine
quiz which determined whether you were a 'Sad Susan' who
doesn't know a thing about dance culture, a 'Techno Tracy' who
raves all the time but indiscriminately, or a 'Vicky Volante' (the
name of the author of the mock quiz) who has the right attitude and
knows how to have fun with style. Significantly, these fanzine articles by female writers are careful to distance themselves from dancing around handbags, Sharon and Tracy (techno or otherwise) (cf.
chapter 3).

While the rave fanzines are certainly outlets for clubber debate,
they are not, as is often assumed, necessarily emergent. Most of the
rave fanzines appeared in the aftermath of the tabloid 'moral panic'
and did little to contribute to the early evolution of acid house. *NME*
tried to explain the absence of fanzines by the fact that the music did
not revolve around artists: 'That there isn't already a massive acid
house fanzine scene is partly down to the anonymity of the idiom.
It's rarely performed live, which is why the DJs who play the
sounds in clubs have a higher profile than the musicians who make
them' (*NME* July 16 1988). But the early fanzines could have focused
on DJs as did the later ones which were full of hagiographic articles
with titles like 'Seventeen things you never knew about Danny
Rampling' (*Herb Garden* April 1992).

All but one fanzine appeared long after British acid house had
been converted into a 'scene' by the subcultural consumer press
because before the niche media baptism, the culture consisted of
little more than a dozen tracks, a few clubs and DJs. Moreover, even
when the numbers of people involved swelled through the summer
of 1988, it was not long before the tabloids were on the case. Professional media are generally faster off the mark, working to monthly, weekly and daily deadlines rather than the slow productions

and erratic schedules of amateur media. Even after their proliferation, then, the fanzines tended to write about events that happened
months prior to their publication and were well behind the consumer press.

Free from the constraints of maintaining readerships, fanzines
don't have to worry about being identified with a scene that has
become passé. Much fanzine copy therefore wallows in nostalgia.
Their writers reminisce about the legendary raves and hanker after
the initial 'vibe'. Conscious of lying in the wake of a historic youth
movement, even when they try to avoid sentimental longing, it
often prevails. For example:

> My purpose is not to describe the pre-Fall idyll, some sonic paradise
> which we should wander as do unreconstructed hippies to Glaston-
> bury [but] rather to lament the way clubland has so quickly become
> self-conscious and unspecial. Acid house was not the be-all and end-
> all, but it was a beginning, and something that was stamped out before
> it was allowed to develop. (*Boy's Own* spring 1990)

To have attended any event which was given notoriety by
the tabloids has its own subcultural capital. Certainly many wished
they had been there – contributing to the news and taking part in
youth cultural history. One of the bigger club organizations, which
obtained more tabloid front pages than any other, was banking
on such nostalgia when it released videos of its 'Sunrise' and 'Back
to the Future' parties. Its advertisement asked, 'Do you remember
the raves of 88 and 89? Capture your cherished memories on VHS
video cassettes, from the days we travelled the orbital and no town,
field or warehouse was safe' (*Clubland* December 1991/January
1992).

Word-of-mouth and fanzines are likely to be residual as much as
emergent means of communication. The idea that subcultural
scenes are seeded with micro-media, cultivated by niche media and
harvested by mass media describes the exception as much as the
rule. There is no *natural* order to cultural development. In competi-
tive economies where sundry media work simultaneously, where
global industries are local businesses and 'all that is solid melts into
air' (cf. Berman 1983), organic metaphors about 'grassroots' and
'growth' eclipse as much as they explain. They are too unitary to

make sense of the complex teleologies of contemporary popular culture. Culture emerges from above and below, from within and without media, from under- and overground.

Flyers are considered by many club organizers as the most effective means of building a crowd in so far as they are a relatively inexpensive way to target fine audience segments. Their distribution is conducted in three ways: they are mailed directly to clubbers (often members) in the form of invitations, handed to people in the street 'who look like they belong' or distributed to pubs, clothing and record shops in order that they might be picked up by the 'right crowd'. While the first method uses the means of the private party, the last two trace young people's routes through the city, exhibiting an understanding of what Michel de Certeau would call their 'practices of space' (de Certeau 1984). Club promoters talk about how the dissemination of flyers is a deceptively tricky business: one must be wary of printing too many and finding them littering the streets; of depositing them in unsuitable places and procuring a queue full of 'wallies'. The dispersal of flyers influences the assembly of dance crowds; the flow of one affects the circulation of the other.

In her book *Design After Dark: the Story of Dancefloor Style*, Cynthia Rose celebrates flyers as 'semiotic guerilla warfare', likening the form to the old political handbill as well as new art forms which play with mass reproduction processes. But while flyers have clear aesthetic significance, they are more accurately seen as direct advertising rather than cultural combat. 'Direct marketing' is the subject of more advertising investment than either magazines or radio, but because it targets tightly, it often feels more intimate and less 'commercial' (*Marketing* 13 August 1992). Moreover, rather than contesting the *status quo*, flyers mainly suggest that the club whose name they bear satisfies questions like the following: 'Where can you find the wildest, craziest, maddest, most hedonistic, HARD CORE, dance experience that takes place every Friday and Saturday night?' (printed on Uproar flyer 1990).

Mailing lists are compiled in a variety of ways. Sometimes, advertisements in fanzines and the subcultural consumer press invite people to send ten pounds to become a member, or one can pay for membership at the door. At other times, the addresses of regulars are requested by the club organizer or, in the case of a club called

Plate 6 A selection of flyers from 1988–89
(*Photograph*: David Swindells)

Rage (held at Heaven in London), people were chosen from amongst the crowd to have their picture taken, then were issued with a photo I.D. and placed on the mailing list.

Key recipients of flyers are local listings magazines which relay their information (along with that of accompanying press releases) to preview or review clubs for their readers. Listings magazines contain at least three gradations of exposure: the relative obscurity of the listings themselves, the discreet disclosure of a column-mention or the open exhibition of a feature in the front pages. The listings are written in a kind of clubber jargon that is often incomprehensible to those who are not already familiar with clubbing. (For example, some American students at the London School of Economics for a term told me that after scouring *Time Out*'s club listings, they were still bewildered about where they ought to go.) When a club is singled out for recommendation or comment in the columns which precede the listings, overviews are offered and terms are occasionally defined. When the magazine runs a feature – usually on a new scene or 'vibe' – labels are translated and codes revealed; the culture is exposed and explained to non-clubbing outsiders.

Published listings need to be negotiated as carefully as flyer distribution. They can stimulate or stifle interest, under- or overexpose. While a crowd needs to be assembled, too much or the wrong kind of coverage can close down a club in a matter of weeks. Just enough and the right kind of publicity, on the other hand, can reserve a place in the annals of club cultural folklore. Shoom, the club retrospectively hailed as the origin of acid house culture, offers a telling case of the cultural logics involved.

The first entry for this Saturday-night club in the London listings weekly, *Time Out*, read as follows:

> NEW! The Shoom Club, Midnight – 5 a.m. If you're lucky enough to get one of their invites then you'll know the location of this underground House party in E1 which was packed and jumping at their Valentine rave and now goes weekly. DJ Danny Rampling and guest DJs the Cold Cut Crew mix the House variations and rap-dance for a very lively crowd of trendies with great decor on the walls. It's fast becoming a legend so become a member before it's too big for its venue. (*Time Out* 24 February–2 March 1988)

The implied thrills of being part of an elect and taking part in the 'hip' and 'happening' are common to club listings; therefore it is two other themes which set this blurb apart from the rest. First, although the club had yet to operate weekly, the listing predicts the club's mythic status: it is 'fast becoming a legend'. Like the sleeve-notes to London Records' *Acid Tracks* compilation which predicted 'moral panic', we might ask, to what extent is this speculation idly prescient or actively self-fulfilling? The comment may only have picked up on a consensual 'vibe', but what if it hadn't? Media confirm, spread and consolidate cultural perceptions – even

Plate 7 DJ Danny Rampling and his devotees at Shoom just after the club changed its name to Joy because it had received too much media exposure. (*Photograph*: David Swindells)

amongst those who were there to experience the event. Their predictions have repeated if unpredictable effects.

The second distinguishing feature of Shoom's listing is that it publicized the secrecy of the night's location; it promoted the club by withholding its address. Tantalizing statements like 'if you're lucky enough to know the location of this underground party' candidly play on the 'hip' capital of being 'in the know'. Mystery locations are one guarantee of being underground and part of the excitement of raves. As raves grew in size and number, listings would announce the event, tell the reader to look out for the flyer upon which was printed a phone number through which they could get tickets, then later get directions to the rave's location on the day of the events. In order to avoid premature closure by the police, the organizers would indicate only the general whereabouts of the rave until the evening of the event, when they would give out directions that would become more and more specific towards midnight. Computer information phone lines were also an innovation of acid house and rave marketing: when one became a member of a club organization, one received a number to call for information about their forthcoming events.

One Shoom strategy was to refuse access to mass media like television news but to tell niche media like the subcultural consumer press all about it. (In the same way record companies occasionally issue music they know will be banned from television or radio in order to generate more print media attention.) The resulting copy was favourably superlative:

> When a BBC camera crew arrived unannounced at Danny and Jenny Rampling's Shoom night, arrogantly pushing their way to the front of the queue, expecting free entry, they were in for a shock. Jenny showed the direction of the door on the spot ... Warehouse parties were all but killed off by overexposure by the media ... so a big round of applause goes out to Jenny Rampling. (*Soul Underground* August 1988)

This event became a key moment in the written and oral history of acid house. Although the reputation of Shoom cannot be wholly explained by the way the Ramplings managed the ebb and flow of information about their club, their gatekeeping is undoubtedly a contributing factor. Like censorship and 'moral panic', the practice of advertising the inaccessible plays a media game which is in harmony with underground ideology. It doesn't betray so much as reveal a mask; it doesn't double-cross so much as indulge in *double entendre*. It doesn't sell *out* so much as identify the people and places that are *'in'*.

One reason why Shoom did such a good job in managing their own exposure was because they had to. By many off-the-record accounts, 'ninety per cent' of the Shoom crowd were taking the drug Ecstasy. Club cultural media could be trusted to handle this information with care; other niche and mass media could not. For example, after *Time Out*'s club editor, David Swindells, had attended the club, the magazine published a different blurb which judiciously both exposed and protected the club:

> Shoom ... is providing the appropriate aural (not to say, astral) atmosphere for the euphoric and whooping crowd to take the idea of dancing to its outer limits, way beyond the confines of the dancefloor and

the two step shuffle. It has the kind of wild, uninhibited style that you'd normally only associate with mixed-gay trendy nights. (*Time Out* 16–23 March 1988)

'Astral', 'euphoric', 'outer limits' – the rationale behind these ob-lique references to drugs is explained by their author in the follow-ing way:

> In a job like mine, you need to be reasonably conscientious. You want to write about it but not destroy it. Scenes are fragile, bloody small and relatively insignificant. You get to know the people involved, develop a cosy relationship and maybe you don't write as objectively or journa-listically as you should. My job is to tell people what is happening without threatening the scene. (David Swindells, interview: 2 September 1992)

Listings magazines are available from any newsagent, so they manage the flow of information with degrees of cryptic shorthand, innuendo and careful omission. Their gatekeeping can often estab-lish the boundaries of the esoteric, protect the feel of the under-ground and mitigate overexposure. Flyers, by contrast, follow the movement of people through the social spaces of the city, then attempt to guide them to future locations. Both are integral to the formation of club crowds.

Another micro-medium that requires discussion is pirate radio. Here, I will focus on one case which is particularly revealing of the logics of subcultural capital – the transition of KISS-FM from pirate to legal radio station, from micro- to niche medium. Until 1990, dance music radio was illegal in Britain; the only stations to offer a hundred per cent dance programming were the 'pirates'. From sharing the same DJ staff through to club tie-ins, reciprocal promo-tions and overlapping audiences, pirate stations and dance clubs had been entangled in a web of financial and ideological affiliations that went back to the sixties. Before founding pirate Radio Caroline in March 1964, for instance, Ronan O'Rahilly had run the Scene, a fashionable Mod hang-out in Soho. And throughout the 1970–80s, reggae, soul then house music pirate stations organized 'blues parties', 'shabeens', warehouse parties, clubs and raves (cf. Chapman 1993).

Pirate radio stations have long been positioned as the antithesis of the official, government-funded Radio One. Despite being for-profit narrowcasters, they are cloaked in the romance of the underground. Like fanzines, they are supposed to be the active voice of subcultures and like graffiti or sampling, their acts of unauthorized appropriation are deemed 'hip'. To a large degree, the stations did indeed cater to those culturally disenfranchised by age and race. The black music press, in particular, championed the pirates; they published listings of their frequencies (even after it had been criminalized), recounted tricks for dodging the police and berated the DTI (Department of Trade and Industry, responsible for licensing the airwaves) as the 'Department of Total Idiots' (*Touch* October 1991; *Touch* March 1991). Moreover, pirate radio was celebrated as 'the bush telegraph of acid house – [it] keeps the revolutionaries informed' (*Soul Underground* December 1989–January 1990).

The Broadcasting Act of 1990, however, changed a long-standing state of affairs and propelled the pirates in one of two directions. By making it a criminal offence to advertise on pirate radio, many stations were driven from partial to total dependence on revenue generated by advertising clubs and raves. As one pirate DJ explained, 'club nights have always been our biggest money maker and they can still be advertised – they can't hold the owners responsible and they have no way of finding the promoter' (*Touch* March 1991). The ties between clubs and pirates tightened to the extent that many stations became little more than communication units of the larger club organizations. The stations even took on the names of club nights and raves; for example, in September 1990, 'Future' 'Fantasy', 'Friends', 'Obsession', 'Lightning', 'Rave' and 'Sunrise' were all on the air.

The course for a few other pirates, however, was legalization. In London, Manchester and Bristol, for example, pirates with sizeable audiences and sufficient legal and financial backing won licences from the Independent Broadcasting Authority (IBA). Changes in government policy have generally been forced by the popularity of illegal radio. Radio One was established in 1967 as a reaction to the off-shore pirates, Radio Caroline and Radio London. While the 1990 Broadcasting Act intended de-regulation, the IBA was reluctant to license a dance music station, refusing KISS FM's first bid in favour of a jazz station to which few people tuned in. (For a detailed

account of the politics of Greater London FM radio licensing, cf.
Barbrook 1990.)

London's KISS-FM was the largest and most celebrated instance
of a pirate station going legal, and consideration of their transition
illuminates the subcultural logic which distinguishes between the
thrill of the illicit and the banality of the condoned. Founded in
1985, the pirate KISS was ranked in 1987 as London's second most
popular radio station, after Capital FM and ahead of Radio One, by
a poll in the *Evening Standard*. With the million pound launch of
KISS's legal version in 1990, Rogers and Cowan, its public relations
firm, and BBDO, its advertising agency, tried to build on this audience by maintaining what they understood to be the station's appeal – its underground credibility and 'street' feel. They issued six
marketing statements including 'KISS-FM reflects the sound of the
street' and three slogans which declared that KISS was 'Radical
Radio', 'The Station on Everyone's Lips' and 'The Voice of the
Underground'. While the trade weeklies had no problem in accept-
ing that 'KISS has deliberately kept its pirate station feel', most of
the youth-oriented press were sure a combination of IBA restriction
and business pressure would compromise KISS (Music Week 17
November 1990). Even amid the positive reviews, they repeatedly
expressed doubt that the station could 'walk the fine line between
credit and credibility' (*City Limits* 30 Aug.–6 Sept. 1990). KISS had
always been 'commercial' but with licence fees, taxes and corporate
backers, it would need to make more. Contrary to assumptions
about the conservative role of bureaucratic bodies like the IBA,
however, KISS-FM's 'Promise of Performance' contract went some
way toward insisting that KISS maintain its underground feel. Their
licence stipulated that at least fifty per cent of their playlist be new
material, that is, pre-chart, on general release but not in the top
forty, pre-release or unreleased in Britain at the time of broadcast
(IBA document 1990).

Nevertheless, Lindsay Wesker, KISS's head of music and main
spokesman, spent much of the station's first year of legal operation
juggling the ideological contradictions between subcultures and
commerce. Wesker repeatedly told the press that KISS both maintained its subcultural feel and offered a substantial target audience
attractive to advertisers, that they were both uncompromising in

their search for authentic dance sounds and unswerving in their accumulation of socially active listeners between fifteen to twenty-four years. Previously, legal radio stations hadn't bothered with 'hip' subcultural trappings because they enjoyed monopoly or duopoly markets. With KISS (and other incremental dance stations around the country), British radio had to confront the discursive inconsistencies for the first time. As the record and publishing industries had been successfully negotiating the knotted problems of youth niches and subcultural capital since the sixties, it is not surprisingly that KISS-FM's main financial backers were three publishers and a leisure group which grew out of a record company.* Moreover, their first key advertiser was the American Coca-Cola Ltd. British advertisers are notoriously suspicious of radio advertising (radio then attracted only two per cent of advertising revenues), but Coca-Cola had faith in the youth niche markets delivered by radio (particularly as their main rival, Pepsi, had an exclusive contract with KISS's main competitor, Capital FM).

Five years after its launch, KISS-FM continues to promote dance events and club nights. They have club and rave listings several times throughout the day and advertisements at night and at the weekend when rates are cheaper. KISS represents a sizeable section of the London dance scene. It gives key club DJs their own evening shows in which to play a conspicuously high number of 'exclusives' and promote their own club nights. It also has a substantial portion of clubbers and ravers among its listeners. To talk about certain London dance subcultures without reference to KISS would be to omit a main point of reference, source of information, assimilator of sounds and disseminator of underground ideology. Of course, every change of staff, playlist policy or mode of address is usually met with accusations that KISS is getting less and less 'street credible' and sounding more and more like Radio One. Although many clubbers and ravers see themselves as further underground than this 'voice of the underground', it is worth noting the

---

* KISS-FM's founding shareholders were Centurion Press (20%), Cradley Group Holding plc (5%) and EMAP Radio Ltd (20%), sister company to the publisher of *Q*, *Select*, *Kerrang* and *Smash Hits*. Virgin Broadcasting, which until early 1992 was a sister company to Virgin Records, owned 15%. The management team also held shares and a number were unsold at the time of the launch.

way in which a station with a weekly reach of a million listeners employs the rhetoric of subculture and maintains so many club cultural links.

Finally, mention should be made of a new micro-medium which has come to the fore since I completed my research but has implications for the future development of music cultures: the internet. Electronic mail is an obvious improvement on traditional 'snail mailing' lists in so far as it is faster, cheaper and potentially interactive. The mailing list of 'UK-Dance' set up by Stephen Hebditch in 1993 is used by a small number of organizers to publicize clubs, by a larger number of clubbers to discuss forthcoming events and to review releases for one another, and even by a few ex-clubbers to discuss aspects of rave culture other than going out. The discussions here have the same personal flavour as the fanzines, with many being about drugs or the practicalities of dance events (like the lack of available water or the repulsive state of the portable toilets). Although this mailing list spawned an archive site, 'UK-Dance on the World Wide Web', the most elaborate site – and probably the first on the net – was Brian Behlendorf's techno/rave archive. First set up at Stanford University, then on Behlendorf's own San Francisco-based server called 'hyperreal', this world wide web site includes pictures of rave flyers, discographies and sound samples, as well as the opinions of its various experts and users.

Despite the preponderance of Americans on the internet, Behlendorf estimates that some forty per cent of visitors to his site come off British or European servers, undoubtedly because interest in techno music and raves is much more widespread in Europe (e-mail to author, 1994). But there is also a high percentage of non-British, particularly American, users of the 'UK-Dance' site. In fact, many British net surfers spend as much, if not more, time communicating with European and American ravers than with their clubbing compatriots. The internet's quintessentially global character, its obliviousness to geographical distances and national borders, will condition the nature of its effect on music communities. As one Finnish raver on the UK-dance mailing list wrote: 'communicating with people around the world has influenced my musical tastes . . . but the net hasn't done much for me as far as supporting the local scene goes'.

All the micro-media discussed here have different influences and impacts: the most venerated are not necessarily the most actively engaged in convening crowds or shaping subcultures. Whatever their exact effects, they are more than just representations of subcultures. Micro-media are essential mediators amongst the participants in subcultures. They rely on their readers/listeners/consumers to be 'in the know' or in the 'right place at the right time' and are actively involved in the social organization of youth.

Niche Media: the Editorial Search for Subcultures

Britain saw a remarkable seventy-three per cent increase in consumer magazine titles in the 1980s – the result of more detailed market research, tighter target marketing and new technologies such as desk top publishing (*Marketing* 13 August 1992). By the end of the decade, about thirty magazines addressed youth, featured music and style editorial and drew advertising from the record, fashion, beverage and tobacco industries. While flyers and listings tend to deal in the corporeal world of *crowds*, and tabloids handle the sweeping and scandalous impact of *movements*, consumer magazines operate in *subcultures*. They categorize social groups, arrange sounds, itemize attire and label everything. They baptize scenes and generate the self-consciousness required to maintain cultural distinctions. They give definition to vague cultural formations, pull together and reify the disparate materials which become subcultural homologies. The music and style press are crucial to our conceptions of British youth; they do not just cover subcultures, they help construct them.

With a few important exceptions, sociologists of popular music have not investigated the relations between media and music formations. Simon Frith is an exception in so far as he has discussed rock writers as 'professional rock fans' who contribute to the development of an 'alternative music ideology' (cf. Frith 1981a: 165–77). The other scholars who have considered the problem have portrayed the media's presence in negative or at least not productive terms. For instance, Dave Laing examines the 'framing' of punk, putting forth, as his metaphor suggests, an essentially repressive model where media are seen to confine or restrain rather than enable or incite the culture (Laing 1985: 99–105). In her admirably thorough overview of the relations between the media and American heavy metal culture, Deena Weinstein contends, in an argument almost diametrically opposed to mine, that only two media – the concert and the record – are 'essential to the constitution' of heavy metal subculture and that the rest of the media 'merely found that subculture and began to supply it' (Weinstein 1991: 194–5).

Subculturalists have given even less systematic attention to the relations between media and youth's cultural formations. In fact, the Birmingham work ignored the *development* of subcultures, considering them only when they were fully mediated and ripe for critical interpretation. They did not investigate the process by which sounds, styles, argot and rituals congealed into clusters which seemed to perfectly reflect the social structure (these were called 'socio-symbolic homologies'). This was an admitted shortcoming of the methodology:

> Homological analysis of a cultural relation is synchronic. It is not equipped to account for changes over time, or to account for the creation or disintegration, of homologies: it records the complex qualitative state of a cultural relation as it is observed in one quantum of time. (Willis 1978: 191)

But the process by which subcultures crystallize is crucial to understanding their meaning and function. Having already discussed some of the means by which crowds come together and put forth some necessary conditions for a movement, this section examines two moments in the formation of acid house subculture. First, it outlines the process by which acid house became a music brand with a distinct sound, ideology and preferred mode of consumption. It therefore contrasts with the many cultural studies that take the existence of genres for granted (as if music organically evolved into kinds and categories). Second, it identifies some means by which disparate cultural materials and specific crowds were appended to the genre. It considers the niche media's role in assembling acid house into a fully-fledged subculture.

Before considering these cases, it is worth asking why consumer magazines are involved in subcultures at all. One reason is that the *aficionados* who become the writers, editors and photographers of the subcultural consumer press have at one time or another been participants in subcultures and still espouse versions and variations of underground ideology. There is a fraternity of interest between the staff *and* readers of these magazines, not only because they are of the same sex, but because they share subcultural capital investments.*

Another reason for the editorial interest in subcultures relates to the magazines' need to target and maintain readerships. The fortunes of the youth press have tended to fluctuate with the popularity of the scenes with which they're affiliated, so the monitoring of subcultures has become a financial necessity.† For instance, *New Musical Express* peaked in circulation in 1980 when punk and postpunk rock held sway, then experienced steady decline until 1989 when its association with, and promotion of, the Manchester scene gave it a new lease on life (by pulling its circulation back above 100,000).

Similarly, *The Face* was an integral part of the New Romantics/ New Wave London club scene in the early eighties. Its contributors roamed around 'clubland', celebrated posing and elaborated a subcultural ideology. By early 1988, the magazine had lost touch with club culture: it no longer contained its stock-in-trade club column and chose covers depicting established film stars (like Steve Martin and Woody Allen) rather than the budding dance acts of its past. Even when acid house started getting media attention elsewhere, *The Face* opted for rare groove and hiphop as if acid house were a fad too fleeting for its attention. It ran the odd blurb or house-

---

* The music weeklies (like *NME, Melody Maker, Record Mirror*, now incorporated into *Music Week*), the music monthlies (*Q, Select, Vox*) and the DJ monthlies (*DJ* and *Mixmag*) have readerships which are 70–85% male. The style monthlies (*Face, i-D, Sky*) have broader editorial policies that include substantial coverage of clothes and have more balanced readerships – approximately 50–65% male (National Readership Surveys 1988–93). Although 'clubzines' (like *Touch, Clubland* and the defunct *Rave*) are not subject to omnibus market surveys, it is likely that they too lean toward male readerships.

† Of course, other factors contribute to shifts in circulation, including the general state of the economy, rates of consumer spending and competition from other magazines in the same market.

oriented cover story (like 'DJs are the New Stars' in October 1988), but the magazine specialized in the 'House Post-Acid' and 'Clubland after Acid' story (*The Face* December 1988; *The Face* December 1990). In a retrospective feature, the publication obliquely acknowledged being the rearguard:

> When acid first arrived, it seemed to be just another passing phase . . . As the scene continued and expanded, the complaints got louder: this was a suburban crowd, not real clubbers, sneered the old guard. They weren't there for the music, they just wanted the high. They couldn't even dance. As it turned out, these were the grumblings of a generation who were being replaced: those who didn't want to go with the flow were in the end, run over by it. (*The Face* December 1990)

This realization and the magazine's subsequent re-positioning, along perhaps with sympathetic publicity acquired in the process of being sued for libelling a Stock/Aitken/Waterman-produced teen idol, arrested *The Face*'s decline in circulation (which had begun in 1986).

The established magazine closest to clubland in 1988 was *i-D*. Though often grouped with *The Face* as a 'style monthly', the two periodicals are significantly different. Whereas *The Face* had come to specialize in personality profiles and celebrity interviews, *i-D* concentrated on scouting out talent and detecting early signs of subculture. The divergence is aptly represented by their front covers: *The Face* displayed familiar faces; *i-D* opted for enigmatic, winking unknowns. Since its inception, the mission of *i-D* has been to find and formulate subcultures. Back issues are a catalogue of club cultures – constructed, encapsulated and packaged. 'Club News' and 'DJ of the Month' columns as well as regular features excavate the youth cultural landscape and establish scenes. *i-D* is self-conscious about the history of youth culture, counter-culture and alternative style but, compared to the nostalgic fanzines, it is uninterested in origins. The monthly has to be careful to search for what's happening and what's next; it needs to ride the crest of cultural trends. (Many rave fanzines cite *i-D* as their model: *Duck Call* thanked '*i-D* for inspiration' while *Herb Garden* parodied *i-D*'s special issue format with its 'Very First Issue' and lampooned their 'DJ of the Month' column.)

Not all youth-orientated magazines are in the business of discovering and developing subcultures. *Smash Hits* is a top-selling fortnightly glossy that loves *Top of the Pops*, publishes poster pin-ups of the younger Radio One DJs and reiterates tabloid gossip with exclamations like 'Really?!!!'. With a target readership of females aged twelve to twenty-two, *Smash Hits* covers dance music but rarely discusses club culture or celebrates undergrounds. While not subcultural in any current sense of the word, these magazines certainly cater to niche taste cultures which are subject to fad and fashion.

Although the phrase 'subcultural consumer magazines' may at first seem to be a contradiction in terms, it accurately describes the editorial business of sustaining readerships by navigating the underground tributaries (which flow into the 'mainstream') as well as the common interpretative community to which staff and subcultural members belong. Another reason for the symbiotic relations between subcultures and the music and style press is that subcultures are a means by which consumer magazines create good copy, tell a story and make meaning out of music and clothes. The press envelop music in discourses (often instigated by relevant PR feeds from record companies) which don't reveal exact conditions of production but rather give acts a picturesque context, locate them agreeably underground, authenticate them with a scene. In other words, consumer magazines accrue credibility by affiliating themselves with subcultures, but also contribute to the authentication of cultural forms in the process of covering and constructing subcultures.

As discussed in chapter 2, authentication by a subculture is particularly important for musics which don't revolve around performing authors and their *oeuvres*. Acid house music was perceived as authentic partly because it was said to come out of Chicago's underground dance clubs. But exactly how did the genre come into being and how did its legend get into general circulation within British dance clubs? The answers to both questions lie with the commercial activities of London Records which coined the genre in the process of their importing, compiling and marketing several DJ International tracks on the third volume of their *House Sound of Chicago* series. Before the compilation's release in January 1988, all that existed was a technological sounding bleep produced by a Roland

TB303 found on the 1987 house music hit 'Acid Tracks' by Phuture.

Hundreds of dance genres are coined every year. While most fail, acid house prospered; it got into circulation, gained currency and started drawing lines on people's aural, aesthetic and social maps. The album's sleeve-notes effectively set the agenda for the music press; they concentrated on three qualities that might be regarded as decisive for the authentication and promotion of a new dance genre. First, as discussed earlier in relation to 'moral panics', they emphasized acid house's drug-orientation and potential to be 'one of the most controversial sounds of 1988'. Second, they gave meaning to identifiable sounds and placed them in a genealogy. This new genre, they argued, took house music 'into an ecstatic, almost transcendental state, where slower rhythms, abstract sounds and expanded lyrics merge together into a kind of phuture funk'. The spelling of '*ph*uture' and the use of the subtitle 'Acid Tracks' deftly put a gestural genealogy in place, retrospectively claiming the 1987 hit as the origin of the genre. Third, acid house was positioned as the soundtrack of an American subculture with firm roots in Chicago: it had an 'underground creed' and 'came out of that city's underground dance studios'.

To be credible, new genres must be more than nominal; they must come across as genuine, seemingly natural, generations of sound. Only one, arguably two, of the compilation's eight tracks and fewer than a dozen singles in general circulation were acid house as the album's own sleeve-notes defined and described it. Moreover, the DJ-artists featured on the album contradicted each other about what was and wasn't 'acid house'. Given this, the success of the genre was no mean feat. Routinely suspicious of new genres, the music press believed in acid house because the existence of a Chicago scene had already been well established by London Records' two previous volumes of *The House Sound of Chicago*. When the company launched the first volume in the summer 1986, they promoted it by taking journalists to the windy city. Eugene Manzi, London's Head of Press, explained the strategy to me:

> When something is not hype, when something real is going on, then you have to show them. We definitely had a story in Chicago. We introduced a pile of British journalists to the artists, producers and lawyers who were all characters – creative but amateurish – and we

generated a lot of good press. (Interview: 24 August 1992)

Here Manzi partly effaces the record company's active role, for one can always find 'something real', but the compilations and the guided tours constructed a particular kind of scene for British consumption. As Stuart Cosgrove, who went on that and other trips to Chicago and wrote the sleeve-notes to the *Acid Tracks* compilation, admitted: 'commercial enterprise constructs as much as it discovers genres and sub-genres' (Interview: 25 August 1992).

London Records formulated a genre which played into underground ideology and framed the sound as authentic, psychedelic and transgressive. Features on a new genre called 'acid house' in *New Musical Express, Melody Maker, Record Mirror* and *Soul Underground* repeated the sleeve's three themes: it was a new generation of music with authentic subcultural roots and a potential for 'moral panic'.* Later, when telling the story of acid house-cum-rave, however, these same periodicals excluded record company involvement from the early history, positioning them as 'bandwagon jumpers' producing last-minute acid remixes and pop singles with applied acid hook-lines. Contrary to the ideologies of both the underground and many subcultural studies, culture industries do not just co-opt and incorporate; they generate ideas and incite culture.

Both the publishing and record industries have sectors which specialize in the manufacture and promotion of 'anti-commercial' culture. This is not to say that acid house-cum-rave culture was not vibrant, nor that its youth were cultural dupes. On the contrary, business involvement does not make young people any less active or creative in their leisure. The argument here is that subcultural gestures are less grand and more contingent than subculturalists have argued. When appropriation is an industrial objective, it is whimsical to regard young people's use of cultural goods as 'profane' or 'subversive' (cf. Willis 1978; Hebdige 1979). Subcultural-

---

* See John McCready 'New Acid Daze' *NME* 6 February 1988; Scott Summers 'Acid Daze' *Record Mirror* 20 February 1988; Simon Reynolds and Paul Oldfield 'Acid Daze' *Melody Maker* 27 February 1988; Darren Deynolds 'Acid House' *Soul Underground* April 1988. An exception to this trend was David Swindells' *Time Out* column which asked DJs Mark Moore and Colin Faver to come up their own definition and list of 'acid house' tracks in response to the Acid Tracks compilation and made no mention of 'moral panic' at this time (*Time Out* 3–10 February 1988).

studies often overstate the homogeneity and conformity of cultural industry output (sometimes, as we have seen, going so far as to call it the 'shit of capitalist production') and, as a consequence, exaggerate the presence of subcultural resistance (Willis 1978: 170).

In early 1988, acid house was little more than an imported type of music with drug associations. It didn't have a definite crowd, a tell-tale wardrobe or a unique blend of dance styles. With the exception of one club called Delirium, 'the only place . . . which accurately re-creates the authentic Chicago setting of acid house', it had few British sites (*Record Mirror* 20 February 1988). Acid house did not yet have a suitable British origin. When the music eventually found a home at Shoom, it was not because the club had any special affiliation to the sound, rather that the club was associated with the hallucinogenic discourses in which the music was enveloped. Shoom was said to 'capture the free spirit of the sixties more than any other' (*Soul Underground* April 1988). Rather than being an organic part of the scene, then, acid house 'simply gave them a musical identity that . . . these particular hippies could relate to, man' (*i-D* June 1988). So admitted the article that conclusively united the music with a club, drug and crowd and fixed the parameters of acid house as a London subculture.

Although many listings and consumer magazines contributed to the construction of the subculture, *i-D* was the most productive. Throughout the early months of 1988, *i-D* ran stories on aspects of what would come to be clustered under the rubric of acid house. On the cover of its first issue of the year, *i-D* sported a winking Smiley face (the insignia which would be banned from high street shops that autumn because of its associations with drug-taking). Inside, a feature described the new penchant for Smiley T-shirts, purple turtle-necks, mutton chop sideburns, floppy fedoras and platform boots. These were the beginnings of the acid house wardrobe, but the garb was associated with rare groove (that is, original and remixed 1970s American funk music) and the crowd was emphatically urban and mixed-race (cf. *i-D* December 1987/ January 1988).

In the ensuing months, *i-D* ran many articles about neo-hippie social types and subcultures. In a parodic manner that admits their creative writing and avoids any 'uncool' earnestness, the magazine portrayed the 'Yappy' or 'Young Artistic Previously Professional Yippy' who was said to fuse the materialism of yuppies with the rebellion of yippies and 'the Baldrics' (named after television character Blackadder's acne-faced sidekick) who were described as the 'psychedelic miscreants ... of Manchester's latest surreal youth cult' and said to wear long hair and flares and 'roam the Haçienda in packs' (*i-D* February 1988; *i-D* April 1988).* Twenty years after 1968, hippie attitudes and attire were in revival among many disparate groups of youth, to diverse soundtracks, with different ideologies – and *i-D* was busy picking scenes out of the cultural morass and labelling them as subcultures.

In their June issue, they ran a piece written by John Godfrey and illustrated by David Swindells which wove these disparate hippie themes through an account of Shoom and effectively transformed a club crowd into a fully fledged subculture. Called 'The Amnesiacs', the article reiterated the much vaunted 'realignment of club attitudes' – the 'return to fun', the pursuit of the 'non-stop party' and introduction of 'happiness into club consciousness' (*i-D* June 1988). It combined this discourse, however, with the revelation of subculture – the 'core crowd had adopted its own language and fashion codes'. Rendered fully newsworthy, the article then proceeded to tabulate the clothing, sounds, sites and argot of the club crowd. It concluded with four top ten lists. 'Happy Fashion' included anything two sizes too big, Smiley or Boy's Own T-shirts, dungarees, headscarves, baggy trousers, patched jeans and sweatshirts (clothing that by previous accounts would not count as subcultural). 'Happy Trax' was non-generic in a way usually considered mainstream, but 'alternative' in so far as it eccentrically included Mory Kante, Mandy Smith, the Woodentops and a few acid house singles. 'Happy Places' catalogued six London clubs and four conveniently remote Ibizan ones. Finally, the most novel and noteworthy list, 'Happy Talk', consisted of drug-oriented argot 'translated' into innocent party speech. An amusing dictionary for those 'in the know', it read:

---

* A year later, 'the Baldrics' scene would be dubbed 'Madchester' by the Happy Mondays and promoted as the 'Manchester scene' by Factory Records and *NME*.

Aciieed!!: the shout at the height of the dance ecstasy
Shoom: the rush of dance ecstasy
Get on one: get into the groove
Matey: a term of greeting
A top one: the ultimate compliment

The subcultural consumer press compile what subculturalists turn around and interpret as revealing homologies. But, while not random, the distinct combination of rituals that came to be acid house was certainly not an unmediated reflection of the social structure. Magazines like *i-D* produced acid house subculture as much as the participating dancers and drug-takers. Like genres, subcultures are constructed in the process of being 'discovered'. Journalists and photographers do not invent subcultures, but shape them, mark their core and reify their borders. Media and other culture industries are integral to the processes by which we create groups through their representation. Just as national media like the BBC have been crucial to the construction of modern national culture (cf. Scannell 1989), so niche media like the music and style press have been instrumental in the development of youth subcultures.

Conclusion

Although acid house and rave are unique phenomena, a few general lessons about music subcultures and the media can be gathered from their case study. First, communications media are inextricably involved in the meaning and organization of youth subcultures. Youth subcultures are not organic, unmediated social formations, nor are they autonomous, grassroots cultures which only meet the media upon recuperative 'selling out' or 'moral panic'. On the contrary, the media do not just represent but participate in the assembly, demarcation and development of music cultures.

Second, the reason for an absolute and essentialist ideological opposition between subcultures and media is, in one sense, simple. The stories that subcultural youth tell about media and commerce are not meant to give accurate accounts of media production processes, but to negotiate issues of subcultural capital and social structure.

Third, the stratifications of popular culture or, at least, these hierarchies of 'hipness' would seem to operate in symbiotic relation to the media. This is not only to say that assorted media act as symbolic goods – bestowing distinction upon their owners/readers/listeners – but also to contend that the media are a network or institution akin to the education system in their creation, classification and distribution of cultural knowledge. In other words, subcultural capital maintains its currency (or cultural worth) as long as it flows through channels of communication which are subject to varying degrees of restriction. The inaccessibility can be physical as in the case of carefully circulated flyers or intellectual in the case of indecipherable subcultural codes. Either way, media are involved in the determinations of cultural knowledge. The prestige of being 'in the know' is one way to make sense of young people's use of and attitudes towards different strata of contemporary communication.

Fourth, this is *not* to deprive clubbers and ravers of their agency or to argue a case for media manipulation. Neither would do justice to the labyrinthine interplay of media representations and authentic cultures, commerce and consumer. Clubbers and ravers are active and creative participants in the formation of club cultures, but myriad media are also involved. They are integral to clubber and raver perceptions of where they belong and to practices of where they actually go.

London may be an 'overexposed city', but it is not one without its darkened doorways, obscure recesses and unmapped circuits (cf. Virilio 1986). Club 'undergrounds' are distinguished by being in the shadow of mass-media spotlights. Unless the culture is cast in the 'negative light' of 'moral panic', such television or tabloid illumination leads to demystification, explication and access (processes often clustered under the negative banner of 'commercialization'). The circumspect highlighting of a culture by niche media and micro-media, however, doesn't threaten as much as shape and sustain the interest and activities of appropriate audiences. One basis for predicting the formation, longevity and even the revival of any British subculture is, therefore, the nature of its association with distinct layers of media.

Finally, although it would be difficult to argue without further historical research, I suspect that youth-oriented media and youth subcultures have proliferated in tandem. In the early 1960s, a 'scene' was 'the newest thing in musical journalism' (*Melody Maker* 10 March 1962). Since then, journalists influenced by key texts like Cohen's *Folk Devils and Moral Panics* (which was for years on the syllabuses of many A-level sociology courses) and Hebdige's *Subculture* (which has been required reading in art school and cultural studies degrees) have authenticated music and placed it within newsworthy narratives by referring not only to 'scenes' but also to 'moral panics' and 'subcultures'. This appropriation and application of academic terms is a component of what Anthony Giddens has called the 'reflexivity of modernity'. In other words, the formation of club subcultures illustrates the way the discourses of sociology 'circulate in and out of what they are about' and in so doing 'reflexively restructure their subject matter' (Giddens 1990: 43). Not an example of postmodernity *per se*, but one of the acceleration and intensification of the tendencies of modernity, the case of acid house-cum-rave embodies the many processes at work in determining the shape of contemporary society, including knowledge about that society as well as primary disseminators of that knowledge like schools and colleges, but also media.

Given this scenario, I am forced to conclude that subcultures are best defined as social groups that have been labelled as such. This is the most convincing way to account for the fact that some cultural groupings are deemed subcultural while others, whose practices may be equally arcane, are not. Scholars need not embark on long-winded attempts to define the indeterminate (like the subculturalists discussed earlier), nor need they explain subcultures out of existence by referring to class dichotomies (like some sociologists of youth). Communications media create subcultures in the process of naming them and draw boundaries around them in the act of describing them. Moreover, it would seem that sociology and cultural studies have furnished at least a couple of convenient concepts to help media make sense of, define and incite young people's cultural activities.

Afterword

Contemporary cultures – high and low – are riddled with dynamics of distinction. Although the canons and classifications of high cultures have been the extensively analysed, the distinction systems of popular culture have yet to be as thoroughly researched. In this book, popular distinctions are explored as means by which people jockey for social power, as discriminations by which players are both assigned social statuses and strive for a sense of self-worth. This perspective envisages popular culture as a multi-dimensional social space rather than as a flat folk culture or as simply the bottom rung on some linear social ladder. Rather than characterizing cultural differences as 'resistances' to hierarchy or to the remote cultural dominations of some ruling class, it investigates the microstructures of power entailed in the cultural disagreements and debates that go on between more closely associated social groups. For example, youth construct elaborate scenarios whereby the superficial or belated activities of *other* young people act as a yardstick of the depth and style of their own culture. The social logic of these distinctions is such that it makes sense to discuss them as forms of *subcultural capital* or means by which young people negotiate and accumulate status within their own social worlds.

Media are fundamental to processes of popular distinction because media consumption is a primary leisure activity and because they are leading disseminators of culture. Media are so involved in the circuits of contemporary culture that they could be conceived of as being part of the material conditions of social groups, in a way not unlike access to education. In the case of youth, the difference between the 'hip' and the banal, honourable and trash culture tends to correlate with amounts and kinds of media exposure – some media legitimate while others popularize, some preserve the esoteric while others are seen to 'sell out'. As subjects of discussion and sources of information, media are deliberate and accidental determinants of cultural hierarchy.

This approach interrogates the 'popular' not just in terms of its etymological root, 'of the people', nor in the sense of being 'prevalent' or 'common', but specifically in the sense of being 'approved', 'preferred' and 'well-liked'. In other words, issues of taste are essential to this conception of *popular* culture. Tastes are fought over precisely because people define themselves and others through what they like and dislike. Taste in music, for youth in particular, is often seen as the key to one's distinct sense of self. Youth, therefore, often embrace 'unpopular cultures' because they distinguish them in ways that the widely liked cannot.

The implications of this approach for the politics of popular culture are contradictory and perhaps best clarified by taking a historical view. A broad comparison of two classic texts – Jock Young's *The Drugtakers* and Dick Hebdige's *Subculture* – offers just such a perspective on the politics of youth culture. The first of these books was researched in the 1960s and is haunted by hippie culture; the second, written during the 1970s, is dominated by the power of punk. Young's book comes out of a tradition of deviance studies and criminology while Hebdige's text, which owes its greatest debts to literary theory, is a contribution to what was then the fledgeling discipline of 'cultural studies'. Both texts locate youth subcultures on the progressive side of the political arena but, in accordance with their disciplinary differences, they position the crux of youth politics in disparate aspects of youth culture.

Jock Young's *The Drugtakers: The Social Meaning of Drug Use* is a sociological investigation which identifies the progressive potential of youth culture in its hedonism – its refusal to settle into work routines and conform to bureaucratic rules. Following in the tradition of Marxists like Herbert Marcuse, Young argues that some youth cultures (particularly drug-taking ones) go beyond the deferred gratifications of 'leisure' and enter the realm of pure 'play'. In other words, they seek worlds of truly subterranean values which are not governed by latter-day versions of the 'Protestant work ethic' or some other ethos of productivity. Young sees this kind of youthful escape into 'alternative forms of reality' as a threat to the social order, to capitalism and conservatism (Young 1971: 136).

Hebdige's *Subculture: The Meaning of Style*, by contrast, is a semiotic interpretation of post-war British youth subcultures which locates the progressive potential of youth culture in the way it flouts, and therefore makes visible, society's aesthetic rules. Drawing on the work of Roland Barthes, Hebdige sees the clothes and music of Teddy Boys, mods, skinheads and rastas as challenges to the symbolic order, which paved the way for the even more aggressive confrontations of punk style. This kind of 'semiotic guerilla warfare' acts as 'noise' in the silent workings of dominant ideology. Subcultures therefore become a 'form of resistance in which . . . contradictions and objections to this ruling ideology are obliquely represented in style' (Hebdige 1979: 133).

Both Young's and Hebdige's definitive commentaries on subcultural politics take the ethos of the key youth movements of their day to their logical, theoretical conclusions. In researching and contemplating the club and rave cultures of the late 1980s and early 1990s, this book also explains the ideals and standards of a main youth movement of its time. With the benefit of historical hindsight, however, it was difficult simply to accept clubber and raver discourses about 'radical' escape and 'revolutionary' style, particularly as these discourses seemed to be entwined in complex ways with concerns for distinction.

Youthful interest in distinction is not new. One could easily reinterpret the history of post-war youth cultures in terms of subcultural capital. In a contemporary context, however, dynamics of distinction are perhaps more obvious for at least two reasons. First, unlike the liberalizing sixties and seventies, the eighties were 'radical' in their conservatism. Change was experienced as a move to the political right, while the left were effectively positioned as reactionary in their intent to preserve the past. Unlike Young's hippies and Hebdige's punks, then, the youth of my research were, to cite the cliché, 'Thatcher's children'. Well versed in the virtues of competition, their cultural heroes came in the form of radical young entrepreneurs, starting up clubs and record labels, rather than the politicians and poets of yesteryear.

The second reason that the pursuit of distinction may be more noticeable today is because sociological debates have shifted our vision of *difference*. For example, despite their many disparate opinions, both Young and Hebdige see the assertion of cultural difference as an essentially progressive gesture, a step in the right direction away from conformity and submission. Difference was cast positively as *deviance* and *dissidence.* If one believes that it is in the nature of power to homogenize – be it in the form of Young's 'consensus' or Hebdige's 'hegemony' – then difference can be seen as a good thing in itself. But if one considers the function of difference within an ever more finely graded social structure, its political tendencies become more ambiguous. In a post-industrial world where consumers are incited to individualize themselves and where the operations of power seem to favour classification and segregation, it is hard to regard difference as necessarily progressive. The flexibility of new modes of commodity production and the expansion of multiple media support micro-communities and fragmented niche cultures. Each cultural difference is a potential distinction, a suggestion of superiority, an assertion of hierarchy, a possible alibi for subordination. In many circumstances, then, the politics of difference is more appropriately cast as *discrimination* and *distinction.*

These shifting notions of the power of difference have informed the main arguments of this book. They have shaped the double-edged way in which I have considered the relations between the 'mainstream' and the subcultural. On the one hand, youth are rebellious in their opposition to the mainstream as a complacent, dominant culture. On the other, the characteristics of the mainstream they repeatedly disparage and subordinate in speech are those of a feminine working-class minority. Here, it is not possible to separate an embryonic critique of the *status quo* from ideas which express and support extant relations of power. They are two sides of the same coin. As Bourdieu writes, subcultural practices 'produce paradoxical effects which cannot be understood if one tries to force them into a dichotomy of resistance or submission' (Bourdieu 1991: 94).

These issues are clouded by the fondness that youth subcultures have for appropriating political rhetorics and frequently referring to 'rights' and 'freedoms', 'equality' and 'unity'. This can be seen as a strategy by which political issues are enlisted in order to give youthful leisure activities that extra punch, that added *je ne sais quoi*, a sense of independence, even danger. In the process of coming to grips with the existential and social circumstances of their lives, youth appropriate the 'political' as a way of making their culture more meaningful. As such, this is not evidence of the politicization of youth as much as testimony to the aestheticization of politics.

The two-sided nature of distinction also clarifies the politics of the youthful will to classlessness. At one level, youth do aspire to a more egalitarian and democratic world. On the other hand, classlessness is a strategy for transcending being classed. It is a means of obfuscating the dominant structure in order to set up an alternative and, as such, is an ideological precondition for the effective operation of subcultural capital. This paradoxical combination of resignation and refusal, defiance and deference would seem to be characteristic of youth subcultures.

The politics of youth are also complicated by the fact that subcultures adore rejection or condemnation by media that seem to represent the *status quo*, like Radio One and the *Sun*. I've discussed this in terms of the thrill of censorship and 'moral panic', processes unrivalled in their ability to authenticate transgression and therefore legitimate a subculture. But we shouldn't assume the presence of political subversion just because a youth culture got a negative response from some part of the media. For, rather than operating with any imperative to repress or oppress, media are motivated by corporate agendas like generating sensational copy to keep up high sales or maintaining their image as a family-orientated public service. In other words, media react to phenomena which don't actually threaten them, and youth cultures (unlike, say, Monopolies and Mergers Commission inquiries) are one such subject.

This is not to say that individual participants in club and rave culture are not active in the arena of Politics proper (rather than the politics with a small 'p' under discussion here) or that club culture has spawned no political movements. On the contrary, clubbers and ravers have been affiliated to two political projects – both of which were concerned first and foremost with the unrestrained pursuit of pleasure. The first was the 'Freedom to Party' campaign which was organized in anticipation of the private member's bill outlawing 'pay parties' in 1990. Here the key MPs to voice support were from the far right, libertarian wing of the Conservative party. The second political venture was opposition to the Criminal Justice Bill which sought to go even further in outlawing gatherings of ten people or more which were accompanied by music dependent on amplification with a pronounced and regular beat. In this case, youth found themselves aligned primarily with Labour MPs. In both cases, the demonstrations organized to oppose these bills hardly constituted defining moments of club and rave culture. They were poorly attended peripheral activities which pale in comparison with the dance activities of any Saturday night.

Rather than de-politicizing popular cultures, a shift away from the search for 'resistance' actually gives fuller representation to the complex and rarely straightforward politics of contemporary culture. The distinctions examined through multiple methods in this book demonstrate the rich creativities and originalities of youth culture as well as their entanglement in micro-politics of domination and subordination. However, this economy of the 'hip' and happening is but one dynamic in a huge array of popular distinctions. In order to give a more comprehensive account of the causes and consequences of popular culture, future studies would do well to investigate the generation, evolution and dissolution of subcultural distinctions.

Bibliography

Abrams, Mark. 1959. *The Teenage Consumer*. Press Exchange, London.

Adorno, Theodor. 1941/1990. On popular music. *On Record* eds S. Frith and A. Goodwin. Pantheon, New York.

——. 1968/1988. *Introduction to the Sociology of Music*. Continuum, New York.

——. 1991. The curves of the needle; The forms of the phonograph record; Opera and the long-playing record. *October* 55.

Allor, Martin. 1988. Relocating the site of the audience: Reconstructive theory and the social subject. *Critical Studies in Mass Communication* V/3.

Ang, Ien and Joke Hermes. 1991. Gender and/in media consumption. *Mass Media and Society* eds J. Curran and M. Gurevitch. Edward Arnold, London.

Arnold, David O. (ed.) 1970. *Subcultures*. The Glendessary Press, Berkeley.

Attali, Jacques. 1985. *Noise: The Political Economy of Music* (trans. B. Massumi). University of Minnesota Press, Minneapolis.

Attallah, Paul. 1986. *Music television*. Working paper in communications. McGill University, Montreal.

Austin, Brian. 1992. The dance club network and the club disc jockey. Unpublished dissertation proposal, *October*.

Austin, Bruce. 1989. *Immediate Seating: A Look at Movie Audiences*. Wadsworth Publishing Inc., Belmont, CA.

Averill, Gage. 1989. Haitian dance bands 1915–1970: Class, race and authenticity. *Latin American Music Review* X/2, fall/winter.

Back, Les. 1988. Coughing up fire: Soundsystems in South-East London. *New Formations* 5, summer.

Banham, Reyner. 1966. Vinyl deviationa. *New Society*, 1 December.

Barbrook, Richard. 1990. Melodies or rhythms?: The competition for the Greater London FM radio licence. *Popular Music* IX/2.

Barthes, Roland. 1972. *Mythologies* (trans. Annette Lavers). Paladin, London.

——. 1977. *Image–Music–Text* (trans. S. Heath). Fontana/Collins, London.

Baudrillard, Jean. 1982. The Beaubourg effect: Implosion and deterrence. *October* 20, spring.

——. 1983a. *Simulations*. Semiotext(e), New York.

——. 1983b. *In the Shadow of the Silent Majorities, or the End of the Social*. Semiotext(e), New York.

——. 1983c. The ecstasy of communication. *The Anti-Aesthetic: Essays on Postmodern Culture* ed. H. Foster. Bay Press, Port Townsend, Washington.

BBC Broadcasting Research. 1990. *Youth Programmes on Television*. BBC Broadcasting Research Information Desk.

Becker, Howard. 1963. *Outsiders: Studies in the Sociology of Deviance*. The Free Press, New York.

——. 1967. Whose side are we on? *Social Problems* XIV/3, winter.

——. 1982. *Art Worlds*. University of California Press, Berkeley.

Benjamin, Walter. 1955/1970. *Illuminations*. Fontana/Collins, London.

Berger, Bennett. 1991. Structure and choice in the sociology of culture. *Theory and Society* XX.

Berman, Marshall. 1983. *All That is Solid Melts into Air: The Experience of Modernity*. Verso, London.

Blum, L.H. 1966. The discotheque and the phenomenon of alone-together-ness: A study of the young person's response to the Frug and comparable current dances. *Adolescence* 1.

Bogdanor, V. and R. Skidelsky (eds) 1970. *The Age of Affluence, 1951–1964*. Macmillan, London.

Bourdieu, Pierre. 1984. *Distinction: A Social Critique of the Judgement of Taste* (trans. R. Nice). Harvard University Press, Cambridge, Mass.

——. 1986a. The forms of capital. *Handbook of Theory and Research for the Sociology of Education* ed. J. Richardson. Greenwood Press, London.

——. 1986b. The production of belief: Contribution to an economy of symbolic goods. *Media, Culture and Society: A Critical Reader* eds R. Collins et al. Sage, London.

——. 1990. *In Other Words: Essays Towards a Reflexive Sociology*. Polity, London.

——. 1991. *Language and Symbolic Power*. Polity, Cambridge.

——. 1993. *Sociology in Question*. Sage, London.

Bourdieu, Pierre and Loïc Wacquant. 1992. *An Invitation to Reflexive Sociology*. Polity, London.

Bradby, Barbara. 1993. Sampling sexuality: Gender, technology and the body in dance music. *Popular Music* XII/2.

Brooks, William. 1982. On being tasteless. *Popular Music* II.

Brubaker, Rogers. 1985. Rethinking classical theory: The sociological vision of Pierre Bourdieu. *Theory and Society* 14.

Brunsdon, Charlotte. 1990. Problems with quality. *Screen* XXXI/1, spring.

——. 1991. Satellite dishes and the landscapes of taste. *New Formations* 15, winter.

Brunt, Rosalind. 1992. Engaging with the popular. *Cultural Studies* eds L. Grossberg et al. Routledge, London.

Bulmer, Martin. 1983. The methodology of the taxi-dance hall: An early account of Chicago ethnography from the 1920s. *Urban Life* XII/1, April.

Burke, Peter. 1980. *Sociology and History*. George Allen & Unwin, London.

Burton, Peter. 1985. *Parallel Lives*. GMP, London.

Calhoun, Craig, Edward LiPuma and Moishe Postone. (eds) 1993. *Bourdieu: Critical Perspectives*. Polity, Oxford.

Carter, Angela. 1968. A prince of cloud-cuckoo land. *New Society*, 18 July.

Caughie, John. 1986. Popular cultures: Notes and revisions. *High Theory/ Low Culture* ed. C. MacCabe. Manchester University Press, Manchester.

Central Statistical Office. 1973, 1977, 1983, 1986. Leisure. *The General Household Survey*. Her Majesty's Stationery Office, London.

Chambers, Iain. 1986. *Popular Culture: The Urban Experience*. Methuen, London.

——. 1987. Maps for the metropolis: A possible guide to the present. *Cultural Studies* I/1.

——. 1990. Popular music and mass culture. *Questioning the Media* eds J. Downing et al. Sage, London.

Chapman, Robert. 1993. *Selling the Sixties: The Pirates and Pop Music Radio*. Routledge, London.

Chippindale, Peter and Chris Horrie. 1990. *Stick It Up Your Punter: The Rise and Fall of the Sun*. Mandarin, London.

Christenson, Peter and Jon Brian Peterson. 1988. Genre and gender in the structure of music preferences. *Communication Research* XV/3, June.

Clarke, Donald. (ed.) 1989. *The Penguin Encyclopedia of Popular Music*. Viking, London.

Clarke, Gary. 1990. Defending ski-jumpers: A critique of theories of youth culture. *On Record* eds S. Frith and A. Goodwin. Pantheon, New York.

Clarke, John, Stuart Hall, Tony Jefferson and Brian Roberts. 1976. Subcultures, cultures and class: A theoretical overview. *Resistance Through Rituals* eds S. Hall and T. Jefferson, Unwin Hyman, London.

Clarke, Paul. 1983. 'A magic science': Rock music as a recording art. *Popular Music* III.

Clifford, James and George Marcus. (eds) 1986. *Writing Culture: The Poetics and Politics of Ethnography*. University of California Press, London.

Cohen, Sara. 1991. *Rock Culture in Liverpool*. Clarendon Press, Oxford.

———. 1993. Ethnography and popular music studies. *Popular Music* XII/2.

Cohen, Stanley. (ed.) 1971. *Images of Deviance*. Penguin, Harmondsworth.

Cohen, Stanley. 1972/1980. *Folk Devils and Moral Panics*. MacGibbon & Kee, London.

Cohen, Stanley and Jock Young. (eds) 1973. *The Manufacture of the News: Deviance, Social Problems and the Mass Media*. Constable, London.

Connor, Steve. 1987. The flag on the road: Bruce Springsteen and the live. *New Formations* 3.

Corbett, John. 1991. Free, single and disengaged: Listening pleasure and the popular music object. *October* 54.

Cosgrove, Stuart. 1989. The zoot suit and style warfare. *Zoot Suits and Second Hand Dresses* ed. A. McRobbie. Macmillan, London.

———. 1989. Acid enterprise. *New Statesman & Society*, 13 October.

Cowie, C. and Sue Lees. 1981. Slags or drags. *Feminist Review* 9.

Crane, Jonathan. 1986. Mainstream music and the masses. *Journal of Communication Inquiry* X/3.

Cressey, Paul. 1932. *The Taxi-Dance Hall*. Greenwood Press, New York.

———. 1983. A comparison of the roles of the 'sociological stranger' and the 'anonymous stranger' in field research. *Urban Life* XII/1, April.

Curran, James and Jean Seaton. 1991. *Power without Responsibility: The Press and Broadcasting in Britain*. Routledge, London.

Curran, James and Colin Sparks. 1991. Press and popular culture. *Media, Culture and Society* XIII.

Cutler, Chris. 1984. Technology, politics and contemporary music: Necessity and choice in musical forms. *Popular Music* IV.

Dannen, Fredric. 1991. *Hit Men: Power Brokers and Fast Money Inside the Music Business*. Vintage, New York.

Davies, Hunter. 1968/1992. *The Beatles*. Arrow, London.

Davies, Kath, Julienne Dickey and Teresa Stratford. (eds) 1987. *Out of Focus: Writings on Women and the Media*. The Women's Press, London.

Davis, Tracey. 1991. The moral sense of the majorities: Indecency and vigilance in Late Victorian music halls. *Popular Music* X/1.

Dearling, Robert. 1984. *The Guinness Book of Recorded Sound*. Guinness Books, London.

De Certeau, Michel. 1984. *The Practices of Everyday Life* (trans. S. Rendell). University of California Press, Berkeley.

——. 1985. Practices of space. *On Signs* ed. M. Blonsky. Johns Hopkins University Press, Baltimore, Maryland.

Delph, Edward William. 1978. *The Silent Community: Public Homosexual Encounters*. Sage, London.

DiMaggio, Paul. 1979. Review essay on Pierre Bourdieu. *American Journal of Sociology* LXXXIV/6, May.

Docherty, David, David Morrison and Michael Tracey. 1987. *The Last Picture Show: Britain's Changing Film Audiences*. BFI Publishing, London.

Doherty, Thomas. 1988. *Teenagers and Teenpics: The Juvenilization of American Movies in the 1950s*. Unwin Hyman, London.

Donovan, Kevin. 1981. *The Place*. Kevin Donovan, Stoke-on-Trent.

Dorn, Nicholas and Nigel South. 1989. Drugs and leisure, prohibition and pleasure: From subculture to the drugalogue. *Leisure for Leisure* ed. C. Rojek. Macmillan, London.

Douglas, Mary. 1991. The idea of a home: A kind of space. *Social Research* LVIII/1, spring, 287–307.

Dubin, Steven. 1983. The moral continuum of deviancy research: Chicago sociologists and the dance hall. *Urban Life* XII/1, April.

Durant, Alan. 1984. *The Conditions of Music*. Macmillan, London.

——. 1991. A new day for music? Digital technologies in contemporary music making. *Culture, Technology and Creativity* ed. P. Hayward. John Libbey, London.

Dyer, Richard. 1992. *Only Entertainment*. Routledge, London.

Ehrenreich, Barbara. 1990. *Fear of Falling: The Inner Life of the Middle Class*. Harper perennial, New York.

Ehrlich, Cyril. 1985. *The Music Profession in Britain*. Clarendon Press, Oxford.

——. 1989. *Harmonious Alliances: A History of the Performing Rights Society*. Oxford University Press, Oxford.

Eisenberg, Evan. 1987. *The Recording Angel: Music, Records and Culture from Aristotle to Zappa*. Picador, London.

Eisenstadt, S.N. 1956. *From Generation to Generation*. Free Press, London.

EMAP Metro. 1988. *Youth Behaviour and Attitudes: A Survey of Britain's 11–20 Year Olds*, August.

Euromonitor. 1989a. The pubs network. *Market Research Great Britain* XXX, March.

——. 1989b. *The Music and Video Buyers Survey: Tabular Report and Appendixes*, November.

——. 1990a. Music buyers. *Market Research Great Britain* XXXI, February.

——. 1990b. Music radio and record purchase. *Market Research Great Britain* XXXI, March.

——. 1990c. Leisure spending among the young. *Market Research Great Britain* XXXI, June.

Evans, Stephen. 1989. Nightclubbing: An exploration after dark. Paper presented to the BPS Scottish Branch of the Annual Conference, University of Strathclyde, Glasgow.

Fabbri, Franco. 1982a. A theory of musical genres: Two applications. *Popular Music Perspectives* eds D. Horn and P. Tagg. Gotenberg and Exeter.

——. 1982b. What kind of music? *Popular Music* 2.

Finnegan, Ruth. 1989. *The Hidden Musicians: Music Making in an English Town*. Cambridge University Press, Cambridge.

Folb, Edith A. 1980. *Runnin' Down Some Lines: The Language and Culture of Black Teenagers*. Harvard University Press, London.

Forty, Adrian. 1986. *Objects of Desire: Design from Wedgwood to IBM*. Pantheon Books, New York.

Foster, Hal. (ed.) 1983. *The Anti-Aesthetic: Essays on Postmodern Culture*. Bay Press, Port Townsend, WA.

Fountain, Nigel. 1968. The telephone mob. *New Society*, 18 January.

Franklin, Sarah, Celia Lury and Jackie Stacey. 1991. *Off Centre: Feminism and Cultural Studies*. HarperCollins, London.

Frith, Simon. 1978. Infinite spaces: Thesis on disco. *Time Out*, 24–30 March.

——. 1980. Music for pleasure. *Screen Education* 34, spring.

——. 1981a. *Sound Effects: Youth, Leisure and the Politics of Rock'n'Roll*. Pantheon, New York.

——. 1981b. *Downtown: Young People in the City Centre*. National Youth Bureau, Leicester.

——. 1981c. 'The magic that can set you free': The ideology of folk and the myth of the rock community. *Popular Music* I.

——. 1986. Art versus technology: The strange case of popular music. *Media, Culture and Society* VIII/3, July.

——. 1987a. The making of the British record industry, 1920–1964. *Impacts and Influences: Essays on Media Power in the Twentieth Century* eds J. Curran et al. Methuen, London.

——. 1987b. Copyright and the music business. *Popular Music* VII/1.

——. 1987c. Towards an aesthetics of popular music. *Music and Society* ed. R. Leppert and S. McClary. Cambridge University Press, Cambridge.

——. 1988a. *Music for Pleasure*. Polity, London.

——. (ed.) 1988b. *Facing the Music*. Pantheon, New York.

——. 1991a. Anglo-America and its discontents. *Cultural Studies* V/3, October.

——. 1991b. The good, the bad and the indifferent: Defending popular culture from the populists. *Diacritics*, winter.

——. 1992a. The industrialization of popular music. *Popular Music and Communication* ed. J. Lull. Sage, London.

——. 1992b. The cultural study of music. *Cultural Studies* eds L. Grossberg et al. Routledge, London.

Frith, Simon and Andrew Goodwin. (eds) 1990. *On Record: Rock, Pop and the Written Word*. Pantheon, New York.

Frith, Simon and Howard Horne. 1987. *Art Into Pop*. Methuen, London.

Frith, Simon et al. (eds) 1993. *Sound and Vision: The Music Video Reader*. Routledge, London.

Frow, John. 1987. Accounting for tastes: Some problems in Bourdieu's sociology of culture. *Cultural Studies* I/1, January.

Gans, Herbert J. 1974. *Popular Culture and High Culture*. Basic Books, New York.

Garnham, Nicholas. 1993. Bourdieu, the cultural arbitrary and television. *Bourdieu: Critical Perspectives* eds C. Calhoun et al. Polity, Oxford.

Garnham, Nicholas and Raymond Williams. 1986. Pierre Bourdieu and the sociology of culture. *Media, Culture and Society: A Critical Reader* eds R. Collins et al. Sage, London.

Garofalo, Reebee. (ed.) 1992. *Rockin' The Boat: Mass Music and Mass Movements*. South End Press, Boston.

Gelatt, Roland. 1977. *The Fabulous Phonograph, 1877–1977* (2nd edition). Cassell, London.

Giddens, Anthony. 1964. Notes on the concepts of play and leisure. *Sociological Review* XII/1, March.

——. 1990. *The Consequences of Modernity*. Polity, Cambridge.

Gillett, Charlie. 1983. *The Sound of the City*. Souvenir Press, London.

Gilroy, Paul. 1987. *There Ain't No Black in the Union Jack*. Unwin Hyman, London.

——. 1993. Between Afro-centrism and Eurocentrism: Youth culture and the problem of hybridity. *Young* I/2, May.

Godbolt, Jim. 1984. *A History of Jazz in Britain 1919–1950*. Quartet Books, London.

Godfrey, John. (ed.) 1990. *A Decade of i-Deas: The Encyclopedia of the 80s*. Penguin Books, London.

Goodwin, Andrew. 1990. Sample and hold: Pop music in the digital age of reproduction. *On Record*. Pantheon, New York.

——. 1992a. Rationalization and democratization in the new technologies of popular music. *Popular Music and Communication* ed. J. Lull. Sage, London.

——. 1992b. *Dancing in the Distraction Factory: Music Television and Popular Culture*. University of Minnesota Press, Minneapolis.

Gordon, Milton. 1947/1970. The concept of the sub-culture and its application. *Subcultures* ed. D.O. Arnold. Glendessary Press, Berkeley.

Gotfrit, Leslie. 1988. Women dancing back: Disruption and the politics of pleasure. *Journal of Education* 170/3.

Greater London Council. 1979. *Disco Rules Okay?* GLC, London.

Griffiths, Vivienne. 1988. Stepping out: The importance of dancing for young women. *Relative Freedoms: Women and Leisure.* Open University Press, London.

Grossberg, Lawrence. 1984. Another boring day in paradise: Rock and roll and the empowerment of everyday life. *Popular Music* IV.

——. 1987. The politics of music: American images and British articulations. *Canadian Journal of Political and Social Theory* XI/1–2.

——. 1992. *We Gotta Get Out of This Place: Popular Conservatism and Postmodernism in Contemporary America.* Routledge, New York.

Grossberg, Lawrence, Cary Nelson and Paula Treichler. (eds) 1992. *Cultural Studies.* Routledge, London.

Hadley, Daniel. 1993. Ride the rhythm: Two approaches to DJ practice. *Journal of Popular Music Studies* V.

Hall, Stuart. 1980. Cultural studies: Two paradigms. *Media, Culture and Society* 2.

Hall, Stuart and Paddy Whannel. 1964. *The Popular Arts.* Pantheon, London.

Hall, Stuart and Tony Jefferson. (eds) 1976. *Resistance Through Rituals: Youth Subcultures in Post-war Britain.* Unwin Hyman, London.

Hall, Stuart, Dorothy Hobson, Andrew Lowe and Paul Willis. (eds) 1980. *Culture, Media, Language: Working Papers in Cultural Studies.* Hutchinson, London.

Halsey, A.H. 1986. *Change in British Society.* Oxford University Press, Oxford.

Hammersley, Martin and Paul Atkinson. 1983. *Ethnography: Principles and Practice.* Tavistock Publications, London.

Hanna, Judith Lynne. 1988. *Dance, Sex and Gender: Signs of Identity, Dominance, Defiance, and Desire.* University of Chicago Press, Chicago.

Harvey, David. 1989. *The Condition of Postmodernity: An Inquiry into the Origins of Cultural Change.* Basil Blackwell, London.

Harvith, John and Susan Edwards Harvith. (eds) 1987. *Edison, Musicians and the Phonograph: A Century in Retrospect.* Greenwood Press, London.

Hayward, Philip. (ed.) 1991. *Culture, Technology and Creativity in the Late Twentieth Century.* John Libbey & Co., London.

Hazzard-Gordon, Katrina. 1990. *Jookin': The Rise of Social Dance Formations in African-American Culture.* Temple University Press, Philadelphia.

Hebdige, Dick. 1979. *Subculture: The Meaning of Style.* Methuen, London.

——. 1987. *Cut'n'Mix: Culture, Identity and Caribbean Music.* Comedia, London.

——. 1988. *Hiding in the Light: On Images and Things.* Routledge, London.

Henley, Nancy. 1977. *Body Politics: Power, Sex and Nonverbal Communication.*

Simon & Schuster, New York.

Henley Centre for Forecasting. 1990a. Time use. *Leisure Futures*, August.

——. 1990b. Postmodernism and leisure markets. *Leisure Futures*, August.

——. 1991. The local future of leisure. *Leisure Futures*, February.

Henry, Tricia. 1989. *Breaking all the Rules: Punk Rock and the Making of a Style*. U.M.I. Research Press, London.

Hey, Valerie. 1986. *Patriarchy and Pub Culture*. Tavistock, London.

Hoher, Dagmar. 1986. The composition of music hall audiences 1850‑1900. *Music Hall: The Business of Pleasure* ed. P. Bailey. Open University Press, London.

Hollander, Anne. 1975. *Seeing Through Clothes*. Penguin, London.

Hollingshead, August B. 1949. *Elmstown's Youth: The Impact of Social Classes on Adolescents*. John Wiley & Sons, New York.

Honneth, Axel. 1986. The fragmented world of symbolic forms: Reflections on Pierre Bourdieu's sociology of culture. *Theory, Culture and Society* III/3.

Hooker, Evelyn. 1969. The homosexual community. *The Same Sex: An Appraisal of Homosexuality* ed. R.W. Weltge. Pilgrim Press, Philadelphia.

Hosokawa, Shuhei. 1984. The Walkman effect. *Popular Music* IV.

Hughes, David. 1964. The Spivs. *The Age of Austerity 1945–51* eds M. Sissons and P. French. Penguin, London.

Hughes, Everett C. 1945. Dilemmas and contradictions of status. *American Journal of Sociology* L/5.

Hughes, Walter. 1994. In the empire of the beat: Discipline and disco. *Microphone Fiends* eds A. Ross and T. Rose. Routledge, London.

Humphreys, Laud. 1970. *Tearoom Trade: Impersonal Sex in Public Places*. Aldine, Chicago.

——. 1972. *Out of the Closets: The Sociology of Homosexual Liberation*. Prentice Hall, Inc., NJ.

Hunter, Nigel. (ed.) 1977. *BPI Yearbook 1977*. British Phonographic Industry Limited, London.

Hustwitt, Mark. 1983. Caught in a whirlpool of aching sound: The production of dance music in Britain in the 1920s. *Popular Music* III.

Huyssen, Andreas. 1986. *After the Great Divide: Modernism, Mass Culture, Postmodernism*. Indiana University Press, Bloomington.

Jameson, Fredric. 1984. Postmodernism, or the cultural logic of late capitalism. *New Left Review* 146, July–August.

——. 1988. Cognitive mapping. *Marxism and the Interpretation of Culture* ed. C. Nelson and L. Grossberg. University of Illinois, Urbana.

Joe, Radcliffe A. 1980. *This Business of Disco*. Watson-Guptill Publications, New York.

Jones, Simon. 1988. *Black Culture, White Youth*. Macmillan, London.

Katz, Elihu and David Foulkes. 1962. On the use of the mass media as 'escape': Clarification of a concept. *Public Opinion Quarterly* XXVI.

Katz, Ruth. 1983. The egalitarian waltz. *What is Dance? Readings in Criticism and Theory* eds R. Copeland and M. Cohen. Oxford University Press, Toronto.

Kavanagh, James. 1990. Ideology. *Critical Terms for Literary Study* eds F. Lentricchia and T. McLaughlin. Chicago.

Kealy, Edward R. 1979/1990. From craft to art: The case of sound mixers and popular music. *On Record* eds S. Frith and A. Goodwin. Pantheon, New York.

Kinsman, Francis. 1990. *UK Leisure Markets: 1990 Survey Prospects to 1995.* Staniland Hall, London.

Klein, Jean-Claude. 1985. Borrowing, syncretism, hybridisation: The Parisian revue of the 1920s. *Popular Music* V.

Kloosterman, Robert and Chris Quispel. 1990. Not just the same old show on my radio: An analysis of the role of radio in the diffusion of black music among whites in the United States of America, 1920 to 1960. *Popular Music* IX/2.

Kopytko, Tania. 1986. Breakdance as an identity marker in New Zealand. *Yearbook for Traditional Music* XVIII.

Kotarba, Joseph and Laura Wells. 1987. Styles of adolescent participation in an all-ages rock'n'roll nightclub: An ethnographic analysis. *Youth and Society* XVIII/4, June.

Krieger, Susan. 1983. *The Mirror Dance: Identity in a Women's Community.* Temple University Press, Philadelphia.

Kroker, Arthur. 1984. *Technology and the Canadian Mind: Innis/McLuhan/ Grant.* New World Perspectives, Montreal.

Kruse, Holly. 1993. Subcultural identity in alternative music culture. *Popular Music* XII/1.

Laing, Dave. 1985. *One Chord Wonders: Power and Meaning in Punk.* Open University Press, Milton Keynes.

——. 1986. The music industry and the cultural imperialism thesis. *Media, Culture and Society* VIII/3, July.

——. 1990. Making popular music: The producer as consumer. *Consumption, Identity and Style* ed. A. Tomlinson. Routledge, London.

——. 1991. A voice without a face: Popular music and the phonograph in the 1890s. *Popular Music* X/1.

——. 1992. Sadeness, Scorpions and single markets: National and transnational trends in European popular music. *Popular Music* X1/2.

Laing, Dave and Jenny Taylor. 1979. Disco-pleasure-discourse: On 'rock and sexuality'. *Screen Education* 31.

Lancaster, Geoff and Lester Massinham. 1988. *Essentials of Marketing.* McGraw-Hill, Maidenhead.

Langlois, Tony. 1992. Can you feel it? DJs and House music culture in the UK. *Popular Music* XI/2.

Lee, Stephen. 1988. The strategy of opposition: Defining a music scene. Paper given at the International Communication Association Conference, New Orleans, 2 June.

Leisure Consultants. 1990. *Leisure Trends: The Thatcher Years*. Leisure Consultants.

Leonard, Diana. 1980. *Sex and Generation: A Study of Courtship and Weddings*. Tavistock, London.

Levin, Thomas. 1991. For the record: Adorno on music in the age of its technological reproducibility. *October 55*.

Levine, Lawrence. 1988. *Highbrow/Lowbrow: The Emergence of Cultural Hierarchy in America*. Harvard University Press, London.

Levitt, Theodor. 1983. The globalisation of markets. *Harvard Business Review* 3, May–June.

Lewis, George. 1992. Who do you love? The dimensions of musical taste. *Popular Music and Communication* ed. J. Lull. Sage, London.

Lewis, Jon. 1992. *The Road to Romance and Ruin: Teen Films and Youth Culture*. Routledge, London.

Lipsitz, George. 1990. Cruising around the historical bloc: Postmodernism and Popular Music in East Los Angeles. *Time Passages: Collective Memory and American Popular Culture*. University of Minnesota Press, Minneapolis.

Lull, James. (ed.) 1992. *Popular Music and Communication* 2nd edition. Sage, London.

Lury, Celia. 1993. *Cultural Rights: Technology, Legality and Personality*. Routledge, London.

Lyall, Sutherland. 1992. *Rock Sets: The Astonishing Art of Rock Concert Design*. Thames and Hudson, London.

Lydon, Michael and Ellen Mandel. 1974. *Boogie Lightning: How Music Became Electric*. Da Capo, New York.

Mabey, Richard. 1969. *The Pop Process*. Hutchinson Educational, London.

MacCabe, Colin. (ed.) 1986. *High Theory/Low Culture*. Manchester University Press, Manchester.

MacDonald, Dwight. 1958a. Eugene Gilbert: A caste, a culture, a market. Part I. *New Yorker* XXXIV/40, 22 November.

——. 1958b. Eugene Gilbert: A caste, a culture, a market. Part II. *New Yorker* XXXIV/41, 29 November.

MacFarlane, Gavin. 1982. *A Practical Introduction to Copyright*. McGraw-Hill Book Co. Ltd, London.

——. 1985. *Copyright Through the Cases*. Waterlow Publishers Ltd., London.

MacInnes, Colin. 1961. *England, Half English: A Polyphoto of the Fifties*. Penguin, London.

Maitland, Sara. (ed.) 1988. *Very Heaven: Looking Back at the Sixties*. Virago, London.

Marcus, Greil. 1989. *Lipstick Traces*. Secker and Warburg, London.

Marvin, Carolyn. 1988. *When Old Technologies Were New*. Oxford University Press, Oxford.

Marsh, Dave. 1985. *The First Rock & Roll Confidential Report*. Pantheon, New York.

Marx, Karl. 1887. 'The fetishism of commodities and the secret thereof'. *Capital: Volume One*. Lawrence and Wishart, London.

Mass-Observation. 1943. *The Pub and the People: A Worktown Study* ed. T. Harisson. Victor Gollancz Ltd, London.

Mays, John B. 1965. *The Young Pretenders*. Michael Joseph, London.

McCaskell, Tim. 1979. We will conquer a space filled with light. *The New Gay Liberation Book* ed. L. Richmond with G. Noguera. Ramparts Press, Palo Alto, CA.

McClary, Susan. 1991. *Feminine Endings: Music, Gender and Sexuality*. Minnesota University Press, Oxford.

McLuhan, Marshall. 1964. *Understanding Media: The Extension of Man*. McGraw-Hill, Toronto.

McRobbie, Angela. 1982. The politics of feminist research: Between talk, text and action. *Feminist Review* 12, October.

——. 1984. Dance and social fantasy. *Gender and Generation* eds A. McRobbie and M. Nava. Macmillan, London.

——. (ed.) 1989. *Zoot Suits and Second Hand Dresses: An Anthology of Fashion and Music*. Macmillan, London.

——. 1991. *Feminism and Youth Culture: From Jackie to Just Seventeen*. Macmillan, London.

——. 1994. *Postmodernism and Popular Culture*. Routledge, London.

McRobbie, Angela and Sarah Thornton. 1995. Rethinking 'moral panic' for multi-mediated social worlds. *British Journal of Sociology*, forthcoming.

Mead, Margaret. 1928/1943. The role of the dance. *Coming of Age in Samoa*. Pelican, London.

——. 1944. Are today's youth different? *The American Character*. Pelican, London.

Melly, George. 1970/1989. *Revolt into Style: The Pop Arts in Britain*. Penguin, London.

Mercer, Kobena. 1987. Black hair/style politics. *New Formations* 3, winter.

Merton, Robert K. 1938. Social structure and anomie. *American Sociological Review* III.

Meyrowitz, Joshua. 1985. *No Sense of Place: The Impact of Electronic Media on Social Behavior*. Oxford University Press, Oxford.

Middleton, Richard. 1990. *Studying Popular Music*. Open University Press, Milton Keynes.

Miller, Daniel. 1987. *Material Culture and Mass Consumption*. Blackwell, Oxford.

Mintel. 1988a. Pub attitudes – North versus South. *Mintel Leisure Intelligence* 1.

——. 1988b. Attitudes to evenings out. *Mintel Leisure Intelligence* 4.

——. 1988c. *Mintel Special Report: Youth Lifestyles*.

——. 1989. Tastes in music. *Mintel Leisure Intelligence* 1.

——. 1990. Nightclubs. *Mintel Leisure Intelligence* 3.

——. 1992. Nightclubs. *Mintel Leisure Intelligence* 3.

——. 1993. Records, cassettes and compact discs. *Mintel Leisure Intelligence* 1.

Modleski, Tania. 1986a. Femininity as mas(s)querade: A feminist approach to mass culture. *High Theory/Low Culture* ed. C. MacCabe. Manchester University Press, Manchester.

——. (ed.) 1986b. *Studies in Entertainment*. Indiana University Press, Bloomington.

Monopolies and Mergers Commission. 1988. *Collective Licensing: A Report on Certain Practices in the Collective Licensing of Public Performance and Broadcasting Rights in Sound Recordings*. Her Majesty's Stationery Office, London.

Montgomery, Martin. 1986. *An Introduction to Language and Society*. Methuen, London.

Morris, Meaghan. 1988. Banality in cultural studies. *Discourse* X/2.

——. 1993. Things to do with shopping centres. *The Cultural Studies Reader* ed. S. During. Routledge, London.

Mort, Frank. 1988. Boys' own? Masculine style and popular culture. *Male Order: Unwrapping Masculinity* eds R. Chapman and J. Rutherford. Lawrence & Wishart, London.

Mowitt, John. 1987. The sound of music in the era of its electronic reproducibility. *Music and Society* eds R. Leppert and S. McClary. Cambridge University Press, Cambridge.

Mukerji, Chandra and Michael Schudson. (eds) 1991. *Rethinking Popular Culture: Contemporary Perspectives in Cultural Studies*. University of California Press, Los Angeles.

Mulvey, Laura. 1975. Visual pleasure and narrative cinema. *Screen* XVI/3, autumn.

Mungham, Geoff. 1976. Youth in pursuit of itself. *Working Class Youth Cultures* eds G. Mungham and G. Pearson. Routledge & Kegan Paul, London.

Murdock, Graham. 1982. Large corporations and the control of the communications industries. *Culture, Society and the Media* eds M. Gurevitch et al. Methuen, London.

——. 1977. Class stratification and cultural consumption. *Leisure and the Urban Society* ed. M.A. Smith. Leisure Studies Association, Manchester.

Murdock, Graham and Robin McCron. 1976. Youth and class: The career of confusion. *Working Class Youth Cultures* eds G. Mungham and G. Pearson. Routledge & Kegan Paul, London.

Murphie, Andrew and Edward Scheer. 1992. Dance parties: Capital, culture and simulation. *From Pop to Punk to Postmodernism: Popular Music and Australian Culture from the 1960s to the 1990s* ed. P. Hayward. Allen & Unwin, Sydney, Australia.

Negus, Keith. 1992. *Producing Pop: Culture and Conflict in the Popular Music Industry.* Edward Arnold, London.

Nelson, Cary and Larry Grossberg. (eds) 1988. *Marxism and the Interpretation of Culture.* University of Illinois Press, Urbana.

Neslen, Arthur. 1990. Acidhouse: Crisis in clubland. Unpublished BA Honours thesis.

Newcombe, Russell. 1992. A researcher reports from the rave. *Druglink,* January/February.

Newton, Francis. 1959. *The Jazz Scene.* MacGibbon & Kee, London.

Norman, Philip. 1993. *The Stones.* Penguin, London.

Nourse, Brian with John Hudson. 1990. *The Glen and I: Bristol's Rock'n'roll Years.* Redcliffe Press, Bristol.

O'Doherty, Brian. 1986. *Inside the White Cube: The Ideology of the Gallery Space.* Lapis Press, Santa Monica.

Ogawa, Hiroshi. 1991. Sociology of karaoke. Unpublished paper.

Ohmann, Richard. 1984. The new discourse of mass culture: Magazines in the 1890s. *University of Hartford Studies in Literature* XVI/2&3.

——. 1988. History and literary history: The case of mass culture. *Poetics Today* IX/2.

Oliver, Paul. (ed.) 1990. *Black Music in Britain: Essays on the Afro-Asian Contribution to Popular Music.* Open University Press, Milton Keynes.

Parsons, Talcott. 1964. *Essays in Sociological Theory.* Free Press, New York.

Pearsall, Ronald. 1976. *Popular Music in the Twenties.* David & Charles, London.

Pearson, Geoffrey and John Twohig. 1976. Ethnography through the looking glass. *Resistance through Rituals* eds S. Hall and T. Jefferson. Unwin Hyman, London.

Peel, Barbara. 1986. *Dancing and Social Assemblies in York in the Eighteenth and Nineteenth Centuries.* National Resource Centre for Dance, University of Surrey.

Peterson, Richard. 1978. Disco! *The Chronicle of Higher Education,* 2 October.

Plant, Mark and Moira Plant. 1992. *The Risk-Takers: Alcohol, Drugs, Sex and Youth*. Routledge, London.

Pleasance, Helen. 1991. Open or closed: Popular magazines and dominant culture. *Off-Centre: Feminism and Cultural Studies* eds S. Franklin et al. HarperCollins, London.

Polsky, Ned. 1967. *Hustlers, Beats and Others*. Penguin, London.

Porcello, Thomas. 1991. The ethics of digital audio-sampling: Engineers' discourse. *Popular Music* X/1.

Pursehouse, Mark. 1991. Looking at the *Sun*: Into the nineties with a tabloid and its readers. *Cultural Studies from Birmingham* no. 1.

Quain, Kevin. (ed.) 1992. *The Elvis Reader*. St Martin's Press, New York.

Qualen, John. 1986. *The Music Industry: The End of Vinyl*. Comedia, London.

Radway, Janice. 1988. Reception study: Ethnography and the problems of dispersed audiences and nomadic subjects. *Cultural Studies* II/3, October.

Read, Oliver and Walter Welch. 1976. *From Tin Foil to Stereo: The Evolution of the Phonograph*. Howard W. Sams, Indianapolis.

Redhead, Steve. 1990. *The End-of-the-Century Party: Youth and Pop towards 2000*. Manchester University Press, Manchester.

Redhead, Steve. (ed.) 1993. *Rave Off*. Avebury, Aldershot.

Riesman, David. 1950/1990. Listening to popular music. *On Record* eds S. Frith and A. Goodwin. Pantheon, New York.

Riesman, David, with Nathan Glazer and Reuel Denney. 1961. *The Lonely Crowd*. Yale University Press, New Haven.

Rietveld, Gonnie. 1991. Living the dream: Analysis of the rave-phenomenon in terms of ideology, consumerism and subculture. BA Honours thesis. Working paper from the Unit for Law and Popular Culture, Manchester Polytechnic.

Rimmer, Dave. 1985. *Like Punk Never Happened*. Faber & Faber, London.

Roberts, Kenneth. 1983. *Youth and Leisure*. Allen & Unwin, London.

Rogers, Barbara. 1988. Pubs: Getting away from the wife. *Men Only: An investigation into men's organisations*. Pandora, London.

Rojek, Chris. (ed.) 1989. *Leisure for Leisure: Critical Essays*. Macmillan, London.

Roman, Leslie G. 1988. Intimacy, labor and class: Ideologies of feminine sexuality in the Punk slam dance. *Becoming Feminine: The Politics of Popular Culture*. Falmer Press, London.

Rose, Cynthia. 1991. *Design After Dark: The Story of Dancefloor Style*. Thames & Hudson, London.

Rosenberg, Bernard and David M. White. (eds) 1957. *Mass Culture: The Popular Arts in America*. The Free Press, Glencoe IL.

Ross, Andrew. 1989. *No Respect: Intellectuals and Popular Culture*. Routledge,

London.

Ross, Andrew and Tricia Rose. (eds) 1994. *Microphone Fiends: Youth Music and Youth Culture*. Routledge, London.

Rust, Frances. 1969. *Dance in Society: An analysis of the relationship between the social dance and society in England from the Middle Ages to the present day*. Routledge & Kegan Paul, London.

Said, Edward. 1985. *Orientalism*. Penguin, Harmondsworth.

Savage, Jon. 1988. The enemy within: Sex, rock and identity. *Facing the Music* ed. S. Frith. Pantheon, New York.

——. 1993. Machine Soul: A history of techno. *Village Voice: Rock'n'Roll Quarterly*, summer.

Scannell, Paddy. 1989. Public service broadcasting and modern public life. *Media, Culture and Society*. X1/2, April.

Scaping, Peter. (ed.) 1982, 1984, 1985, 1986, 1987, 1988/89, 1989/90, 1991. *BPI Yearbook*. British Phonographic Industry Limited, London.

——. (ed.) 1992. *BPI Statistical Handbook 1992*. British Phonographic Industry Limited, London.

Scaping, Peter and Nigel Hunter. (eds) 1978. *BPI Yearbook 1978*. British Phonographic Industry Limited, London.

Schlecter, Theodore and Paul Gump. 1983. Car availability and the daily life of the teenage male. *Adolescence* XVIII/69, spring.

Silverstone, Roger. 1994. *Television and Everyday Life*. Routledge, London.

Silverstone, Roger and Eric Hirsch. (eds) 1992. *Consuming Technologies: Media and Information in Domestic Spaces*. Routledge, London.

Silverstone, Roger and David Morley. 1990. Families and their technologies: Two ethnographic portraits. *Household Choices* eds C. Newton and T. Putnam. Futures Publications, London.

Silverstone, Roger, Eric Hirsch and David Morley. 1992. Information and communication technologies and the moral economy of the household. *Consuming Technologies: Media and Information in Domestic Spaces* eds R. Silverstone and E. Hirsch. Routledge, London.

Smith, Mark K. 1992. The changing position of young people. Unpublished paper.

Smucker, Tom. 1980. Disco. *The Rolling Stone Illustrated History of Rock & Roll*. Picador, London.

Sontag, Susan. 1966. Notes on camp. *Against Interpretation and Other Essays*. Farrar Straus & Giroux, New York.

Spencer, Paul. (ed.) 1985. *Society and Dance: The Social Anthropology of Process and Performance*. Cambridge University Press, New York.

Spigel, Lynn. 1988. Installing the television set: Popular discourses on television and domestic space, 1948–1955. *Camera Obscura* XVI.

Stallybrass, Peter and Allon White. 1986. *The Politics and Poetics of Trans-*

gression. Methuen, London.

Stearns, Marshall and Jean. 1968. *Jazz Dance: The Story of American Vernacular Dance*. Macmillan, New York.

Stratton, Jon. 1983. Capitalism and romantic ideology in the record business. *Popular Music* III.

Straw, Will. 1990. *Popular music as cultural commodity: The American recorded music industries 1976–85*, PhD thesis. McGill University, Montreal.

——. 1991. Systems of articulation, logics of change: Communities and scenes in popular music. *Cultural Studies* V/3, October.

Street, John. 1986. *Rebel Rock: The Politics of Popular Music*. Blackwell, Oxford.

——. 1992. Shock Waves. The authoritative response to popular music. *Come On Down? Popular Media Culture in Post-war Britain* eds D. Strinati and S. Wagg. Routledge, London.

Struthers, Stephen. 1987. Technology in the art of recording. *Lost in Music* ed. A. Levine White. Routledge, London.

Sturmer, Corinna. 1993. MTV's Europe. An imaginary continent? *Channels of Resistance: Global Television and Local Empowerment*. BFI, London.

Theberge, Paul. 1989. The 'sound' of music: Technological rationalization and the production of popular music. *New Formations* 8, summer.

——. 1991. Musicians' magazines in the 1980s: The creation of a community and a consumer market. *Cultural Studies* V/3, October.

Thomas, Helen. (ed.) 1993. *Dance, Gender and Culture*. Macmillan, London.

Thompson, John B. 1990. *Ideology and Modern Culture*. Polity, Cambridge.

——. 1991. Editor's Introduction. *Language and Symbolic Power*. Polity, Oxford.

Thomson, Raymond. 1989. Dance halls and dance bands in Greenock 1945–55. *Popular Music* VIII/2, May.

Thornton, Sarah. 1990a. Club class. *New Statesman & Society*, 16 November.

——. 1990b. Strategies for reconstructing the popular past. *Popular Music* IX/1.

——. 1994. Moral panic, the media and British rave culture. *Microphone Fiends: Youth Music, Youth Culture* eds A. Ross and T. Rose. Routledge, London.

Toop, D. 1984. *The Rap Attack: African Jive to New York Hiphop*. Pluto Press, London.

Torp, Lisbet. 1986. 'Hip hop dances' – Their adoption and function among boys in Denmark from 1983–84. *Yearbook for Traditional Music* XVIII.

Tuchman, Gaye. 1978. *Making News: A Study of the Construction of Reality*. The Free Press, New York.

Tyler, Stephen A. 1986. Post-modern ethnography. From document of the occult to occult of the document. *Writing Culture: The Poetics and Politics of Ethnography* eds J. Clifford and G.E. Marcus. University of California Press, Berkeley.

Van der Kiste, John. 1985. *Singles File: The Story of the 45 rpm Record*. A&F Publications, South Brent.

Veblen, Thorstein. 1899. *The Theory of the Leisure Class*. Penguin, New York.

Venturi, Robert. 1966. *Complexity and Contradiction in Architecture*. Museum of Modern Art, New York.

Venturi, Robert, Denise Scott Brown and Steven Izenour. 1977. *Learning from Las Vegas*. MIT Press, Cambridge, Mass.

Virilio, Paul. 1986. The overexposed city. *Zone* I/2.

Wallis, Roger and Krister Malm. 1984. *Big Sounds from Small Peoples*. Constable, London.

Wark, McKenzie. 1989. Elvis: Listening to the loss. *Art & Text* 31, December–February.

Warren, Carol. 1974. *Identity and Community in a Gay world*. John Wiley & Sons, London.

Weeks, Jeffrey. 1985. *Sexuality and its Discontents: Meanings, Myths and Modern Sexualities*. Routledge & Kegan Paul, London.

Weinstein, Deena. 1991. *Heavy Metal: A Cultural Sociology*. Maxwell-Macmillan, Oxford.

Weyeneth, Robert. 1984. Immoral spaces: Saloon, dance hall and street. *Moral Spaces: Reforming the Landscape of Leisure in Urban America, 1850–1920*, PhD thesis. University of California, Berkeley.

Whitehead, Ann. 1976. Sexual antagonism in Herefordshire. *Dependence and Exploitation in Work and Marriage* eds D. Leonard Baker and S. Allen. Longman, London.

Williams, Raymond. 1961. *The Long Revolution*. Penguin, London.

——. 1974. *Television: Technology and Cultural Form*. Schocken, New York.

——. 1976. *Keywords*. Penguin, London.

——. 1978. The press and popular culture: An historical perspective. *Newspaper History* eds G. Boyce et al. Constable, London.

——. 1981. *Culture*. Fontana, London.

Williams, Rosalind H. 1982. *Dream Worlds*. University of California Press, Berkeley.

Williamson, Judith. 1986. *Consuming Passions: The Dynamics of Popular Culture*. Marion Boyars, London.

Willis, Paul. 1977. *Learning to Labour*. Routledge & Kegan Paul, London.

——. 1978. *Profane Culture*. Routledge & Kegan Paul, London.

Willmott, Peter. 1966. *Adolescent Boys in East London*. Pelican, London.

Wilson, Elizabeth. 1985. *Adorned in Dreams: Fashion and Modernity*. Virago, London.

——. 1988. Memoirs of an anti-heroine. *Radical Records: Thirty Years of Lesbian and Gay History* eds B. Cant and S. Hemmings. Routledge, London.

Winnicott, D.W. 1971. *Playing and Reality*. Routledge, London.

Wolfe, Tom. 1968a. *The Electric Kool-Aid Acid Test*. Bantam, London.

——. 1968b. *The Pump House Gang*. Farrar, Straus & Giroux, New York.

——. 1974. Funky chic. *Rolling Stone*, 3 January.

Wolff, Janet. 1981. *The Social Production of Art*. Macmillan, London.

Wollen, Peter. 1987. Fashion/Orientalism/the body. *New Formations* I/1, spring.

Wylson, Anthony. 1980. *Design for Leisure Entertainment*. Newnes-Butterworths, London.

Young, Jock. 1971. *The Drugtakers: The social meaning of drug use*. Paladin, London.

——. 1973. The Hippie solution: An essay in the politics of leisure. *Politics and Deviance* eds I. Taylor and L. Taylor. Penguin, Harmondsworth.

Zillman, Dolf and Azra Bhatia. 1989. Effects of associating with musical genres on heterosexual attraction. *Communication Research* XVI/2, April.

Index

acid house, 6, 9, 73, 75, 88, 89,
  100, 106, 116, 120, 129, 130–1,
  132–6, 139–40, 143–6, 152,
  153–4, 155–60
Adorno, Theodor, 1, 34, 94, 109
Afro-American, Afro-Caribbean
  music culture, *see* black music
  culture
age, 5, 7–8, 11, 12, 14–25, 53–5,
  101–3, 113
alcohol, 20–1, 57
American comparisons, 3, 16–20,
  44, 45–6, 53, 54–6, 136
archival disc cultures, 69–70
aura, 27–8, 30–1, 69–70, 74, 76,
  80–1, 85, 125

ballrooms, 36, 39–40, 45, 47, 53–5,
  58
banning, *see* censorship
Baudrillard, Jean, 1, 33, 42–3, 52
BBC, 36, 53, 122–3, 129–31, 145,
  160; *see also* Radio One; *Top of the
  Pops*
Becker, Howard, 8–9, 119
Benjamin, Walter, 27, 52, 69–70

Birmingham cultural studies
  tradition, 8–10, 24–5, 110, 118–
  19, 121, 152
black music culture, 7, 15, 16–17,
  30, 44, 47, 68, 69–70, 71–6, 105,
  108, 113, 147; *see also* race
Bourdieu, Pierre, 10–14, 92, 99,
  101–3, 113, 117, 166
broadcasting, 122, 124; *see also*
  BBC; Radio One; *Top of the Pops*

cars, 16–17
CDs, 63–4
censorship, 129–31, 145
chartpop, *see* pop
charts, 58–9, 100, 123, 130
cinema, *see* film
class and classlessness, 12–13, 15,
  55–6, 90–1, 93–6, 101–3, 105,
  167
clothes, 55, 99, 113–14
Cohen, Stanley, 119–20
commodities, 28, 36
compilation albums, 118
concert designers, 79
copyright, 37–41, 49, 50, 85

Cosgrove, Stuart, 157
cover/copy bands, 28, 81

dancehalls, *see* ballrooms; Mecca
dancing, 4, 12, 14–16, 21, 35–6,
  52, 57, 58, 60, 62, 65, 71, 93, 103,
  106
disc jockeys, 4, 29, 30, 59–66, 112,
  139
disco music, 2, 43–4, 47, 59, 69, 71
discotheque, as an institution, 1,
  14, 24, 28, 54; mobile, 46–7; *see*
  also interior design
DJs, *see* disc jockeys
door policies, 24, 113–14
drugs, 21–2, 57, 79, 88–91, 105,
  123, 130–5, 138, 145–6, 150,
  164–5

electronic mail, 150
enculturation, 28–9, 33–5, 58, 60,
  66
ethnography, *see* methodology

Face, The, 87, 153–4
fads, 2, 22, 43, 46, 98, 122, 132, 153,
  155
fanzines, 118, 122, 134, 137, 138–41
fashion, *see* fads
film, 19, 37, 46, 57, 68
flyers, 122, 137, 141–2
formats, 58–60
Frith, Simon, 29, 36, 95–7, 125, 151

gatekeeping, 130, 145
gay and lesbian club culture, 6, 16,
  30, 44, 69, 72, 73, 75, 96, 99, 105,
  108, 111–12, 113, 146; *see also*
  sexuality
gender, 5, 8, 13, 15, 21, 56, 72, 95,
  99–100, 103–5, 113, 139
genre, 66, 70–6, 100, 106, 152,
  155–8
globalization, 3, 21, 46, 54–5, 70,
  150; *see also* imports
Grossberg, Lawrence, 97–8

Hebdige, Dick, 9, 93–4, 114, 164–5
hiphop, 20, 71, 72, 113, 153
Hitman and Her, The, 109, 126–7
house music, 31, 63, 71–6, 125, 126

i-D, 154, 158–60
imports, 3, 53, 54, 66–7, 68–9, 155,
  156–7, 158; *see also* globalization
interior design, 51, 53–7, 125–6
internet, 150

jazz, 7, 66–7
jukebox, 36, 45–6, 56, 58
jungle music, 71, 73

KISS-FM, 146–50

labelling, 8, 53, 104, 106, 119, 143,
  159, 162
leisure, 19, 20, 91, 101–2, 129, 157
lesbian clubs, *see* gay and lesbian
  club culture
listings, 137, 142–6
live music, 4, 20, 26–7, 29–31, 32–
  3, 37, 41–4, 47–51, 66, 67–8, 70,
  76–85, 125–6
London Records, 150

McLuhan, Marshall, 33, 70
McRobbie, Angela, 8, 21, 65, 94–5
magazines, 120, 122, 123, 130, 132–
  4, 136, 151–60, 162
Manzi, Eugene, 156–7
marketing, 120, 121, 125, 141
Mecca dancehalls/clubs, 93–4, 99,
  107–8
Melody Maker, 133
methodology, 2–3, 87–98, 105–10,
  114–15, 118, 120–1, 152
Monopolies and Mergers
  Commission, 49
moral panic, 119–20, 129, 131–7,
  145
MTV, 18, 122, 124, 126
Mungham, Geoff, 93–4, 96, 113
music press, *see* magazines

Musicians' Union, 32, 35, 38–43, 49–50, 52

narrowcasting, 122, 147; *see also* *Hitman and Her (The)*; KISS-FM; MTV
New Musical Express (NME), 132
newspapers, 131; *see also* tabloid newspapers
Northern Soul, 69–70
nostalgia, 70, 140

participant observation, *see* methodology
performance, *see* live music
personal stereo, *see* Walkman
Phonographic Performance Limited (PPL), 38–9, 49–50
pirate radio, 122, 137, 146–50
politics, 137, 164–8
Polsky, Ned, 9, 105
pop, 13, 20, 72, 99, 104
postmodernity, 7, 97, 121, 160–2
public appearance (PA), 31, 82–5
pubs, 20–2

race, 7, 15, 16–17, 24–5, 30, 44, 68, 72–6, 105, 113, 147; *see also* black music culture
radio, 13, 36, 68, 109, 122, 123, 129–31, 146–50
Radio One (1FM), 129–31, 147
Rampling, Danny, 139, 143, 145
rare groove, 69, 153, 158
raves, 3, 9, 14, 22–5, 29–30, 47, 55–6, 57, 60, 83–4, 88–9, 90–2, 100, 116, 135, 139, 140, 144–5
record hops, 4, 28, 44, 52–4
record industry, 12, 35–8, 46, 48, 50, 61, 136; *see also* copyright; London Records; Monopolies and Mergers Commission; Phonographic Performance Limited; Virgin Records
reggae, 68–9
rock, 31, 70–1, 76–85

rock'n'roll, 67–8, 71

samplers/sampling, 2, 72
segregation, 22–5, 111–14
selling out, 123–5, 128, 136, 145
sexuality, 6–7, 30, 99, 105, 111–13
Shoom, 143–6, 158–9
singles sales chart, *see* charts
social stratification, 5, 7–8, 10, 92–8, 101–2, 166
sound quality, 44, 58
sound-systems, 47, 68–9
Stock/Aitken/Waterman, 99, 100, 109, 126–7
Straw, Will, 59, 110
street, the, 18, 138, 141, 148
style, *see* clothes
subcultural capital, definitions of 11–14, 98–105
subculture, definition and development of, 8–9, 117, 119, 152, 158–62
Sun, the, 109, 121, 129, 131–5

tabloid newspapers, 75, 100, 120, 121, 122, 129, 131
taste in music, 2, 13, 19–20, 43–4, 53, 112–13, 164
techno, 31, 72–7, 100, 125, 129
telephone, 17–18
television, 13, 18, 53, 68, 109, 121–2, 123–9
Time Out, 143–6
time/temporality, 51–3, 69–70
Top of the Pops, 109, 121, 123–6, 128, 129, 155
top ten, top forty, *see* charts
twelve-inch single, 58–60, 66, 117–18

video, 57, 79–80, 123–6, 127, 140
vinyl, death of, 63–4
Virgin Records, 74–5
virtual reality, 110

Walkman, 19–20
Waterman, Pete, 126–7; *see also*
 Stock/Aitken/Waterman
white labels, 69, 117–18; *see also*
 twelve-inch single
Willis, Paul, 9, 152

women, *see* gender
work, 90–1, 101–2

Young, Jock, 21, 164–5
youth, *see* age

MUSIC / CULTURE

A series from Wesleyan University Press
Edited by George Lipsitz, Susan McClary, and Robert Walser

My Music by Susan D. Crafts,
Daniel Cavicchi, Charles Keil, and the
Music in Daily Life Project

*Running with the Devil: Power, Gender,
and Madness in Heavy Metal Music*
by Robert Walser

*Subcultural Sounds: Micromusics
of the West* by Mark Slobin

*Upside Your Head! Rhythm and Blues
on Central Avenue* by Johnny Otis

*Dissonant Identities: The Rock 'n' Roll
Scene in Austin, Texas* by Barry Shank

*Black Noise: Rap Music and Black
Culture in Contemporary America*
by Tricia Rose

*Club Cultures: Music, Media and
Subcultural Capital* by Sarah Thornton

Popular Music in Theory
by Keith Negus

*Listening to Salsa: Gender, Latin
Popular Music, and Puerto Rican
Cultures* by Frances Aparicio

*Any Sound You Can Imagine:
Making Music/Consuming Technology*
by Paul Théberge

*Voices in Bali: Energies and Perceptions
in Vocal Music and Dance Theater*
by Edward Herbst

Music, Society, Education
by Christopher Small

*A Thousand Honey Creeks Later: My Life
in Music from Basie to Motown—and
Beyond* by Preston Love

*Music of the Common Tongue: Survival
and Celebration in African American
Music* by Christopher Small

*Musicking: The Meanings of Performing
and Listening* by Christopher Small

*Singing Archaeology: Philip Glass's
Akhnaten* by John Richardson

*Metal, Rock, and Jazz: Perception and
the Phenomenology of Musical
Experience* by Harris M. Berger

Music and Cinema
edited by James Buhler, Caryl Flinn,
and David Neumeyer

*"You Better Work!" Underground
Dance Music in New York City*
by Kai Fikentscher

*Singing Our Way to Victory: French
Cultural Politics and Music during the
Great War* by Regina M. Sweeney

*The Book of Music and Nature: An
Anthology of Sounds, Words, Thoughts*
edited by David Rothenberg and
Marta Ulvaeus

*Recollecting from the Past: Musical
Practice and Spirit Possession on the East
Coast of Madagascar* by Ron Emoff

*Global Noise: Rap and Hip-Hop outside
the USA* edited by Tony Mitchell

Banda: Mexican Musical Life across Borders by Helena Simonett

The 'Hood Comes First: Race, Space, and Place in Rap and Hip-Hop by Murray Forman

Manufacturing the Muse: Estey Organs and Consumer Culture in Victorian America by Dennis G. Waring

The City of Musical Memory: Salsa, Record Grooves, and Popular Culture in Cali, Colombia by Lise A. Waxer

Music and Technoculture edited by René T.A. Lysloff and Leslie C. Gay, Jr.

Angora Matta: Fatal Acts of North-South Translation by Marta Elena Savigliano

False Prophet: Fieldnotes from the Punk Underground by Steven Taylor

Phat Beats, Dope Rhymes: Hip-Hop Down Under Comin' Upper by Ian Maxwell

Locating East Asia in Western Art Music edited by Yayoi Uno Everett and Frederick Lau

Identity and Everyday Life: Essays in the Study of Folklore, Music, and Popular Culture by Harris M. Berger and Giovanna P. Del Negro

The Other Side of Nowhere: Jazz, Improvisation, and Communities in Dialogue edited by Daniel Fischlin and Ajay Heble

Wired for Sound: Engineering and Technologies in Sonic Cultures edited by Paul D. Greene and Thomas Porcello

Setting the Record Straight: A Material History of Classical Recording by Colin Symes

Making Beats: The Art of Sample-Based Hip-Hop by Joseph G. Schloss